# THE SPANISH CIVIL WAR

*Twentieth-Century Wars*
General Editor: Jeremy Black

*Published titles*

| | |
|---|---|
| David L. Anderson | *The Vietnam War* |
| D. George Boyce | *The Falklands War* |
| Gerard DeGroot | *The First World War* |
| Peter Lowe | *The Korean War* |
| Francisco J. Romero Salvadó | *The Spanish Civil War* |
| Spencer C. Tucker | *The Second World War* |

**Twentieth-Century Wars**
**Series Standing Order ISBN 0-333-77101-X**

You can receive future titles in this series as they are published. To place a standing order please contact your bookseller or, in the case of difficulty, write to us at the address below with your name and address, the title of the series and the ISBN quoted above.

Customer Services Department, Macmillan Distribution Ltd
Houndmills, Basingstoke, Hampshire RG21 6XS, England

# THE SPANISH CIVIL WAR
## ORIGINS, COURSE AND OUTCOMES

Francisco J. Romero Salvadó

946.081
Rom
pb

First published 2005 by
PALGRAVE MACMILLAN
Houndmills, Basingstoke, Hampshire RG21 6XS and
175 Fifth Avenue, New York, N.Y. 10010
Companies and representatives throughout the world

PALGRAVE MACMILLAN is the global academic imprint of the Palgrave
Macmillan division of St. Martin's Press LLC and of Palgrave Macmillan Ltd.
Macmillan® is a registered trademark in the United States, United Kingdom
and other countries. Palgrave is a registered trademark in the European
Union and other countries.

ISBN-13: 978-0333-75435-1     hardback
ISBN-10: 0-333-75435-2        hardback
ISBN-13: 978-0333-75436-8     paperback
ISBN-10: 0-333-75436-0        paperback

This book is printed on paper suitable for recycling and made from fully
managed and sustained forest sources.

A catalogue record for this book is available from the British Library.

A catalog record for this book is available from the Library of Congress.

10   9   8   7   6   5   4   3   2   1
14   13  12  11  10  09  08  07  06  05

Printed in China

In memory of my grandfathers, José Romero Prats and
Cipriano Salvadó Solsona

# Contents

# Maps

# Preface

More than sixty-five years after its conclusion, the Spanish Civil War continues to exert a particular fascination. The thousands of monographs, memoirs, novels, documentaries and films generated by this conflict bear witness to its enduring impact and put its study on a par with other key events of the twentieth century: the Russian Revolution, the rise and fall of the Third Reich and the Second World War.

The Spanish Civil War was above all a domestic conflict, a brutal attempt to solve by military means a host of social and political issues that had divided Spaniards for generations. Questions such as land reform, centralism versus regional autonomy and the role of the Catholic Church and the armed forces in a modern society came to a head in the attempted military coup of July 1936 which precipitated the civil war. This cruel three years of fratricidal struggle was a traumatic experience which directly touched the lives of every family and even saw brothers fighting on opposite sides. The triumphant Nationalists then ensured that this climate of hatred and division lasted for 40 years.

However, the war was not just a domestic conflict but also one that transcended national barriers and aroused passions and acrimonious debate throughout Europe. All the great powers intervened and, to a large extent, determined the course and outcome of the conflict. The Soviet Union supported the Republic not so much as proof of ideological solidarity but as an attempt to build an international alliance against Fascism. Before the *Anschluss* with Austria and the Sudetenland crisis in Czechoslovakia in 1938, Spain was a glaring example of Western appeasement. All evidence of the blatant involvement of the Fascist powers in Spain, including their mass bombing of cities and indiscriminate sinking of merchant vessels, was ignored. Stalin learnt the lesson of the West's strategy and, in August 1939, signed the Non-Intervention Pact with Nazi Germany that made war on the continent all but inevitable.

It was, however, the appeal to the common people that gave the Spanish Civil War a special romanticism. In 1936 Spain was a microcosm that encapsulated the ferocity, radicalism and polarisation of an era. No other conflict has ever aroused the passion of citizens and artists to such a degree. Works such as Pablo Picasso's *Guernica*, Ernest Hemingway's *For Whom the Bell Tolls* (later filmed in Hollywood, with Gary Cooper in the starring role), George's Orwell *Homage to Catalonia* and André Malraux's *L'Espoir* have become classics. Even in the legendary film *Casablanca*, the adventurer Rick (played by Humphrey Bogart) confesses that prior to settling in Morocco he had been fighting for the Republic in Spain.

Nevertheless, despite the high profile of poets, artists and writers, they represented only a tiny minority of the flood of volunteers who fought in Spain. Those who sided with the Nationalists believed that theirs was a struggle in the defence of Christian civilisation against Communist barbarism. For the thousands who volunteered to fight for the Republic, Spain was the 'last great cause' – the last-ditch stand against the seemingly invincible forces of Fascism and political reaction which had swept the continent in the inter-war years.

The Spanish Civil War is far from being an exhausted subject but remains today a fresh, vast topic of analysis and debate. For 40 years its study remained part of the long and bitter 'war of words' that marked the Francoist regime. In Spain, the apologists for the dictatorship portrayed the fratricidal strife as a heroic crusade against the usual suspects: Masons, Reds, Jews and separatists. However, the vanquished also provided a Manichean view in which the war was explained as the subjugation of the Spanish people by a minority of clerics, generals and capitalists. Of course, owing to their contemporary divisions and subsequent mutual recriminations, the Republicans could never offer the monolithic and homogeneous image presented by the Nationalists. It was only abroad that the Spanish tragedy could be analysed with a degree of objectivity. However, although foreign scholars could write without the censorship existent in Spain, their conclusions were limited by their inaccessibility to primary sources.

It has only been since the late 1970s, following the death of Franco and the dismantlement of his dictatorship, that an explosion of scholarship has been able to correct the historical distortions which were part of the Francoist legacy. This new and ground-breaking historiography has only confirmed the complexity, richness and depth of the Spanish Civil War. Drawing on the abundance of such monographic works and printed primary sources, this text seeks to provide an up-to-date

analytical study and to offer the reader a clear path through what the
English author Gerald Brenan once termed 'the Spanish Labyrinth' and
what the Austrian writer Franz Borkenau, in his eyewitness account of
the war, called 'the Spanish Cockpit'. A crucial aim of this book is to
uproot the myths, manipulations and easy conclusions that have often
accompanied this fascinating subject. Of course, in view of its scope,
many interesting issues (such as gender, daily life behind the lines, the
social experience of the collectives, etc.) cannot be addressed in depth,
and the bitter legacy of the Civil War is only synthetically dealt with in
its epilogue. A chronological order has been adopted so as to facilitate
a sense of evolution.

This work lays particularly emphasis on the genesis of the conflict.
Many studies start their analysis of the Spanish Civil War in the
summer of 1936 or, at the most, cast a brief look back to the years
of the Second Republic (1931–6). In fact, the origins of the Spanish
tragedy are far more deeply rooted in the country's history. At best one
might say that even the immediate seeds of the conflict should be
described as having been sown during the half-a-century existence of
the previous regime, the restored Bourbon monarchy of December 1874
to April 1931. The political radicalism, social upheaval and praetorian
interventionism of 1930s Spain were the legacy of the monarchist governing classes of the Restoration era who failed to initiate democratic
reform from within. Indeed, the persistence of a traditional oligarchic
rule when confronted by the arrival of mass politics and the demands
of newly mobilised sectors of the population initiated an almost unprecedented age of social warfare and political polarisation that led to
the replacement of the Liberal regime by a military dictatorship in
1923 and to the fall of the monarchy itself eight years later.

Despite the course of the war being the central theme under study,
this work refutes any idea of historical determinism and the inevitability of the conflict. Thus, despite the rebel officers' assertions, the
war was not inevitable but was the product of an illegal coup and of its
subsequent partial failure. For all the errors committed by the Republican governing class, the pretexts of the conspirators to justify their
rebellion were spurious. There was, certainly, social turmoil and street
violence in 1936. However, it was not necessarily worse than at other
times under the monarchy. Furthermore, very much like the Fascist rise
to power in Italy and Germany, the breakdown of public order was, to
a large extent, caused by rightist thugs. Even more ludicrous was the
suggestion, spread by elements close to the military insurrection, that
the army officers had acted to pre-empt a formidable international Red

conspiracy; in fact, from the evidence of the first days of the civil war, it was clear that the different Republican militias, from the Communists to the CNT, lacked weapons, military training and even the desire to seize state power.

Many texts view the outbreak of hostilities as proof of the Republic's bankruptcy; the opposite is true. The Republic's success was borne out by the defeat of the military uprising in nearly two-thirds of mainland Spain. With a few notable exceptions, the rebellion only succeeded in those areas that had traditionally voted for right-wing parties. Unlike many other European countries whose constitutional systems had been overthrown with relative ease by right-wing forces, the Republic fought back and it took 33 months of brutal struggle to crush its resistance.

This text concentrates on the two camps at war. However, the monolithic view of a fiercely divided Spain is misleading. As Paul Preston, Enrique Moradiellos and other authors in their recent analyses have demonstrated, the majority of Spaniards did not welcome the war. On the contrary, they were overwhelmed and regarded with horror the tragedy unfolding before their eyes. It was geography in most cases which dictated the side on which most people would have to fight. Furthermore, as Hugh Thomas noted in his pioneering study of the Civil War, there were not two but a thousand Spains in the summer of 1936. Following the failure of the coup, the fratricidal contest was not a clash between two clearly homogeneous camps but a variety of bitter local conflicts.

This work also seeks to draw a comparative picture of the evolution in the two camps, particularly in the fields of repression and internal organisation. In regard to repression, all civil wars, as proven by recent conflicts in the Balkans and Eastern Europe, are extremely cruel affairs. The Spanish cockpit was no different. Both sides offered an equally shameful spectacle of the persecution and slaughter of thousands of fellow Spaniards. The Nationalist camp was not the 'city of God' described by Bishop Enrique Pla but one dominated by an obscurantism and religious fanaticism reminiscent of the worst times of inquisitorial Spain. In turn, in Republican Spain priests and property-owners were being hunted down and shot. Members of my own family faced the brutality of both sides. However, they were more fortunate than many others. My paternal grandfather, José Romero Prats, knowing that FAI patrols had been making enquiries about him, had to spend a good part of the war in hiding, in the cinema beneath his flat. His 'crime' was to have been a secretary in the town hall of Valencia during the monarchy. Anarchists arrested his brother-in-law, Manuel Pérez, a judge. Only the rapid mobilisation of the family saved him. A distant cousin, who was an influential member of one of the many street militias, found out where he had been jailed and managed to free him from his captors. Manuel Pérez escaped, but not before he had received a beating that would leave him crippled for life. My maternal grandfather, Cipriano Salvadó Solsona, fought for three years in the Republican army in Cataluña and, like thousands of his comrades, fled across the border in early 1939 and found himself in a French concentration camp from which he escaped a few months later to return to Spain. After crossing the Pyrenees on foot, he and his companions soon enjoyed a taste of the new order when they were harassed and robbed of their few belongings by a group of Falangists. To them, my grandfather's group were not only former members of the vanquished Red Army but also 'Catalan scum'! Still, they were not shot and the Falangists' fun was limited to insulting them and forcing them to sing, with their arms raised in salute, the Falangist anthem – 'Cara al Sol' ('Facing the Sun').

No political party of either camp could plead innocence regarding the bloodshed that took place in nearly every corner of Spain. It is no longer possible to apportion all the blame to criminal elements and call them *incontrolados* (the uncontrolled ones). Jorge Reverte's recently published book on the siege of Madrid, for example, provides shocking evidence of the collusion between Anarchists and the Socialist Youth in the liquidation in late 1936 of hundreds of Nationalist prisoners who were supposed to be transferred to other jails from the besieged capital. However, there existed a vital difference in the waves of terror carried out by both sides.

From the beginning, there were loud voices in Republican Spain, including that of President Azaña, which expressed regret for the killings and demanded their end. The re-creation of the Republican state effectively terminated this brutal kind of mob rule by early 1937. It would only reappear again when the Republic's governmental machinery crumbled in the last months of the war. By contrast, the carnage never diminished in Nationalist Spain. If anything, it worsened over time. Vigilantism could have been effectively limited, if not eliminated altogether, by the military commanders. They not only failed to do that but also even encouraged the violence. Most of them being colonial officers, they merely put into practice the brutal methods that they had learnt from years of vicious campaigns against the 'heathen natives' in Morocco: the enemy had to be exterminated and the potentially hostile population paralysed by sheer terror. In turn, the

Catholic establishment blessed the orgy of blood, since, in its eyes, the Nationalists were engaged in a holy crusade against the Godless heretics of the 'anti-Spain'.

In regard to the evolution and organisation of the two camps, this work underlines how the rise to power of General Franco and Largo Caballero (and later Negrín) and the settling of the internal differences in the spring of 1937 (the Nationalists in April in Salamanca and the Republicans one month later in Barcelona) can be seen as parallel attempts by both sides to centralise, co-ordinate and mobilise all the human and material resources at their disposal to deliver victory. This proved much easier for the Nationalists. Despite their different agendas, there was a tradition of collaboration between the different forces of the right. Their shared authoritarian values the 'fascistisation' undertaken by all of them during the 1930s – and tacit agreement to subordinate their activities to the authority of the army facilitated the task. By contrast, the infighting that had historically plagued the left continued unabated until the last days of the war. The Republican camp never achieved the community of objectives and efforts of the opposite side. The competing aims of the central government with those of the Basque and Catalan administrations, the left's traditional aversion to militarism and centralisation, and the clashes between reformists and revolutionaries, Marxists and libertarians, among others, fragmented the different forces fighting for the Republic and were never satisfactorily resolved.

The uniformity achieved by praetorian discipline over its political constituency provided the Nationalists with a clear advantage. Franco could build an efficient army, a unified rear and a relatively cohesive and centralised state and economy with which to wage the war effort. However, to explain the Republic's ultimate implosion and capitulation in terms of its own internal squabbling only provides part of the story. This work stresses how the link between the domestic reality and the international context was also a crucial reason for Franco's decisive victory. Foreign intervention and so-called 'non-intervention', determined, to a large extent, the course and outcome of the war. At the very outset, in July 1936, it was only the timely Italo-German airlift of Franco's Army of Africa that transformed a failing coup into a successful march towards Madrid. Equally, the arrival of Soviet aid and the mobilisation by the Comintern of thousands of volunteers in the autumn of 1936 saved the Spanish capital and helped prolong the war.

One must never forget that a war is fought with tanks, planes and bullets. In Spain, a country lacking any significant arms industry, the regular and steady procurement of weapons from abroad proved crucial. It is, therefore, ludicrous to continue to offer the old cliché that Stalin's perfidy was responsible for the Republic's defeat. Of course, the Soviet Union did not intervene in Spain for altruistic reasons. It was well paid for its services and tried to impose a political agenda favourable to its own interests within the Republican camp. However, it was the only major power which, throughout the conflict, was prepared to sell arms to the Republic and send military advisers. Without Soviet weapons and support to mobilise the Republic's financial resources, the war would have ended much sooner. It was Fascist bombs and troops, combined with Western hypocrisy, which dictated the ultimate outcome of the Spanish tragedy. Moreover, the disturbing conclusion that emerges from examining Italian and German sources is that neither of the Fascist dictatorships was prepared to risk a major confrontation over Spain. Had the Western powers acted with genuine impartiality, the war might have ended in a very different fashion – and certainly not with Franco's outright victory. It is telling that both Azaña and Negrín blamed Britain and not the Axis for the Republican defeat. The Baldwin administration began by turning a blind eye to blatant Italian intervention in Spain and, later, sealed the monstrous farce of the non-intervention agreement that not only placed the legal government of Spain on a par with the army rebels but also effectively imposed a one-sided arms embargo. Later, under Chamberlain, the British government prayed for Franco's victory. But the sacrifice of 'Red' Spain for the sake of appeasing the dictators proved hollow, as it did not preserve peace on the continent. On the contrary, Western appeasement might have even accelerated the march towards the horrors of the Second World War. During their common Spanish adventure, Germany and Italy sealed the Axis pact and perfected their military techniques, while their territorial ambitions were only emboldened by the impunity with which their tanks, planes and troops acted, despite the existence of a non-intervention agreement. The Western stance certainly ensured that Spaniards would 'enjoy' a Francoist future.

# Acknowledgements

In the years it has taken me to write this book, I have incurred many debts. First of all, I should like to express my gratitude to the Cañada Blanch Centre at the London School of Economics, a research facility that never fails to provide an ideal environment for any Hispanist working in London. Its director, Professor Paul Preston, has always been a source of inspiration to me, offering steadfast support and encouragement. Indeed, this book is heavily indebted to his enlightening work on the Spanish Civil War. I should also like to thank the staff of the Fundación Pablo Iglesias in Madrid and the Centre d'Estudis d'Historia Contemporánia (Biblioteca Figueras) and the Ateneu Enciclopèdic Popular in Barcelona for their assistance.

During my research in Spain I was fortunate to interview a number of people who had lived through the war. Their accounts were always moving and helped me understand the madness and passions triggered by the conflict. I am deeply indebted to Carmen Salvadó, Ramón Castelló and Miquel Serrano in Lleida; Rafael Puerta and Alberto Guerrero in Madrid; and Ana Torres, Angel Romero, Juan Ferrer, Lidia Bosch and Domingo Monsuri in Valencia for sharing their memories with me.

I am also grateful to several friends and colleagues: first of all, I am indebted to Jonathan Smele for his meticulous proof-reading of and helpful suggestions on the entire text; I was also extremely fortunate to have draft chapters of this book read and commented upon by two of the foremost experts on the subject, Helen Graham and Enrique Moradiellos; and I should also like to thank Jerry Blaney, Angela Cenarro, Christopher Ealham, Darren Olley and Agustí Salvadó for their advice and help, and Carlos Puerta, Paula Pinto, Joan Miquel Reichs and Montserrat Salvadó for their cordial hospitality during my visits to Spain.

Finally, I could never express the debt I owe to my wife, Alison Pinington. She not only consented to read and offer suggestions on every draft of this book but also accepted with her unique good humour and unfailing support my constant research trips abroad, my heavy workload and my variable moods.

Without the help, support and encouragement of all these friends and colleagues, this book would probably never have been completed. Of course, any errors in the text are entirely mine.

# Abbreviations

ACNP    *Asociación Católica Nacional de Propagandistas* (National and Catholic Association of Propagandists) – the influential Catholic lay association created in 1909 which played a leading role in the establishment of the CEDA and the pursuit of a legalist strategy to take control of the Republic.

AR    *Acción Republicana* (Republican Action) – the party of progressive Republicans led by Manuel Azaña.

CEDA    *Confederación Española de Derechas Autónomas* (Spanish Confederation of Autonomous Rightist Parties) – the coalition of rightist and Catholic groups founded in 1933 and led by Jose María Gil Robles.

CGT    *Confédération Générale du Travail* (General Confederation of Labour) – the main French trade union.

CNCA    *Confederación Nacional Católica Agraria* (National Catholic Confederation of Agrarians). Founded in 1917 and closely connected to the ACNP, this organisation provided the mass base for the CEDA.

CNT    *Confederación Nacional del Trabajo* (National Labour Confederation) – the Anarcho-syndicalist trade union, founded in 1910.

CRT    *Confederación Regional del Trabajo* (Regional Confederation of Labour) – the Catalan branch of the CNT.

CTV    *Corpo di Truppe Volontarie* (Volunteer Troop Corps) – Italian forces sent to Spain to fight for the Nationalists during the Civil War.

FAI    *Federación Anarquista Ibérica* (Iberian Anarchist Federation) – a group created in 1927 by Anarchists with the objective of imposing their principles on the CNT.

FET    *Falange Española Tradicionalista* (Spanish Traditionalist Falange) – the Francoist party, also known as the 'National Movement', created by the merging of different right-wing groups in April 1937.

FNTT    *Federación Nacional de Trabajadores de la Tierra* (National
Federation of Land Workers) – the agricultural workers'
section of the UGT.

IR    *Izquierda Republicana* (The Republican Left) – the political
force which emerged from the merger in April 1934 of
Azaña's *Acción Republicana*, the left-wing section of the
PRRS and other smaller parties such as the Galician
Republican Party of Santiago Casares Quiroga.

IRA    *Instituto de Reforma Agraria* (Institute of Agrarian
Reform) – the state body established in 1933 with the
objective of financing and supervising the implementation of
the agrarian reform.

JAP    *Juventudes de Acción Popular* (Popular Action Youth) – the
youth section of the CEDA.

JSU    *Juventudes Socialistas Unificadas* (United Socialist Youth) –
Formed in the spring of 1936 by the amalgamation of the
Socialist and the Communist Youth, this group effectively fell
under the control of the Communists.

NIA    Non-Intervention Agreement – the pact adhered to by 27
European nations in September 1936 with the objective of
ensuring the isolation and arms blockade of the Spanish
Civil War.

NIC    Non-intervention Committee. Based in London, this was the
supervising body of the NIA. It was staffed by the
ambassadors of every signatory.

NKVD    *Narodnyi Komissariat Vnutrennikh Del* (People's
Commissariat for Internal Affairs) – the Soviet secret police.

PCE    *Partido Comunista de España* (Spanish Communist Party) –
the party that resulted from the merger of the two original
and small Spanish Communist parties in November 1921.

PNV    *Partido Nacionalista Vasco* (Basque Nationalist Party) – the
leading Nationalist group in the Basque Country. It was
founded by Sabino Arana in 1895.

POUM    *Partido Obrero Unificado Marxista* (Workers' Party of
Marxist Unification) – the small revolutionary Marxist
group formed in 1935 by the merger of two parties of
Communist dissidents, the Left Communist Party led by the
former Trotskyist Andreu Nin and Joaquín Maurín's Bloc of
Workers and Peasants.

PRRS    *Partido Republicano Radical Socialista* (Radical Socialist
Republican Party) – the Jacobin and anti-clerical party

|        | |
|--------|---|
|        | which formed part of the governmental coalitions of 1931–3. Divided in 1933, its left wing joined Azaña to form *Izquierda Republicana* and the right joined Diego Martínez Barrios to set up *Unión Republicana*. |
| PSOE   | *Partido Socialista Obrero Español* (Spanish Socialist Workers Party) – founded in 1879. |
| PSUC   | *Partido Socialista Unificado de Cataluña* (United Socialist Party of Cataluña) – Formed in July 1936 by the fusion of four parties, the PSUC included the Catalan section of the PCE and that of the PSOE. However, the most important component was the Catalanist Unió Socialista de Catalunya. |
| SIM    | *Servicio de Investigación Militar* (Military Intelligence Service) – the Republican intelligence service created in August 1937. |
| SOMA   | *Sindicato de Obreros Mineros Asturianos* (Union of Asturian Mineworkers) – Established in 1910, this was one of the most important sections of the UGT. |
| SSOO   | *Sindicatos de Oposición* (Opposition Trade Unions) – a combination of different unions, mostly from Valencia and Barcelona, which were expelled from or which abandoned the CNT during the radicalisation of the years 1932–3. In 1936 some rejoined the CNT but others went over to the UGT. |
| UGT    | *Unión General de Trabajadores* (General Union of Labourers) – the main Socialist-controlled trade union, created in 1889. |
| UP     | *Unión Patriótica* (Patriotic Union) – the political movement created in the 1920s to support the dictatorship of General Primo de Rivera. |
| UR     | *Unión Republicana* (Republican Union) – the party led by Diego Martínez Barrios and formed in September 1934 by those Radicals who had followed him in the split with Lerroux's Radical Party and a section of the PRRS. |

# Maps

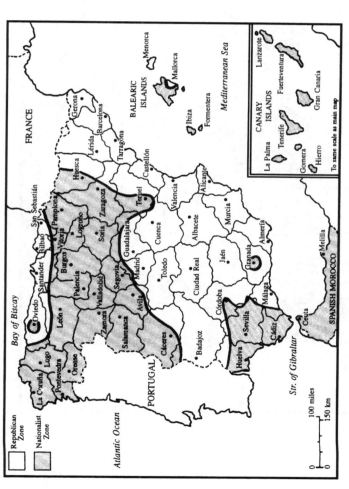

Map 1  *The division of Spain, end of July 1936*

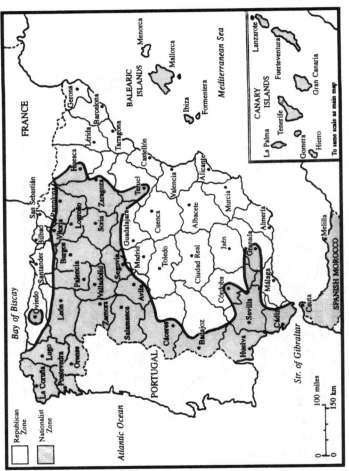

Map 2   *The division of Spain, August 1936*

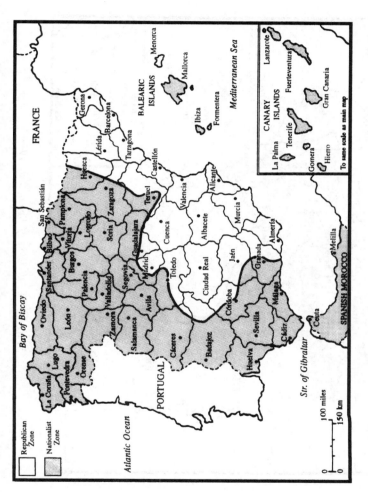

Map 3 *The division of Spain, October 1937*

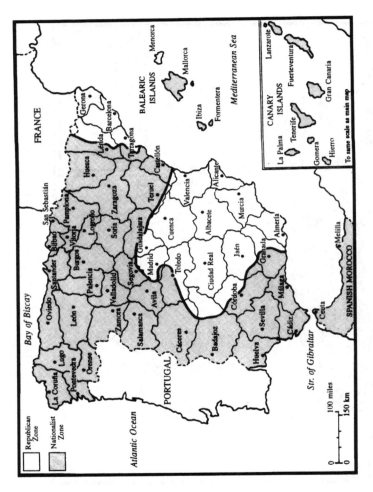

Map 4   *The division of Spain, July 1938*

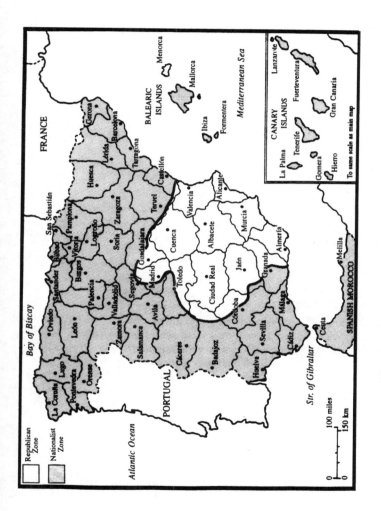

Map 5   *The division of Spain, February 1939*

# 1

# The Painful Road to Modernity

So far this year, more than 20 people have been killed by the Civil Guard ... In fact, Spain lives in a state of perpetual civil war: on the one hand, the people who fight peacefully for their livelihood and rights, on the other, the authorities that deny them their livelihood and rights at gun-point.[1]

## The fading charm of Spanish Liberalism

The origins of the Spanish Civil War are deeply rooted in the country's history. The religious fanaticism and fierce rhetoric surrounding the conflict were largely borrowed from the legendary *Reconquista*, the almost 800-year struggle to expel the Moors from the peninsula. The clash between state centralism and peripheral nationalisms also evoked the War of Succession of the early eighteenth century, when the Bourbons crushed Catalan autonomy. Equally, the cruelty and passion displayed by both sides mirrored the fierce brutality of the nineteenth-century civil wars fought between Carlists and Liberals.[2] Nowhere else in Europe had the transition from feudalism to capitalism produced such a protracted and merciless conflict. Closer in time, the failure of the Restoration Monarchy (1874–1931) is of paramount importance in understanding the political radicalism and social polarisation that finally exploded in the carnage of 1936–9.

The return of the Bourbons to the throne in December 1874 seemingly inaugurated a period of political stability based on a modern constitutional order. Yet elements of the *ancien régime* were still dominant in political and civil society, and their persistence, in an era of rapid cultural and economic modernisation, led to the social and political upheaval that in Spain (as elsewhere in Europe) characterised the inter-war years. In this context, the Spanish fratricidal conflict was

1

the fiercest battle in a European civil war, which had been raging on the continent since the Bolshevik seizure of power in October 1917, and included, amongst other events, the consolidation of Soviet Russia, the rise of Fascism in Italy, the Nazi takeover in Germany and the establishment of royalist and military dictatorships throughout central and eastern Europe.[3]

By the end of the nineteenth century, Spain, once the largest colonial empire in the world, was a country relegated to the sidelines of Europe. Her stunning defeat by the United States in 1898 brought to an end the last glimmers of imperial splendour. In an era of Social Darwinism, when the health of nations appeared to be marked by the acquisition of colonies, Spain seemed sick and troubled. The loss in that war of most of the overseas territories (Cuba, the Philippines, Puerto Rico, Guam, etc.) exposed her overall inability to remain on a par with the leading powers of the Western world.

In this moment of trauma and decline, the nation seemed united by the new magical formula: *Regeneración*, or the thorough overhauling of Spain's social, economic and ideological foundations. With the country enjoying an artistic and literary golden age, it was the intellectuals who, by concentrating their attention on Spain's maladies, undermined the moral legitimacy of the regime. The so-called 'Generation of 1898' was formed by an eclectic group of novelists, poets and philosophers who contemplated Spain's obscurantism and backwardness with pessimism. Their prescribed solutions ranged from Pío Baroja and Miguel de Unamuno's progressive belief in mobilisation from below to José Ortega y Gasset's search for a moral elite and Joaquín Costa's call for a strong figure, 'an Iron Surgeon', to extirpate the corruption of politics and carry out national regeneration from above.[4] These approaches constituted the two roads to modernity, the democratic and the authoritarian, whose final clash would take place in 1936.

In all external aspects, *fin de siècle* Spain possessed a modern parliamentarian system. Following the restoration of the Bourbons after a military coup in December 1874, the architect of the regime, the Conservative Antonio Cánovas del Castillo, brought to an end the strife of previous decades by conceiving a political formula through which the governing elites could enjoy power without the need to resort to praetorian intervention as the only instrument of change. He agreed to alternate in office with another political party, the Liberals, led by Práxedes Mateo Sagasta. The 1876 Constitution consolidated the fundamental freedoms of expression and association; Catholicism was declared the state religion but private practice of other faiths was allowed; political parties and trade unions were permitted to exist and to voice their views in a large number of local and national newspapers. With the introduction in 1890 of universal male suffrage and trial by jury, Spain appeared to be in the vanguard of Europe's modern political orders. In reality, two dynastic or monarchist formations, Conservatives and Liberals, enjoyed a monopoly of power, alternating in office so systematically that the practice was known as *turno pacífico* (peaceful rotation).[5] However, they were hardly parties in the modern sense of the word. Apart from timid anticlericalism and a greater emphasis on civil values on the part of the Liberals, there was little difference between them. Both were groups of notables linked by clientelism and endogamy. Stunning levels of nepotism resulted in parliaments resembling committees of friends exchanging verbose speeches and avoiding clashes over real issues.[6] This governing elite was linked with the ruling economic classes, the landed and financial elites, while the commercial and industrial bourgeoisie was the junior partner.[7]

At the apex of the Liberal order was the Crown. In Restoration Spain, the principle of national sovereignty shared by monarch and parliament concealed the potential for autocracy.[8] The king was the commander-in-chief of the armed forces and, as head of state, could dissolve parliament, appoint or dismiss governments, veto legislation and sign international treaties. He also possessed vast powers of patronage with the conferment of titles and rewards. During the Restoration, the alliance of altar and throne was re-created. As religious congregations expanded, the clergy experienced a revival in power and wealth, obtaining almost total control of primary and secondary education, as well as a leading role in social functions such as the operating of charitable trusts and the running of orphanages and hospitals. If the Church was the ideological guardian of the monarchy, the armed forces were its praetorian guard. The second clause of the Law of the Constitution of the Army, of 29 November 1878, stated that the military had as its primary function the defence of the nation from its internal enemies. Thus, any social unrest was followed automatically by the suspension of the constitution and the declaration of martial law, granting the army final control over the maintenance of public order.[9] José Berruezo, a leading Anarcho-syndicalist in 1920s Santa Coloma de Gramenet (Barcelona), experienced the clerical intolerance and police abuse of those who pursued social or political alternatives to the established canon. Aged 14, he was grabbed by a civil guard and branded 'a son of a whore' when trying to convince miners to attend classes in the local workers' institute. In his small town, the most prominent opponent of proletarian cultural centres was none other than the local priest, Don Celeste.[10]

The functioning of Liberal Spain hinged on electoral falsification, widespread political apathy and, when necessary, physical violence. Elections in Spain did not produce governments: rather each administration rigged the results in advance and ensured a working majority in the next Cortes or parliament. Fundamental in underpinning the electoral results were the so-called *caciques* (local political bigwigs). Varying in composition from province to province, the *caciques* could be made up of moneylenders, landowners or their agents, civil servants and even priests. They were the link between the distant and alien state and the estranged localities.[11] They delivered the votes of their constituency and, in return, were allowed to run their areas as private fiefdoms and to bend legislation to benefit their clientele and punish the recalcitrant.

*Caciquismo* in the country and the governing oligarchy in Madrid relied upon a background of slow economic development, low political awareness and widespread cultural backwardness. The endurance of that situation was a deterrent to national modernisation and resulted in the unchallenged domination of the vested interests, as well as in a socially and economically fragmented Spain. By leaving education largely in the hands of the Church, the Liberal state did not forge a national mechanism to give a common sense of belonging to the citizenry.[12] Nor could the army fulfil this function. It lacked the prestige of its Prussian counterpart or the revolutionary tradition of the French army. Social imperialism – successfully used in other European states to divert domestic tension – could not be used in Spain.[13] The unfair recruitment system (*quintas*), by which the wealthy could buy themselves out of the military service, the frequent use of the armed forces to quell social unrest and the slaughter of some 60,000 soldiers from humble origins in the disastrous colonial wars of the 1890s quashed any patriotic sentiment within the working classes.

Judged by Western Europe's standards, *fin de siècle* Spain lagged far behind in terms of economic modernisation. The short-term planning of most administrations, coupled with the need for quick pecuniary relief, led to a significant part of the rich mineral rights falling into the hands of foreign companies. By 1910, 66 per cent of the population were engaged in the primary sector of the economy; rates of illiteracy were around 56 per cent, with only 26 per cent of those aged 18 or under receiving proper school tuition; and infant mortality was about 200 per thousand.[14]

The transition from feudalism to modern capitalist production failed to modernise effectively the agrarian sector. The transformation of the land into a commodity that could be bought or sold freely, the so-called *desamortización*, offered the traditional landed elites the opportunity to turn their feudal privileges into capitalist rights of private property, converting former dues into rents and rationalising the overall exploitation. This benefited both the landed magnates and those well-off farmers, urban speculators and financiers who took advantage of the situation to buy the land. Thus, an enlarged oligarchy of wheat-growers and wine and olive oil producers closely connected with the country's financial elites emerged as the new powerful ruling class. Many of them became absentee landowners, who regarded their property as a source of prestige, neglected investment and left administrators to run their estates. Communal and ecclesiastical land was sold in large chunks to the highest bidder at public auction and thereby aggravated even further the unequal distribution of land-ownership in the country. Labourers lost their long-term leases and the ancestral rights that had been enshrined in the feudal order and were left to the mercy of market forces. As a result, agriculture did not produce food surpluses to feed the growing urban population, and seasonal employment and starvation wages ensured a lack of demand for manufactured products. These conditions severely restricted the possibility of an industrial take-off on a national scale.[15] Furthermore, economic development was an uneven process that exacerbated the structural differences between north and south, city and countryside. The fertile north, with its abundant rain, green pastures and livestock, and the east, with a dynamic, export-oriented market-gardening sector, consolidated a class of small tenants and farmers. Their distrust of the central state made them support political options ranging from Carlism to federal republicanism and regionalism. In the poorer, central cereal-growing region of Castilla, the agrarian norm was the co-existence of large landowners with peasant smallholders and farmers. Here, the inherent Catholicism of the peasantry tended to produce more conservative social attitudes and to diminish social conflict. The Church's pastoral activity and loan provision gained mass support for its Catholic trade union, the *Confederación Nacional Católica Agraria* (CNCA). The Castilian peasants would form later the popular echelons of the right-wing parties in the 1930s and the cannon fodder of the Nationalist armies.

By contrast, Spain's southern half (Southern Castilla, Extremadura and Andalucía) was marked by the huge economic gap between landowners and landless peasants. Historically, the best land had been partitioned between the warring nobility and ecclesiastical orders in the last stages of the *Reconquista*. During the Liberal reforms (1830s–1850s), the aristocracy (now joined by a class of urban speculators and merchants) confirmed their property rights as owners of the *latifundios* (large estates) and retained their influence in national politics. The vast majority of the population remained a pool of cheap labour, subject to the whimsical authority of the administrators of the absentee landowners. Given that monoculture was the norm, peasants were usually dependent on a single source of employment which, even then, was only available for part of the year – at planting and harvesting times. Not surprisingly, the southern *braceros* (literally, those working with their arms, or *brazos*) or *jornaleros* (those working for a fixed salary, or *jornal*) enjoyed the lowest living standards in Spain, working in terribly hot weather, from sunrise to sunset, for starvation wages. The lack of any substantial rural middle class exacerbated class divisions and the Church was perceived as the institution that legitimised this quasi-feudal oppressive order. Consequently, the south became the centre of an almost primitive type of social conflict, experiencing frequent and violent outbursts of anticlerical and insurrectional Jacqueries that were put down with equally brutal ferocity by the paramilitary police, the Civil Guard.[16]

By the turn of the century, in contrast, a modern capitalist economy had developed around the cotton-textile industry of Cataluña, the iron and steel factories of the Basque Country and the mining concerns of Asturias. The emergence of these industrial enclaves resulted in a dual economy and underlined the cultural and social differences within Spain. Indeed, the contrast between the progress of urban centres and the backwardness of the countryside was staggering. By 1910, Barcelona and Madrid had surpassed half a million inhabitants, Valencia had over 200,000, and ten other cities had populations of about 100,000. These urban communities enjoyed the accoutrements of a modernising world: trams, cars, the telegraph, the telephone, electricity, gas, etc. Equally, these societies presented a richer social stratum – a commercial and financial bourgeoisie, a middle class made up of the liberal professions, a petty bourgeoisie of artisans and shopkeepers, and a growing proletariat. These social divisions often translated into a topographic separation of the residents. The medieval walls of cities were pulled down and *ensanches* (large extensions) were built to accommodate the rising population. These new areas were designed with all modern facilities to lodge the wealthy classes. By contrast, the workers were pushed into the suburbs or into inner-city slums where they had to pay high rents and endure overcrowded tenements that frequently lacked the most basic services.

A lack of social legislation, low wages, food shortages and a regressive fiscal system fuelled class conflict.[17] Workers' strikes co-existed with more traditional forms of popular protest, such as *motines de subsistencias* (food riots) and local revolts against *consumos* (taxation on foodstuffs) and *quintas* (military recruitment). However, in an overwhelmingly rural and socially fragmented society, there was no nationwide political movement that could benefit from widespread discontent. Popular unrest hardly went beyond its locale and was, therefore, easily dealt with as a question of public order. Matters began to change, however, by the turn of the century, when the slow but steady growth of social mobilisation, economic modernisation and political awareness threatened the hegemony of the elites and the *caciques*.

After the short-lived experiment of the First Republic (1873–4), Republican parties survived as little more than small rival factions. Yet after 1898 they began to make modest but important strides in some cities where it was becoming increasingly difficult for the dynastic governments to fix the election results. They enjoyed the support of the progressive middle class, saw a large number of intellectuals join their ranks and retained considerable sympathy amongst some working-class sectors.

Socially exploited and politically neglected, the proletariat and the peasantry constituted the largest and most obvious dissenting groups. However, their effective organisation only began to take shape in the last quarter of the nineteenth century and their division – both at an ideological and at a geographical level – characterised their evolution. Indeed, a libertarian tendency flourished in the south and east, while Marxism became dominant in the centre and north. Both shared the belief that emancipation had to come through a process of education. Socialist *Casas del Pueblo* (People's Houses) and Libertarian *Ateneos Racionalistas* (Rationalist Centres) sought to raise the class-consciousness of the workers and to dissuade them from harmful pastimes such as gambling and drinking. Yet, the bitter rivalry between Marxists and anarchists made the unity of the proletariat, even in crucial moments, ephemeral.

The arrival in 1868 of the Italian Giuseppe Fannelli, a disciple of the leading Russian Anarchist Mikhail Bakunin, gave that political current an early start. Consequently, the two pioneer Spanish workers' organisations were under Anarchist control: the Spanish Regional Federation (FRE, 1870–81) and the Regional Federation of Spanish

Workers (FRTE, 1881–8). Socialism arrived later, in December 1871, in the hands of Paul Lafargue, Karl Marx's son-in-law. The Spanish Socialist Party (PSOE) was not established until 1879, and its trade union, *La Unión General de Trabajadores* (UGT), was founded in 1888. Spanish Socialism experienced a steady but painfully slow development and, unlike its European counterparts, failed to become the clearly dominant force of the labour movement. Both the party and the trade union normally shared the same authoritarian leadership, whose rigid interpretation of Marxism bore little relation to the Spanish situation. They overlooked the agrarian question and their deterministic views led them to an innate belief in the necessity of the class struggle and the inevitability of the final triumph of the proletariat. Yet while the official rhetoric was full of radicalism, in practice they laid more emphasis on questions of organisation and daily social disputes. What was the point, they asked, in planning the destruction of capitalist society – and especially of making sacrifices in readiness for its coming – if it was going to happen anyway?[18]

Socialism's gradualist strategy proved successful amongst the so-called 'labour aristocracy' of the small-scale concerns and skilled craftsmen of Madrid and other Castilian cities. Patient organisational skills gained the Socialists vital inroads into key industrial areas, such as the Asturian mines and the Basque steel, shipping and iron works, where the local leadership often followed more militant tactics than those prescribed by the Executive Committee.[19] Between 1900 and 1913, following its consolidation in the industrial northern areas and its success in organising, at a national level, miners and railway workers, the UGT's membership shot up from 15,000 to almost 150,000.[20] However, the absence of an agrarian strategy prevented its expansion in the rural south. The Socialists' efforts also failed in Cataluña, the leading industrial region and, by default, in the neighbouring regions of Valencia and Aragón. There the Socialists' dogmatic isolation from other left-wing Republican groups clashed with the more pragmatic approach of a long-established, moderate Catalan trade-unionism. Equally, their reluctance to participate in many strikes, such as the massive general stoppage of 1902, left them alienated from a radicalised proletariat. This feeling of estrangement was greatly enhanced when the Socialists made the glaring mistake, in 1899, of moving the UGT's headquarters from Barcelona to Madrid, the nation's political but not industrial capital.[21] Furthermore, their fixation with politics led them to enter, albeit with admirable courage, into the electoral contest. However, a political system where ballot falsification was endemic, together with the Socialists' determination to preserve the isolation of the movement from other 'bourgeois' forces, led to dismal outcomes. However, Socialist councillors did begin to be elected (in small numbers) in the 1890s in the Basque Country and in Madrid in 1905, when the party's leader, Pablo Iglesias, and two others obtained seats in the municipal administration. Ironically, though, they had to resort, in the capital, to the same fraudulent methods that their opponents had always used to secure election, including the forging of ballot papers.[22]

By contrast, the Libertarian movement enjoyed periods of feverish activity followed by others of repression and clandestine activity. Anarchist 'apostles' carried the new gospel from village to village. There they converted the downtrodden labourers by heralding the arrival of a new era of justice, liberty and land redistribution. Anarchist ideas seemed to provide an ideological coherence to a tradition in which the popular classes, distrusting the state and politics, relied on direct action to redress their grievances.[23] It was, indeed, a more logical appeal than the reformist approach offered by the Socialists. However, the Anarchists' loathing of organisational issues led to constant and badly planned revolutionary outbursts that were easily quelled and that led to heavy casualties.

Also, the Anarchists' inability (or unwillingness) to overcome a subculture marked by the legendary heroism and violence of the so-called groups of affinity or groups of action (a small number of comrades who shared anarchist goals) proved costly to the proletariat. The activities of these groups, the so-called 'propaganda by the deed', facilitated the activities of agents provocateurs and provided the authorities with the excuse to carry out stern reprisals. Thus, in the volatile Andalusian countryside, a spate of crimes led in 1881 to police claims of the existence of a secret society, *La Mano Negra* (The Black Hand), whose objective was to murder the main landowners. After thousands of arrests and several executions, the southern Anarchist organisations were shattered. In the 1890s, Barcelona saw a spiral of bombings and merciless repression, including widespread torture and falsified charges that sent many innocents to the gallows.[24] Additionally, workers had to endure a violent offensive by the employers that concluded with the collapse of the moderate textile trade union, *Las Tres Clases del Vapor*. Soon thereafter the Catalan labour movement suffered a massive setback with the defeat of the General Strike in 1902 and only showed signs of revival with the creation, in 1907, of *Solidaridad Obrera*. This new organisation adopted the revolutionary syndicalism of the French *Confédération Générale du Travail* (CGT) which rejected both electoral politics and anarchist individualist violence. Instead, it attempted to organise workers into strong trade unions (*sindicatos*) with which to lead the economic struggle by means of direct action, including sabotage, boycotts and strikes.

The turn of the century also saw the consolidation of anti-centralist political forces. In the Basque case, the *Partido Nacionalista Vasco* (Basque Nationalist Party, PNV), founded by Sabino Arana in 1895, was an anti-modernist reaction against the dangers to the alleged 'purity' of the Basque race and culture that had been brought about by industrialism and Spanish immigration. It inherited from Carlism its ultra-Catholicism and nostalgia for the past, summed up in the motto 'God and Ancient Laws' (*Fueros*), which was now combined with quasi-separatist positions. Catalan nationalism enjoyed more rapid success to become a hegemonic force locally, and even a considerable factor in national politics. Up to the 1920s, the dominant Catalanist formation was the *Lliga Regionalista*, founded in 1901 (the year in which it obtained an astounding electoral victory in Barcelona). Having lost their lucrative colonial markets, sectors of the Catalan industrial bourgeoisie moved away from a regime that could not defend their economic interests. Led by Francesc Cambó, the *Lliga* always trod a pragmatic road, oscillating between a fierce criticism of the political monopoly held by the southern and central landed elites to an ambition to be part of the governing class, so as to ensure an axial role for Catalan industrial interests.[25]

The lethal combination of a radicalised proletariat, a nationalist movement, an intransigent employer class and a restless officer corps resulted in Barcelona, Spain's largest industrial metropolis, becoming the main centre of political conflict. To add insult to injury, since 1901 the Catalan capital had witnessed the rise of a Republican demagogue, Alejandro Lerroux. A skilful orator and organiser, Lerroux took advantage of the demoralisation of the labour movement to build up a formidable political machinery with which his Radical Party gained a foothold in municipal politics. His skill in mobilising the lower classes, at least until 1914, earned Lerroux the nickname of the 'Emperor of the Paralelo', the proletarian quarter of the city. His followers were roused with crude anticlericalism, anti-Catalanism and vague promises of a forthcoming revolution following the establishment of a republic. Lerroux's incendiary pamphlets, calling among other things for the burning of convents, further polarised the situation. Yet, for all his radicalism, Lerroux's efforts enjoyed the goodwill of Liberal administrations in Madrid, who were not unwilling to back such a shady character if he could help stem the rising tide of Catalanism. Lerroux's unprincipled opportunism and dubious deals not only underlined the murky foundations of Restoration Spain but would also spell trouble when, in the 1930s, his party became dominant in national politics.[26]

After 1898 the stability of the regime was jeopardised by the frequent praetorian intervention in politics. In 1900 the Spanish army boasted 499 generals, 578 colonels and over 23,000 officers for some 80,000 troops (six times more officers than in France, which had an standing army of 180,000 soldiers). This represented a cancer for a state that devoted over 40 per cent of its budget to defence. However, 70 per cent of it went on officers' salaries, thereby hindering the modernisation of the armed forces. Furthermore, by now embittered and traumatized by the colonial defeat, the officer corps grew sensitive to any civilian criticism.[27] Alienated from society, it began to claim the role of guardian of the sacred values of the nation: that is, the unity of the fatherland and the preservation of social order. The military saw the existing constitutional practices as inadequate to crush the pernicious effects of regionalism and class conflict. In this it found a ready ally in the new monarch. Crowned in 1902, Alfonso XIII, raised by Catholic and army preceptors, generally sided with his officers in their disputes with the politicians and frequently used his constitutional prerogatives to appoint and dismiss prime ministers, thereby furthering factionalism.[28]

In November 1905, some three hundred officers assaulted the offices of the satirical Catalanist journal *Cu-Cut*, having been enraged by its publication of an anti-militarist cartoon.[29] The existing Liberal government, led by Eugenio Montero Ríos, caught between the solidarity of the army corps and widespread Catalan outcries, was dismissed by the King and replaced by another Liberal administration, under Segismundo Moret, which was more ready to placate the army. Thus, in March 1906, the Law of Jurisdictions was introduced. Henceforth, any offence against the army, the monarchy or the fatherland was to come under military jurisdiction.[30] Civil supremacy had bowed to praetorian pressure, thereby heralding an ominous future. The indignation was such in Cataluña that all political parties, from the Carlists to the Regionalists, sealed a political alliance, the *Solidaridad Catalana*. The only exception was Lerroux's faction, which in January 1908 abandoned the other Republicans to form a separate Radical Party.

In the summer of 1909, Spain's involvement in a new colonial adventure in Morocco triggered days of widespread unrest that subsequently became known as the Tragic Week.[31] With memories of 1898 still fresh, the call-up of reservists to put down a native rebellion led to popular anger. A general strike against the war was easily pre-empted everywhere except in Barcelona, where events exploded: barricades went up and the previous years of violent anticlerical propaganda led to the burning of some fifty churches, convents and religious schools, as well as such macabre scenes as the exhumation of nuns' corpses. In turn, the state's response was brutal. Military courts tried 1725 individuals, sentencing 17 to death. Five of them were executed, including Francisco Ferrer Guardia, the well-known Anarchist director of the rationalist school *La Escuela Moderna*. This caused a major scandal, both in Spain and abroad. Ferrer was falsely accused of being the mastermind behind the insurrection, and his death sentence was based on the deposition of some Radicals eager to pin the blame on someone else. For many he remained a martyr, a man judicially assassinated for his revolutionary personality and his alleged part in a failed attempt against the King's life years earlier.[32]

Although not a political assault against the regime itself, the importance of the Tragic Week cannot be underestimated.[33] On a small scale, it foretold the savagery of the civil war: anti-military mutinies and anticlerical violence as an expression of the frustration of the working classes were drowned in the ensuing bloodbath. At the time, it also furthered the internal factionalism of the two ruling parties and strengthened the role of the Crown. So, the Liberals, with the agreement of the King, ousted the Conservative prime minister, Antonio Maura, from office in October 1909.[34] Maura, the most outstanding dynastic politician of the era, had pursued an agenda of political reform, alienating in the process many of the governing classes. According to his son Gabriel, Maura was astounded when the monarch accepted a resignation that he never tendered. Upon Maura's return from the royal palace, Gabriel even saw his father burst into tears for the first time. In 1913, when he refused to carry on with the *turno* fiction, Maura was abandoned by the bulk of his party. A minority followed the dismissed leader and created the *Maurista* movement, thus splitting the Conservatives. The *Mauristas* never formed a coherent party, but were a broad church united by their devotion to Maura, their monarchism and their bitter criticism of dynastic corruption. Its two currents, a Christian Democratic faction and a nationalist and anti-liberal tendency, could be said to have represented the two alternatives of modern right-wing politics in Spain.

The Tragic Week, by debunking its 'radicalism', also initiated the eclipse of the Radical Party amongst the Catalan proletariat.

*Solidaridad Obrera* decided to expand to the rest of the country in open competition with the UGT. Thus, the Anarcho-syndicalist trade union *La Confederación Nacional del Trabajo* (CNT) was created in a founding congress in Barcelona (30 October–1 November 1910). The Socialists abandoned their traditional sectarianism and established a *conjunción* (electoral alliance) with the Republicans, in the hope of establishing a progressive, bourgeois republic. Success came, in May 1910, when Pablo Iglesias became the first Socialist elected to parliament.

### The making of a revolution

It was the outbreak of the First World War which acted, as it did elsewhere in Europe, as a catalyst and accelerator of unprecedented levels of economic transformation and social mobilisation in Spain. The war heralded the arrival of mass politics, undermining those Liberal orders that hitherto had depended on the subservice of a large percentage of the population.

Spain did not enter the war but the war certainly entered Spain – and with a devastating impact. Initially, there was a consensus on neutrality. However, this soon broke down. Most dynastic politicians avoided taking sides, in a vain effort to ignore and be ignored by the events taking place on the continent. However, for other, non-dynastic political forces and for the cultural elites, the European conflict became a question of obsessive concern. For them, the war was perceived as an ideological clash, in which each of the warring factions came to symbolise certain transcendent values. Essentially, the right-wing political parties (the *Mauristas* and the Carlists), the landed classes, the court, the army and the clergy identified with the Central Powers: they were regarded as symbols of social order, hierarchical politics and monarchism. In contrast, the intellectuals, the professional middle classes, and those political groups who were against the existing status quo – Republicans, Socialists and Regionalists – were Francophiles: they believed that the triumph of the Entente would bring about democracy throughout Europe.[35]

The quarrel between the partisans of the Allies and those of the Central Powers generated such a violent debate that it acquired the quality of a moral civil war: a verbal clash between two Spains and a portent of the real civil war that lay a generation in the future.[36] This bitterness was exacerbated by the growing interference of the warring sides in the Spanish arena. In particular, shortages of paper gave the combatants the opportunity to fund (or even to buy) newspapers and thereby to influence editorials and public opinion. German intelligence services were certainly the most active. They organised the smuggling of weapons to Morocco to foster a rebellion in the French zone, funded Anarchist engagement in strikes and disruption of industrial production that was servicing the Entente war effort, hired gunmen to assassinate pro-Allied producers and bribed local officers for information on vessels carrying cargo to Allied ports (which would then be torpedoed by submarines).[37] Not only were Entente ships their prey; in fact, they destroyed over 30 per cent of Spain's merchant fleet.

Parallel to ideological polarisation, the war dramatically altered Spain's economy. Her neutral status facilitated sales to both camps, generating a period of fabulous profits in commercial and industrial sectors. But the impact of this was uneven and it exacerbated social and structural realities. The explosion in external demand, the drastic cut in imports, the hoarding of staple products, the collapse of the transport system and the increase in the amount of money in circulation brought about galloping inflation, shortages and a demographic flood from the depressed countryside to the buoyant cities, where recently-arrived workers had to endure appalling living conditions as well as derisory wages. Salaries could not keep up with mounting prices.[38] Thus, the disparity between the gloom of the proletariat and the extravagant lifestyle of the bourgeoisie fuelled food riots and an upsurge in strike activity. The severity of the crisis was such that, responding to grass-roots pressure, the UGT and the CNT sealed a labour pact in July 1916.[39]

Public sector workers (including army officers), whose economic conditions were equally ravaged by inflation and shortages, also began to organise themselves to defend their living standards. In 1915 the officers began to create the so-called *Juntas Militares de Defensa*, a kind of officers' trade union. Incensed by the prospective introduction of reforms and cutbacks in the officer corps, the military had become fiercely critical of the corruption of the ruling system, as well as of the favouritism exhibited by the regime, and the fast promotions which it awarded to the *Africanistas* – that is, those serving in Morocco.[40] Simultaneously, the Catalan industrial bourgeoisie sought to translate its recently gained economic strength into political terms. When the Liberal minister of finance, Santiago Alba, attempted to tax the war-related profits of trade and industry but not those of agriculture, the *Lliga* led the mobilisation of national industrial interests. In parliament it introduced, for the first time, the question of Catalan autonomy and directed with success the opposition to Alba's projects.[41]

During 1917, intertwined domestic and international events produced the crisis of authority of the regime. Republicans and the labour movement greeted with enthusiasm the fall of tsarism in March. At the end of the month, the UGT and the CNT signed a manifesto threatening to topple the ruling system with a general strike. In April, the King forced his prime minister, the Liberal Count Romanones, out of office when he attempted to follow the US example and break diplomatic relations with the Central Powers. When replaced by a rival Liberal administration, the Liberals split.[42] With the debate over neutrality heating up, a frightened monarch ordered his government to dissolve the *Juntas*. He could not help but draw parallels with the 'betrayal' of Tsar Nicholas II by many of his officers. However, the refusal of the *Juntas* to disband forced the collapse of the government after less than two months in office, and seemed to open the gates for political change. The widespread impression that the regime had reached a dead-end gained momentum when the King entrusted the Conservative leader, Eduardo Dato, with the task of forming a new administration. In theory, Alfonso was merely abiding by the constitution. However, these were not normal times. Endorsing the *turno* fiction at this critical moment meant the denial of the glaring necessity for reform. The Catalanist leader, Francesc Cambó even declared at this time that the most conservative thing to do was to be a revolutionary.[43] On 19 July the *Lliga*, with the support of the Republicans and the Socialists, organised an assembly of parliamentarians in Barcelona. Reminiscent of the early days of the French Revolution, it demanded the end of the old system and the summoning of a Constituent Cortes, to be convened by a national government whose members should represent the real will of the nation.[44]

Following the officers' defiance and then the parliamentarian rebellion, many believed in the summer of 1917 that the Bourbon dynasty was about to follow the fate of the Romanovs. Simó Piera, a leading Catalan Anarcho-syndicalist, wrote that everywhere – in cafés, on trams and in markets – a revolutionary atmosphere could be breathed.[45]

In the summer of 1917 it was far from clear whether Dato was the right man to save the regime. Unlike Maura, who was known for his forceful style and personal charisma, Dato was regarded as a compromiser and a court lackey and, therefore, not the ideal person to take tough decisions. Yet working in tandem with his minister of the interior, José Sánchez Guerra, his government was to prove more resourceful than others expected. Bearing in mind the danger posed by a possible collaboration of middle-class parties, the proletariat and the army, the Dato administration took a gamble: it decided to provoke the labour movement into an ill-timed revolutionary strike, so as to scare the middle classes and to provide an excuse to use the army to quell the disturbances. The government could then claim to be the saviour of Spain and the guarantor of law and order.[46]

During the 'hot summer' of 1917, the government managed to outwit a Socialist movement which, blinded by euphoric confidence, was willing to forego its traditional prudence and therefore paid the price of its revolutionary inexperience. The outbreak of a transport strike in Valencia in July provided the opportunity. The Socialists went to painful lengths to avoid the expansion of the transport conflict, but they constantly ran into the intransigence of the company – an intransigence which was supported, if not inspired, by the administration. Under pressure from their CNT partners, the PSOE and the UGT Executive Committees agreed to link the transport dispute with a revolutionary general strike. The Socialists believed that if the railway workers went ahead on their own, their organisation – built up so painfully over the previous years – would be destroyed and the whole labour movement would suffer the consequences. Additionally, there was such optimism that – for once – they did not pay heed to Pablo Iglesias, who from his sickbed argued strongly against it. Julián Besteiro and Andrés Saborit (for the PSOE) and Francisco Largo Caballero and Daniel Anguiano (for the UGT) were appointed members of the leading strike committee in Madrid. They then communicated the decision to their Republican and CNT allies in the rest of the country. After the stance of the officers and the gathering of parliamentarians, they believed that the regime would collapse like a house of cards.[47]

This moment represented the baptism of fire for Socialism as a leading political force in Spanish politics. It was, indeed, not only the first serious attempt to usher in democratic modernisation but also the first bid for power of those who had hitherto been perennially forced to remain in opposition. The intensity of the struggle and the hopes of the revolutionaries – as well as the cruelty of the repression – foretold the civil-war confrontation between the two Spains which was still looming on the horizon.

However, the general strike of August 1917 failed to spread beyond the main urban centres and, except in Asturias, was crushed in less than a week. Any hopes that the army would refuse to defend the regime were soon dashed. Unlike in Russia, the Spanish peasant soldiers had not been demoralised by years of defeats and war weariness. Consequently, they obeyed the orders of their superiors who, in turn, forgot all their reformist language of the previous two months. Economic concessions to the military, together with rumours spread by the government that foreign gold was behind the disturbances, removed the army's last hesitations: it was better to shoot workers in Spain, they concluded, than to dig trenches in France. The military response was shocking in its brutality. Cannons were used against workers' centres and popular demonstrations were machine-gunned, leaving dozens of casualties across the country.[48] Soon thereafter, frightened by the August events, the *Lliga* performed a sudden about-face and, in November 1917, joined a dynastic coalition government. With this act they effectively killed the reformist hopes that had been raised by the Assembly of July in Barcelona.[49]

## Rehearsal of a civil war

The violent suppression of the revolutionary movement not only dashed democratic hopes but also, ironically, sounded the death-knell of the Liberal regime in Spain. That it had been forced to rely upon military repression to survive underlined both the estrangement of the system from the rest of society and the consolidation of praetorian interference at the centre of decision-making. In fact, with social stability worsening, the constitutional order was effectively subverted as the army was not only increasingly needed to maintain public order but also, in alliance with the Crown, acted as an anti-constitutional force with power of veto over cabinets. Meanwhile, mounting inflation and worsening living standards fuelled constant working-class militancy and political turmoil. Assaults on shops and bakeries and strike activity reached a peak in the years 1919 to 1920. At the same time, in the aftermath of the First World War, Bolshevism threatened to sweep westwards across the continent, thus increasing revolutionary euphoria and initiating the richest period of revolutionary activity in Europe since 1848.

Fear of Bolshevism gripped all European governments. The establishment of the Communist International (Comintern) in March 1919, followed by the creation (albeit short-lived) of Soviet Republics in Hungary and Bavaria intensified that panic. In Spain, massive industrial and rural unrest rang alarm bells. With the post-war economic recession looming, employers planned to resort to the usual tactics of massive lay-offs and production cuts. Yet this could not easily be carried out in the face of a combative working class. Hence, a miniature civil war was in the offing. The carnage of this social conflict was to be a dress rehearsal of the violent class struggle of the 1930s.

From late 1918 many foreigners, in particular Russians and Germans, were being rounded up and deported from Spain.[50] Incidentally, Comintern agents, led by the Russian Mikhail Borodin, arrived in Spain in December 1919. Yet their attempts to create a strong Communist organisation met with very poor results.[51] Traumatised by the experience of 1917, most Socialist leaders were firmly against embarking upon fresh revolutionary adventures. Only some members of the Socialist Youth were prepared to oppose their seniors and to form a tiny Communist Party in April 1920. A more serious split took place one year later when the PSOE refused to endorse the Moscow International and a minority of its members broke away. Yet the Communists' membership and influence was fairly limited – even after the creation of a unified Communist Party (PCE) in November 1921. They found it impossible to offer a clear-cut programme to lure workers from the two established traditions of reformist socialism and radical Anarcho-syndicalism.[52] Their only significant inroads were in the UGT's Basque and Asturian strongholds, where the local leadership was split over their strategy against a concerted bourgeois offensive of cutting salaries in mines and factories. Consequently, 1922 and 1923 saw a massive wave of strikes in the coal and iron mines and steel foundries of these regions. Violence often flared between Communists endorsing confrontational tactics and Socialists seeking a negotiated solution. By 1923, after a bitter series of defeats of Communist-led strikes, Socialism was still dominant.

It was mainly the CNT that capitalised on the rising discontent of the post-war years. Unlike the Socialists, the *Cenetistas* concluded, after the defeat of 1917, that workers should intensify direct action at the workplace and abandon compromises with political parties. From mid-1918, rebellion flared up all over the agrarian south. News of the Bolshevik victory and the subsequent expropriation of landed estates in Russia provided the impulse to trigger an upheaval in the restless Spanish countryside. During the so-called *Trienio Bolchevique* (Three Bolshevik Years), workers' centres and unions sprang up, land was seized and strikes launched. The movement was only crushed after months of pitched battles in which the full might of the Civil Guard and the army was used.[53] Yet, it was in its urban strongholds where the CNT became most formidable. In the summer of 1918, Catalan

Anarcho-syndicalists abandoned the old craft trade unions and instead adopted the model of modern industrial unions (*Sindicatos Unicos*). Well-organised strikes, undertaken by fewer but much larger unions, soon resulted in astonishing victories for the proletariat. The turning-point took place in February 1919, when a dispute broke out at the Anglo-Canadian hydroelectric concern known as *La Canadiense*. The authorities and the employers were stunned by the strength of the Catalan proletariat. In a general strike lasting for 44 days, Barcelona was totally paralysed. To add insult to injury, the trade union of graphic artists even introduced 'red censorship' – the prevention of any publication hostile to the workers' position. The CNT's victory was unprecedented: the government promised an eight-hour working day and the company agreed both to accept the rehiring of its employees without penalties of any kind and to raise wages.[54] When the CNT held a congress at the *Teatro de la Comedia* in Madrid in December 1919, the organisation was at the peak of its power. By then, it claimed over 700,000 members, three times more than the UGT. The structure of the *Sindicato Unico* was adopted nationally and, amidst revolutionary optimism, the CNT voted for provisionally adhering to the Comintern.[55]

From 1919, social conflicts turned into veritable class warfare, as an alliance between the bourgeoisie, para-military groups and the army was sealed behind the back of a series of impotent governments in Madrid. In April 1919, Jaime Miláns del Bosch, Captain General of Barcelona, with the enthusiastic endorsement of the local economic elites, ordered the civil governor and his chief of police, whom he deemed to be 'too soft', to catch the train for Madrid. An old bourgeois rural militia dating from medieval times, *El Somatén,* was established in the cities and its members were granted permission to carry weapons, patrol the streets and arrest strikers. Meanwhile, industrialists hired gangs of thugs, whose task was to beat up, harass and even shoot leading Anarcho-syndicalists. In November 1919 the Catalan employers launched a massive lockout that lasted two months and left 200,000 workers jobless. One month later, a group of mostly Carlist workers founded the so-called *Sindicatos Libres*. Favoured by the local authorities, they were on a collision course with the CNT.[56]

With social disputes being solved by naked violence, many Spanish cities became battlefields. The carnage in Barcelona was such that it was dubbed the 'Chicago of the Mediterranean'. In this atmosphere of terror, the action groups began to take control of the CNT. Industrialists, foremen and rival trade-unionists were targets for their guns and bombs. In turn, CNT members were rounded up and deported to distant provinces (making the journey on foot and in chains) or were assassinated. The appointment of General Severiano Martínez Anido as civil governor of Barcelona in November 1920 marked the climax of this repression. For two years he ran Barcelona as his private fiefdom and counter-terrorism received official protection. Gunmen of the *Libres* were armed in military barracks and the notorious *Ley de Fugas* (that is, the shooting of captured Anarcho-syndicalists 'while trying to escape') was introduced. The CNT was decimated as hundreds of its best cadres were imprisoned or assassinated. Not surprisingly, most of them were the best-known 'moderate' Anarcho-syndicalist leaders. In March 1923 the most charismatic Catalan labour activist, Salvador Seguí, reputed for his opposition to the unrestrained activities of the groups, was killed. In this cycle of tit-for-tat retaliations, Prime Minister Dato, the Archbishop of Zaragoza and two former civil governors, amongst others, were shot dead. Seldom did a day pass without the newspapers reporting fresh assassinations or new acts of violence.[57]

To make matters worse, devastating news from the half-forgotten Moroccan adventure shocked the country in the summer of 1921. After the Spanish army had been defeated at Annual by the natives, the hasty retreat of its troops soon became a rout. Some 9,000 soldiers were killed and hundreds were taken prisoner. In a few days, all the territory conquered since 1909 was lost and the natives were at the gates of Melilla. Massive reinforcements were called up in an initial reaction of patriotism and revenge. However, as the troops became bogged down in a bloody campaign and politicians argued about the long-term strategy to follow, those feelings turned, in 1922, into calls for the heads of those responsible for this new disaster. The publication of the investigation undertaken by General Juan Picasso confirmed massive political and military flaws. A parliamentary commission was formed to discuss the issue of responsibilities. Its two Socialist members, Indalecio Prieto and Julián Besteiro, became leading voices in the criticism of a regime that had presided over the debacle. The close relationship between the King and *Africanista* officers (in particular his alleged encouragement of General Manuel Silvestre, the commander-in-chief of the forces at Annual) even personally implicated Alfonso.[58]

In this unabated climate of social violence and colonial mishap, the ruling economic classes began to demand an authoritarian solution as right-wing editorials praised the rise of Fascism in Italy and the Europe-wide political reaction which had followed the revolutionary push of the previous years. When, in September 1923, Miguel Primo de

Rivera, Captain General of Barcelona, staged a military coup, the Liberal regime collapsed without resistance.

## Regeneration from above

The *pronunciamiento* was the ultimate outcome of both growing praetorian meddling and military criticism of the Liberal order. Now the officers no longer seized power as the representative of a political faction but claimed to be above partisan politics: they saw themselves as defenders of the sacred values of the nation (unity of the fatherland, public order and property) which were being imperilled by the mismanagement of politicians in a moment of revolutionary danger. This therefore established a dangerous precedent for the future: that of the anti-liberal road to modernity in which the army assumed the role of national saviour. Indeed, Primo de Rivera claimed for himself the role of 'Iron Surgeon', the strong leader prepared to adopt drastic measures in order to cure the maladies destroying the fatherland.[59]

The King (who had toyed with the idea of fulfilling that role himself) did not prevent the collapse of the old order. If technically innocent of being behind the military rebellion, Alfonso was well aware of its preparations. The possibility of being incriminated in the colonial disaster confirmed his opinion that the sterile dynastic parties offered him no protection against the enemies of the throne. Consequently, in the crucial hours of the night of 13 September, the monarch took a deliberately long time to arrive in Madrid, refused to back any exceptional measures against the coup and made it clear that his primary allegiance was to 'his army'. Once in the capital, he rapidly dismissed the cabinet and invited Primo de Rivera to form a military government.[60]

The dictatorship was, above all, a solution demanded by the frightened dominant classes in a society that was in transition between oligarchic and democratic politics.[61] It was Spain's formula of social control when traditional liberalism crumbled, much as had been the case in Italy in 1922. As Captain General of Barcelona in 1923, Primo became the hero of the Catalan bourgeoisie, who endorsed enthusiastically his bid for power and accompanied the general in his triumphal departure from the train station, bound for Madrid, to form a new administration.[62] Spain's agrarian and industrial bodies and chambers of commerce, as well as the Catholic Church, were not far behind and greeted the new regime with joy.[63] In return, the dictatorship granted high protectionist tariffs to shield national production from external competition and to enforce social peace. With Martínez Anido in charge of the Ministry of the Interior, martial law lasted until May 1925. The PCE and the CNT were banned and hundreds of their militants were imprisoned.

State repression, although quite moderate in terms of bloodshed compared with the previous years, did not solely explain the decline in labour unrest that was witnessed in these years. The economic bonanza and active interventionism in the economy ensured an era of industrial expansion in the 1920s. Financed by an extraordinary budget, the dictatorship invested heavily in public works, such as road construction, railways and other infrastructures. Substantial economic modernisation co-existed with original social initiatives. Far from being persecuted, the UGT was drawn into collaboration with the state. The opposition of sectors of the PSOE, headed by Indalecio Prieto, was defeated by the alliance between the leader Pablo Iglesias and, after his death in 1925, Julián Besteiro, and the trade-unionist wing led by Francisco Largo Caballero. They welcomed the opportunity to establish socialist hegemony in the labour movement and, consequently, UGT members accepted paid jobs in the bureaucratic machinery of the regime.[64]

Industrial workers in general benefited from growing economic development and from state paternalism.[65] Borrowed from fascist corporatism, the establishment of the so-called *comités paritarios* (arbitration committees of employers' and workers' representatives) to promote social legislation and to solve conflicts was the most far-reaching social experiment. Yet, unlike in Italy, trade-union freedom was respected and a single fascist union did not represent workers. In fact, the UGT acquired the lion's share of labour representation, above the *Libres* or the Catholic trade unions. Moreover, while employers bore the burden of financing the committees and had to abide by decisions largely favourable to the workers, the proletariat still had the right to resort to strike action. Even the CNT's old guard, led by Angel Pestaña, contemplated the idea of participating in the regime's corporatism and accepting its arbitration machinery. However, this was furiously opposed by the Anarchist hard-liners. The latter founded, in a secret meeting in Valencia in July 1927, the *Federación Anarquista Ibérica* (FAI), with the objective of capturing the leadership of the organisation once it could resume its activities legally.[66]

The restoration of social peace, the fierce criticism of the corruption of the discredited previous regime and the successful pacification of Morocco ensured a certain popularity for the dictatorship.[67] However, lacking any ideological coherence or solid political foundations, the regime soon began to disintegrate. In an attempt to turn his rule from a military- into a civilian-based system, in 1924 Primo founded a political party, *Unión Patriótica* and, one year later, several civilians joined the government. Yet, unlike the dynamism of Italian Fascism, the *Unión Patriótica* never went beyond being an artificial imposition from above that was mostly joined by careerists thirsty for jobs and official protection.[68]

As political uncertainty mounted, widespread censorship, constant arbitrary decisions and a clear favouritism towards the Catholic Church led to growing opposition amongst intellectuals and students. The 1920s brought about a significant acceleration in the process of cultural modernisation, with the beginnings of mass production, the introduction of radio, and widespread attendance in cinemas, which affected the middle classes in particular. Feeling alienated and unrepresented, they began to move in droves towards the Republican camp. In Cataluña, repressive measures banning its language and its symbols saw the hegemony of Catalan Nationalism passing from the *Lliga* to left-wing groups, including the quasi-separatist *Estat Catalá*, led by Francesc Maciá. Also, sectors of the army which were enraged by Primo's attempts to cut the military budget and to deal with the promotion system began to conspire. Most of these plots, involving politicians of the old regime, were easily dismantled. Yet they revealed the glaring divisions within the armed forces, who were the ultimate guarantor of the monarchy.[69] By 1929, the King had grown tired of a regime in which he played a secondary role. The onset of the world economic depression, added to military discontent, provided Alfonso with the excuse to exert pressure on Primo to retire quietly. Landowners and industrialists rejected a fiscal policy that would have paved the way for more progressive taxation and, in a clear vote of no confidence, refused to contribute the loans that the regime was desperate to raise.[70] The same groups who had hailed the coup in 1923 now became its outspoken detractors. A sick and isolated Primo de Rivera finally resigned on 28 January 1930. Three months later he died in Paris.

**The twilight of an era**

In vain, the Crown sought to disassociate itself from the dictatorship. By having cast his lot in with the praetorian takeover, Alfonso had thought that he was securing his throne. In fact, he was destroying his constitutional underpinnings and joining his fate with that of Primo. The monarchy had readily accepted the military coup in 1923 because the oligarchic system could no longer function. However, in 1930 the attempt to bring back the old Liberal order as if nothing had happened proved ludicrous. The impact of the previous seven years could not be erased overnight. In that period, the dictatorship had presided over a period of rapid economic and cultural modernisation that significantly altered Spain's social fabric. Between 1923 and 1930, over a million people migrated from the countryside to large cities such as Barcelona, Madrid, Valencia, Bilbao and Zaragoza. Agriculture, although still the largest employment sector of the economy, fell from 57.3 to 45.5 per cent of the workforce, while the industrial and service sectors grew from 21.9 and 20.8 to 25.6 and 27.9 per cent respectively. Increasing urbanisation was accompanied by a similarly dramatic rise in literacy, a spectacular development of the railway and road system and the production of telephones, radios and other signs of modernity.[71] The obvious consequence was that the old elitist system, which had already proven moribund in 1923, was a total anachronism in the much more modern and advanced Spain of 1930.[72]

Having become fragmented long before Primo's *pronunciamiento*, and then being kept out of public office and vilified in the press during the dictatorship, the old dynastic parties were in total disarray. Moreover, only some of the monarchist notables responded with enthusiasm to their sovereign's call to save the throne. Many others either joined the Republicans or avoided backing a monarch who had identified himself with a regime that denigrated them. By contrast, Republicanism had never seen better days. According to the former *Maurista* Angel Ossorio, even his cat was now a Republican.[73] The dictatorship's censorship, as well as its other arbitrary measures mobilised thousands of small entrepreneurs, intellectuals and members of liberal professions who had not previously revealed any interest in politics. They agreed that, far from being a guarantee of stability, the continuity of the monarchy was a source of conflict and clerical obscurantism.[74]

While Monarchists soon engaged in squabbling over spheres of power, Republicans were marked by their coherence and unity. On 17 August 1930, representatives of different Republican groups, including Catalans, and (in a private capacity) the Socialists Indalecio Prieto and Fernando de los Ríos held a crucial meeting in the northern town of San Sebastián, where they agreed to collaborate in an electoral campaign to bring about a Constituent Cortes that would lead to the proclamation of a republic and the granting of autonomy to Cataluña. With the full incorporation of the Socialists into the Pact in October, a provisional government was established, in which the Socialists were given three portfolios. However, in order to dissipate the fear among the middle classes that a Republican takeover would mean a thorough social revolution, the crucial posts of prime minister and minister of the interior were left to two well-known former monarchists, Niceto Alcalá Zamora and Antonio Maura's son, Miguel.[75]

While members of the CNT, legalised in April 1930, were conspiring with Catalan Republicans and a small number of discontented young army officers, chastened by the bitter memories of 1917, Socialists and Republicans were treading with extreme caution. After many postponements, they agreed to stage an insurrection on 15 December 1930. Predictably, following the usual dismal record of Spanish rebellions, it was an utter disaster. Three days before the accorded date, the impulsive Captain Fermín Galán rose up in the isolated northern garrison of Jaca (Huesca) in the belief that his daring action would be the spark to ignite an all-embracing revolutionary movement. The authorities acted rapidly, arresting most members of the provisional government. Most compromised officers remained passive, with the exception of a minority who took over the airbase of Cuatro Vientos outside Madrid and confined their actions to flying over the capital and dropping some anti-monarchist leaflets before escaping abroad. Galán himself was captured and, together with his second in command, was summarily executed within 24 hours.[76] The Republic now had its martyrs and the monarchy could be presented as a cruel regime. The subsequent trial of the provisional government, in March 1931, revealed in full how dramatically the times had changed since 1917. The president of the military court, General Burguete, had been one of the fiercest repressors of the revolution of 1917 in Asturias. Now he allowed the accused to travel to the courthouse from prison in private cars and during the trial never contained the cheering of a vast pro-Republican audience. The verdict was a virtual acquittal: the minimum sentence of six months and one day was imposed but the accused were then set free and greeted as heroes by enthusiastic crowds. Burguete even commented that he, personally, had voted for their total absolution.[77]

In order to have time to rebuild its networks, the government decided to organise municipal elections for 12 April 1931, but the results stunned the nation. The Monarchists obtained overwhelming majorities in the countryside but 47 out of the 52 provincial capitals voted for the Republican–Socialist coalition. Clearly, where public opinion could be expressed freely it had voted massively against the regime. The rural vote had no serious meaning, being just a case of the traditional sheep-like obedience orchestrated by the still omnipotent local *caciques*.[78] It was not so much Republican strength as Monarchist defeatism that proved decisive. During the following crucial 24 hours, the regime simply collapsed. Unlike so often in the past, there was not even any attempt to present the manufactured overall majority as a proof of victory. The bewildered Monarchists conceded defeat and deserted en masse. As jubilant crowds celebrated the proclamation of Spain's Second Republic in the streets of the main cities, Alfonso, identified as the main obstacle to modernity, fled the country, abandoned by his politicians and by an army reluctant to intervene, as it had in 1923.[79]

# 2
# The Second Republic (1931–1936): A Brief Essay in Democracy

The Republic is the crucible where revenge turns into justice, the class struggle into one of ideas, and the bourgeoisie and the proletariat into harmonious forces to create social justice.[1]

## The honeymoon period

On 14 April 1931, unprecedented festivities erupted in Spain. As King Alfonso fled into exile, people danced and embraced each other. Republican flags appeared overnight, adorning balconies, lampposts and public buildings.[2] However, there existed latent and profound social conflicts barely concealed by the national celebrations. They were only momentarily submerged but would reappear in full once the initial euphoria was over. Five years later, the same boulevards and squares would become battlegrounds, as festivities gave way to hatred and resentments.

In fact, the proclamation of the Republic could not have come at a worse moment: 1931 was the beginning of an era of unprecedented political radicalism, ideological extremism and worldwide economic crisis. Spain seemed to be going against the current of the times. Whereas the Republic represented Spain's first exercise in democracy, elsewhere the political trend was towards dictatorships and Fascism. The fall of Primo de Rivera was a unique case, the only authoritarian government in Europe in the inter-war years to lead to democracy. Furthermore, although the relative backwardness of the Spanish economy, combined with the depreciation of the peseta, softened the impact of the international economic crisis, the new administrations had to face severe financial constraints. Unemployment soared, as trade plummeted and available capital dried up. Amongst the worst affected were the construction industry and the dynamic export sectors of metals, minerals and citrus fruits, whose levels of production had almost halved since 1929.[3]

Within this international context of political radicalism and economic crisis, the new regime's modernising objectives fuelled the country's polarisation. Notwithstanding the reformist zeal of the new ministers, the impossibility of borrowing capital from abroad, added to the huge debt inherited from the dictatorship's years of lavish expenditure, meant that they lacked the financial resources to carry through many of their projects. Consequently, when the rising expectations in traditionally aggrieved groups were not matched by reality, popular disenchantment gained momentum. Yet, at the same time, this very same legislation was regarded as intolerable by the wealthy classes as, if fully implemented, it would threaten their economic and social hegemony.

Thus, with the Republic coming under attack from both sides of the political spectrum, the honeymoon period was short-lived. Had the monarchy been overthrown by violent means, as opposed to the rapid and bloodless transition of April 1931, the balance of power might have been radically different. In fact, by deserting the King out of sheer expediency, the principal pillars of the old regime (the army, the Church and the land-owning oligarchy) not only managed to preserve their social and institutional might, but were also able to act as a constraint upon change.[4] Republicans soon faced the harsh reality of implementing legislation in distant corners of Spain, where social and economic power remained largely in the hands of the traditional elites.

The weakness of the republican parties led to political instability and even deadlock. Indeed, republicans were divided into several groups whose alliance had been cemented only through their common opposition to the monarchy. Now, however, with power within their grasp, they would be torn apart by personal rivalries and conflicting agendas. To make matters worse, their national grass-roots support was relatively small and concentrated amongst the urban middle classes. Real mass support was for non-republican formations: Socialists and *Cenetistas* on the left and Catholics and, to a lesser extent, Carlists on the right.

Initially, the Republic could bank on the existing enthusiasm. The hegemony of the parties converging in the San Sebastián Pact was confirmed by their landslide victory in the general elections of June 1931. Out of 470 seats, several left-wing Republican groups returned 180 deputies; amongst the centre-right Republicans, the Radicals (with

90 seats) became the second largest group in the chamber; Alcalá's party failed to attract the moderate vote, obtaining only 22 seats, with another 20 going to some minor parties. Save for notable exceptions, the old dynastic parties were literally swept away.[5] The new right-wing parties could muster only 41 deputies, with Monarchists and Catholics forming the so-called 'Agrarian minority' and Carlists and Basque Nationalists, the Basque–Navarrese coalition.[6] The PSOE, with 116 seats, emerged as the largest party. However, the Socialists were still plagued by an internal debate regarding ministerial responsibility. Their official leader, Julián Besteiro, defended a strategy of leaving government to Republicans, with the Socialists supporting from the backbenches so as to ensure the passing of progressive legislation. He was defeated by a combined front of the bulk of the party's trade-unionist wing (headed by Largo Caballero) and the parliamentary Socialists (led by Indalecio Prieto), who both wanted to remain at the centre of cabinet decision-making and make Socialism the bedrock of the new order. Thus the Socialists retained three portfolios (Largo in Labour, Prieto in the Treasury and Fernando de los Ríos in Justice). Besteiro himself was not averse to accepting the prestigious role of speaker in the Constituent Cortes.[7]

After decades of elitist government, the state machinery was now in the hands of a new governing class, formed mainly from the urban professional middle classes and committed to the modernisation of the country through a vast programme of reforms that, its members believed, could only survive if accompanied by a profound cultural transformation.[8] Crucial to this mission was the construction of the intellectual and symbolic foundations for a secular and democratic society. In other words, they endeavoured to destroy the monarchist and clerical ties that made Spaniards 'subjects' instead of 'citizens'. The essence of the transformation was education, to which they ascribed almost mystical powers. This was hardly surprising, of course, given the presence of so many university professors, writers and journalists in the first Constituent Cortes.[9] Indeed, an education that stressed independent thinking, freedom from religious indoctrination and rejection of hierarchy would perform the double function of preparing people for their role in the new society and of helping to construct its foundations.[10] Schoolteachers would become the main force of this democratic revolution: they were the transmission belt, carrying 'modern', civic values to the furthest corner of rural Spain.[11]

Indeed, one of the most laudable republican achievements was the commitment to and financial investment in public education. Between

1931 and 1933, 13,580 new teaching posts were created. Additionally, the Ministry of Education funded cultural enterprises such as the so-called *Misiones Pedagógicas* (Pedagogical Missions) or theatrical companies like García Lorca's *La Barraca*.[12] These modern missionaries were the shock troops to usher in a new egalitarian era replacing Catholicism – hitherto the ideological motor of social hierarchy – with secular humanism and social justice. They travelled to remote villages and hamlets where they showed films, read poetry and lectured on democratic principles. Upon their departure, they left behind a library well stocked with literary classics.

Despite its great idealism, the republican's top-down, paternalist approach was akin to building a house by starting with the roof. While it alienated the Catholic middle classes, it was also not entirely in tune with the basic demands of the population. Indeed, a more thorough emphasis on economic and social reform would have consolidated greater popular support for the regime. Bread and jobs rather than songs and poems were what villagers desperately needed.[13] Furthermore, stocking libraries in destitute areas with works by the likes of Tolstoy, Balzac and Zola was a noble but misguided effort. It was not only a daunting task for a barely literate peasantry to read tomes of classic literature but also it was of much less practical use than reading technical manuals on agriculture.

Also crucial in the modernisation of the country was the introduction of a package of military reforms by the war minister, Manuel Azaña, the dynamic leader of the small party *Acción Republicana*. The objective was to transform the armed forces from the monarchy's praetorian guard into a professional institution that abided by and defended Spain's constitutional order. However, Azaña's initiatives would stimulate serious opposition and resentment within the officer corps. The infamous Law of Jurisdictions of 1906 (which gave the military judicial authority over civilians) was abolished and officers had to take an oath of loyalty to the Republic or face discharge. The question of 'responsibilities' for the disaster in Morocco was reopened and some of the military were tried. Measures to deal with the inflated officer corps were also approved, including encouraging senior officers to take early retirement on full pay (over ten thousand accepted the offer), and promotion by war merits was frozen.[14]

While republicans were more concerned with cultural and political measures, the PSOE's foremost concern was the introduction of social legislation aimed at ameliorating the appalling living conditions of ordinary workers. The labour minister, Largo Caballero, helped by the justice minister, de los Ríos, devised the new measures. Salaries were increased and rents were frozen so that, in a deflationary period, real wages for urban workers increased by 16 per cent between 1931 and 1933 and in the countryside they virtually doubled.[15] Employees now obtained seven days of paid holiday per annum and the right to strike could not lead to dismissal. There were other important advances in the field of social security, such as maternity, retirement and insurance against labour accidents. Primo's arbitration committees were renamed *jurados mixtos* and extended to the countryside. The eight-hour working day was introduced to cover all types of labour. Finally, in order to solve unemployment in rural Spain, the Law of Municipal Boundaries (forbidding employers from bringing in outside workers until those in a given municipality had jobs and hence preventing strike-breaking) and of Obligatory Cultivation (forcing owners of land, under penalty of its possible confiscation, to use it for arable purposes) were passed.[16]

The crowning of these first months of reformist zeal was the approval of a new constitution in December 1931. Spain was defined as a 'republic of workers of all categories' and as a democratic, lay and potentially decentralised regime. Individual rights, including the protection of private property, were included in the constitution but Article 44 accepted the possibility of expropriation on grounds of social utility. Two of the most controversial issues, the concession of autonomous power to historical regions, in particular Cataluña,[17] and the introduction of the awaited agrarian reform, were implicitly approved but the details of legislation were left in the hands of parliament. All elections were to be conducted by universal, direct and secret suffrage in which, for the first time, women could participate.[18] There was to be a single lower chamber and a Tribunal of Constitutional Guarantees (a kind of supreme court) charged with the duties of determining the constitutionality of laws and of mediating in any conflicts between the central and autonomous governments. Parliament was to elect, for a term of six years, a president of the Republic with important but limited powers. He could appoint and remove prime ministers, dissolve the chamber twice and play an advisory role in the matter of legislation. However, his decisions had to be endorsed by parliament, which could also oust him.

In less than a year, Spain had advanced further down the road to modernity than it had in the previous two centuries. However, fast change in such a short time caused deep traumas to the traditional fabric of society.

Divergences within the ruling coalition were glaring even by the summer of 1931. The anticlerical legislation, added to differences over the agrarian reform, led in October to the departure from government of the two leading conservative republicans: Alcalá Zamora and Miguel Maura. Nevertheless, the election of Alcalá in December as first president of the Republic served to postpone existing antagonisms. More threatening was the confrontation between the two largest parties, the Radicals and the Socialists. The Radicals' shady reputation was such that, in 1930, all those participants in the San Sebastián Pact had agreed that the party should not be given any portfolio related to economic matters. The idea of making Lerroux minister of justice had also to be abandoned, as Maura suggested that the Radicals would then be found auctioning court sentences in the centre of Madrid. Nevertheless, the Radicals' significant support in the urban middle-class constituencies could not be ignored. They were key members of the so-called *Alianza Republicana*, a republican alliance formed in February 1926, and had to be accommodated in the provisional government as necessary – if deeply undesirable – allies.[19]

After the elections of June 1931, the Radicals could claim the mantle of being not only the most senior republican party but also the one with the largest parliamentary minority. Yet whereas their partners in the *Alianza* and in government, the Radical-Socialists (PRRS) and *Acción Republicana* (AR), were embracing a progressive programme, the Radicals had moved dramatically from their former revolutionary stance. Lerroux now presented himself as the guarantor of a socially conservative republic. Furthermore, the Radicals were more successful than the other republican parties in creating a national organisation by expanding from their urban strongholds into the countryside, where they had hitherto been weakly represented. To a large extent, this was achieved by absorbing a number of existing *cacique* networks. Former Monarchist notables (such as Santiago Alba) joined the Radicals; others (like Manuel Burgos y Mazo, José Sánchez Guerra and even Count Romanones) instructed their clienteles to do so. This infiltration by former monarchists and reputed *caciques*, who were hoping to safeguard their influential position under the cover of 'republican respectability', affected all parties but it certainly affected the Radicals by far the most. They claimed that, for the sake of the Republic, the incorporation of sectors of the old regime was better than their alienation. The obvious drawback was that many local authorities remained in the hands of former monarchists who were likely to oppose any meaningful reforms and so accentuated the Radicals' rightward shift.[20]

In October 1931 the Socialists and the Radicals continued to avoid an open clash by jointly backing the candidacy of Manuel Azaña for new prime minister. However, it was no secret that Lerroux believed this to be a temporary measure and that he, as leader of the largest republican party, should hold that post once the constitution had been approved. When, in December, Azaña made clear that the Cortes would not be dissolved and that, with Socialist backing, he would retain the premiership, the Radicals suddenly abandoned the government.[21] By 1932, personal and ideological disputes had resulted in the virtual collapse of the San Sebastián Pact. An embittered Lerroux gradually began to move into opposition, calling for the removal of Socialists from office and the installation of an all-republican government.[22] From then on, ominously, the largest republican party was openly against the 1931 settlement.

As the initial governmental coalition began to break up, the Republic's anticlerical content ensured the uncontained hostility of the Catholic Church. For so long an unreconstructed institution, its reform was not only long overdue but also necessary to transform Spain into a modern democratic and secular state. The new legislation introduced divorce and civil marriage, the eradication of religious symbols from public buildings and terminated the clergy's special fiscal status. State subsidies were to end in two years and the Church had to disclose its assets and revenue which, for the first time, would be liable to taxation.[23]

The republicans' anticlerical zeal (which was far stronger than that of the PSOE), although largely provoked by a traditionally intolerant Church, was not only politically unwise but also self-defeating. The Republic could have adopted a more cautious approach and instead made social and economic legislation its priority. Dislodging the clergy from its paramount grip on education was nevertheless required for cultural modernisation. Yet, the republicans did not just promote alternative state schooling. Alleging that it was a question of public safety, they banned all teaching by religious orders.[24] This was a naive measure. The vacuum left by the ending of Catholic education could not be filled for years owing to budgetary constraints, whilst it put the new regime on a headlong collision course with the Church. This, along with unnecessarily punitive directives (such as forbidding religious burials and celebrations) provided the anti-republican Right with an ideal banner – that of persecution – around which to rally opposition to the regime.[25]

Certainly, provocative outbursts such as the pastorals of the Cardinal Primate of Spain, Pedro Segura, in May 1931, redoubled the anticlerical feelings of the government. Of course, many high-ranking clerics could not resign themselves to seeing the Church, the very symbol of old Spain, experience the modernisation that had been undertaken in nearly all the Western world. Rooted aversion to democracy had long been embedded in the ecclesiastical hierarchy and had recently borne conspicuous fruit in its active support for the dictatorship and in its role as the bulwark of the monarchy. It was the Catholic Maura who soon thereafter decreed the expulsion of Cardinal Segura and the Bishop of Vitoria, Mateo Múgica.[26] However, many local parish priests were not, in principle, against the new regime. Some leading figures, such as the Papal Nuncio Monsignor Tedeschini, were prepared to seek a compromise, and the Bishop of Málaga, Ilundain, had publicly endorsed the Republic.[27] But the anticlerical republican discourse alienated these moderates and played into the hands of the hardliners within the Catholic hierarchy.[28]

When Azaña declared, in October 1931, that Spain had ceased to be a Catholic country, he was correct in objective terms but his evaluation ignored the still awesome might of that institution.[29] Even though overall levels of church attendance were in decline and Catholicism was losing ground in the urban centres, it still held sway over significant sectors of the middle classes and had a mass following amongst the rural farmers of Castilla, the Basque Country and Navarra. In 1930s Spain, Catholic practice was more characteristic of the north than the south, of property owners rather than manual workers, of the better educated rather than the poorly educated and of women rather than men.[30] Furthermore, the Church enjoyed a vital control over publications and media. Indeed, leading Catholics, such as the highly influential *Asociación Católica Nacional de Propagandistas* (ACNP), played a crucial role in reorganising right-wing politics, which was in a state of total disarray in 1931. Led by Angel Herrera, this organisation (which consisted mainly of students of former Jesuit schools) owned the largest and most powerful chain of newspapers and radio stations. Herrera himself was the editor of *El Debate*, the most important Catholic newspaper.[31] It echoed the vitriolic attacks of the Catholic hierarchy. The Republic was portrayed by it as the embodiment of anti-Spain: godless, satanic and evil. The expulsion from the country of anti-republicans, such as Cardinal Segura and, later, the Jesuits, was proof that the government revelled in crushing the defenceless clergy. Simultaneously, the Catholic press also sought to win the support of the armed forces. The concession of autonomy to Cataluña was described as the beginning of the break-up of the fatherland and Azaña's reforms were distorted to make them appear as an attempt to crush the army. The hammering home of apocalyptic messages, describing the Republic as an unpatriotic regime dominated by Reds, atheists, Masons[32] and separatists, was intended to link with the military's own feelings. Particularly receptive were the *Africanistas*, who were already enraged by the reopening of the responsibilities issue and by the freezing of battlefield promotions awarded during the Moroccan wars.[33]

The dominant economic classes and institutions joined the anti-republican offensive. Urban employers (the *Patronal*), however, were far from presenting a monolithic front. Some revealed their contempt towards the new regime by their exporting of capital.[34] Yet there were others that even welcomed the Republic after the monarchy's final troublesome years. However, by 1932, most were exasperated as declining profits and rising wages hit thousands of small and medium-sized businesses. They focused their anger mainly on the arbitration committees that, presided over by the Ministry of Labour's appointees, were seen as a type of socialist dictatorship imposing contracts and conditions always favourable to the working classes. Although not necessarily seeking the overthrow of the Republic, the *Patronal* wanted a drastic reform of its political orientation. In July 1933 the assembly of employers demanded the prompt removal of Socialists from government. Their hopes were pinned on a new Radical-dominated administration.[35]

Unlike their urban counterparts, the rural oligarchy was united in its efforts to restore the social order that had prevailed before 1931. The countryside had never seen the introduction of social reformist legislation before. Hitherto, control of local power through their appointees and with the compliance of the Civil Guard ensured the big landowners' almost absolute sway over the thousands of landless workers. Now, for the first time, they watched their hegemony collapse. The new social legislation, although far from revolutionary, if implemented could have far-reaching consequences in rural Spain. The smooth functioning of the *latifundios* depended on a vast pool of surplus labour working endless hours for miserable wages. Apart from the pending threat of a thorough agrarian reform, labourers now not only worked fewer hours but their wages were also increased. Owners had to pay overtime whenever they required a longer workday, as they almost inevitably did during harvest. In the context of a world depression, with agrarian prices and exports falling, this meant a very significant redistribution of wealth. With Socialists dominating the arbitration committees, the working contracts were bound to be favourable to the labourers. Additionally, landowners were no longer able to keep wages down by bringing in cheap labour from outside; nor could they carry out rural lockouts by leaving vast tracks of land uncultivated.[36] The landowners' resistance to change, added to the hopes raised by the new regime amongst the local labourers, meant that the countryside became the bitterest battleground.[37] Incidents such as the lynching of four civil guards by villagers in Castilblanco (Extremadura) in December 1931, followed, in January 1932, by the indiscriminate shooting and killing of 11 people in Arnedo (Logroño) by members of the Civil Guard revealed the vicious character of the social conflict in rural Spain.[38] In southern Spain, always a potential powder keg owing to the staggering misery of a large percentage of the population, the new horizons opened by the republican regime fuelled ancient hatreds. Republicans, Socialists and Catholics quarrelled for control of local power. The Anarcho-syndicalist CNT and, to a lesser extent, the Communists of the PCE launched constant strikes that ended in savage clashes with the Civil Guard but also in a murderous confrontation with the Socialist UGT. Sevilla (the PCE's main stronghold) experienced an authentic gang war between Communists and Anarcho-syndicalists.[39]

After 1931, the composition and character of the UGT was altered drastically. With Socialists in the government, thousands of southern landless labourers joined the Socialist landworkers' union, the *Federación Nacional de Trabajadores de la Tierra* (FNTT). Consequently, the UGT was transformed from a relatively small organisation of the capital's labour aristocracy and of northern dockers, miners and metalworkers into a powerful mass movement, where nearly 40 per cent were southern and radicalised peasants, thereby displacing the CNT as the main representative of the rural proletariat.[40] By contrast, despite its inter-class rhetoric, the Agrarian Catholic Confederation (CNCA) remained an organisation controlled by big landowners working closely with bishops and local priests.[41] Under the leadership of Jose María Gil Robles, it became the strongest anti-republican force, mobilising hundreds of thousands of small landholders, *arrendatarios* (sharecroppers) and farmers. Not only had the anticlerical laws roused their Catholic susceptibilities but they also felt overlooked by the agrarian reform and hurt economically by the high salaries imposed by the Socialist-dominated arbitration committees.[42] By describing in apocalyptic terms the government's pursuit of land collectivisation as an attempt to deprive them of their properties, the CNCA easily persuaded these Catholic farmers that they shared the same interests as those of the rural oligarchy.[43]

Hostility towards the Republic was not limited, however, to right-wing political forces. Both the Communists and the Anarcho-syndicalists were also in opposition to the democratic Republic. For the Communists, there was no difference between the old and the new regime. In their Manichean view, the Republic was just a smokescreen to divert the masses from the true revolutionary path. The PCE's analysis was clearly influenced by the Comintern's own view of the Socialists as 'social fascists', class collaborators and enemies of the true interests of the proletariat.[44] Nevertheless, although the Communists waged a revolutionary offensive against the Republic, with the exception of Seville and, to a lesser extent, Asturias and Vizcaya, their nationwide influence was minimal. By the autumn of 1932, their meagre impact on the masses resulted in a purge of the leadership, including its secretary, José Bullejos, who was replaced by the more docile José Díaz.[45]

In its turn, having been forced into a clandestine existence during the Primo dictatorship, the CNT was in the process of reconstruction by the time of the proclamation of the Republic. It was far from a monolithic organisation, and its loose libertarian principles made it extremely difficult for it to hone a common strategy. It grouped some very different tendencies: southern millenarian anarchists, pragmatic trade-unionists from Cataluña and Valencia and the *exaltés* of the action groups now flocking into the more radical Anarchist organisation (FAI) with important roots in Cataluña and Aragón.[46]

Initially, under the leadership of the old guard, headed by the national secretary, the veteran Angel Pestaña, the CNT welcomed the Republic as a popular regime that seemingly inaugurated a period of hopes and liberties.[47] In Cataluña, particularly, years of common persecution and collaboration between left-wing Catalan republicans and *Cenetistas* seemed to herald a period of good relations. The leaders were, however, soon under attack by the hardliners. One of the FAI's most charismatic members, a young veteran from the 1920s action groups, Joan García Oliver, stated:

Faced with the surrendering attitude of the old Anarcho-syndical-ists, we considered the Republic a bourgeois institution that had to be replaced by libertarian communism. This made imperative a wave of insurrectionary activities that, in turn, would be fought [against] by the bourgeoisie. This had to go on until the collapse of the bourgeois republic. We had to create in our militants the habit of revolutionary actions, so as to overcome their fear of the repressive forces of the state. This systematic practice of insurrectionary practices was 'revolutionary gymnastics'.[48]

The battle to seize control of the CNT became fierce at its congress of June 1931. Booed and harassed, the old guard obtained a temporary victory with an agreement for the establishment of national trade unions.[49] However, fiercely combated by the Anarchists, who feared that this would lead to the growth of an internal bureaucracy and the destruction of the federalist character of the local organisations, the measure was never implemented.[50] The balance of power soon began to tilt in favour of the FAI. By its own libertarian principles, the CNT was inherently suspicious of the republican top-down paternalism that was more in tune with Socialist gradualism. Instead, the Anarcho-syndicalists believed in direct action and mobilisation from below to advance, through the grass-roots and neighbourhood committees, populist and consumer issues such as rent strikes. The activists were also sometimes involved in criminal activities, including armed robberies.[51] The presence in government of the CNT's historic enemies, the Socialists, intensified existing apprehensions. Socialist, state-sponsored reforms, if successful, threatened the CNT's survival as a leading organisation in Andalucía and other parts of Spain.[52]

Certainly, anarchist violence itself contributed to the persecution of the CNT. Azaña revealed the dichotomy of the government when he declared that it was impossible to help a CNT which refused to be aided and whose extremism rejected any reformist legislation, as the organisation held that this would diminish the insurrectionary spirit of the militants.[53] However, republican shortcomings in dealing with the economic crisis and the application of a tough public order policy played into the hands of the hardliners. Popular expectations were unfulfilled as governments pursued monetarist, budget-balancing, liberal economic policies. Hence there was no room for welfare benefits and public works for the jobless during a time when the spread of unemployment overwhelmed local charitable initiatives and munici-pal projects.[54] Additionally, collective protest was met with the same unreformed habits of martial law and police impunity as under the monarchy. The hated, militarised Civil Guard remained in place, unchanged, and the only novelty was the creation of a new corps, the Assault Guards (themselves led by army officers), to police the cities.[55] Throughout 1931, strikes and riots induced by *Cenetistas* or

Communists led to huge numbers of arrests and even, in July in Seville, to the use of artillery and then the application of the brutal *Ley de Fugas* (shooting while trying to escape) to four prisoners. The CNT was soon accusing the Republic of converting Spain into a slaughter-house.[56] Economic recession and restrictive budgetary practices, added to police repression, left large sectors of marginal workers attracted to the FAI's uncompromising messages. For them, the state arbitration principles preached by the UGT were of little use.

The passing of the *Ley por la Defensa de la República* (Law for the Defence of the Republic), in October 1931, which formalised excep-tional measures (including the banning of spontaneous strikes and the arrest of suspects and even their deportation), confirmed to many *Cenetistas* that the Socialist-dominated Republic wanted their destruc-tion.[57] Legislation that seemed to condone the shooting of workers and marginalised the CNT left little room for manoeuvre for the old guard. Thus, under the violent guidance of the FAI, the CNT embarked upon the path of the so-called 'revolutionary gymnastics'. According to the veteran Anarcho-syndicalist Simó Piera, it was extremely painful for those who had led the CNT in its early years to see how all the solid work of people such as Seguí was being destroyed by the existing pseudo-revolutionary euphoria.[58] Thirty of the most significant leaders published, on 1 September 1931, a statement condemning the reckless activities of the extremists. For Camil Piñón, the leading *Cenetista* who had organised the massive Barcelona transport strike of 1923, this was a manifesto against the constant, senseless robberies, killings and bombings practised by 'those of the daily revolution' who only achieved widespread havoc.[59]

In January 1932 a first massive insurrection began in Alto Llobregat (Barcelona). It was quickly defeated and about a hundred *Cenetistas* were deported to Equatorial Guinea in Africa.[60] Throughout the rest of the year, this suicidal strategy of open confrontation with the state continued unabated. The CNT's undisciplined character condemned it to costly failures with a heavy toll of casualties. In the meantime, accused of reformism, many members of the old guard were hounded out of their posts; some even were expelled, while others left the CNT to form a rival organisation, the *Sindicatos de Oposición* (SSOO), with a following of 80,000 members, mostly from Cataluña and Valencia. Pestaña him-self founded the Syndicalist Party and others, such as Piera, joined *Ezquerra*.[61] In little more than two years, the CNT had paid the price for its adventurism, losing some 300,000 members out of the 800,000 of the autumn of 1931, two-thirds of them from its Catalan stronghold.[62]

By unleashing an all-out revolutionary offensive, the CNT and, to a lesser extent, the PCE became the second part of the pincer in which the Republic became ensnared. Indeed, the right-wing media could only be pleased to announce that the new regime was presiding over a reign of anarchy. Simultaneously, throughout 1932, the right-wing parties fought a well-concerted campaign to prevent the passing of the legislation on agrarian reform and Catalan autonomy. While their press described these measures as a threat to the national economy and the fatherland, the conservative deputies engaged in obstructionism in the chamber, introducing amendments and complicated technical questions for every clause of the new bills. They managed to delay the legislation while also increasing the exasperation of the labouring classes.

Ironically, the government was rescued from the frustrating parliamentary deadlock by an aborted *pronunciamiento*. On 10 August 1932, the former head of the Civil Guard, General Sanjurjo, still smarting from his sacking after the Arnedo's events, rebelled in Sevilla in order to 'rectify' the extreme revolutionary character which the Republic was adopting. Badly organised, the conspirators lost nine men in a desperate rising in Madrid and only temporarily succeeded in the Andalusian city. The role played by Lerroux during these events was ambiguous. The Radical leader had been in close touch with Sanjurjo before the coup and even, in a vehement speech he had made one month prior to the coup, seemed to have been attempting to justify such an insurrection. However, the cabinet preferred to avoid investigating, in the belief that it could have a devastating effect on public opinion.[63]

The rebellion's impact was the opposite of what Sanjurjo had intended. It redoubled republican enthusiasm and ended the legislative paralysis. With right-wing deputies in disarray and the Radicals momentarily playing up their reformist commitment, the agrarian reform and the Catalan statute were passed in September.[64] On 30 November, Maciá's *Esquerra* won a landslide victory in the first elections to the Catalan parliament and he was elected president of the Catalan government (*Generalitat*). However, the agrarian reform was far from successful. While failing to fulfil the expectations of the workers, it terrified the landowners (even though compensation was to be paid at market values). After two years of successive drafts, its extraordinary complexity and many vague provisions marked the final law. It was clearly aimed at southern Spain (where more than one-third of the total land area and about half of the cultivated area fell into one of the categories of expropriable land) but it neglected measures which could have won over smallholders and sharecroppers. The agriculture minister, the Radical-Socialist Marcelino Domingo, was a good-hearted but weak man who knew very little about agrarian matters.[65] Like most progressive Republicans, he was mostly concerned with political legislation and not with economic matters. Worst of all was the fact that the institution established to carry through the law, the Institute of Agrarian Reform (IRA), was provided with only 50 million pesetas (or 1 per cent of the budget) and, therefore, lacked the technical and financial resources to compensate landowners and resettle peasants with even the minimum means required to make their plots productive. In one year, of the planned 60,000 families who should have obtained land, only 10 per cent had acquired it. Yet, for landowners, this was an assault on the sacred right of property and encouraged them to bide their time to reverse the reform.[66]

The aborted military coup proved to be a watershed in the subsequent right-wing strategy. It brought about the end of *Acción Nacional*,[67] the umbrella organisation formed in April 1931. Unreconstructed Monarchists, unwilling to reject the conspiratorial route, set up their own political party, *Renovación Española*, under the leadership of the former dictatorship minister José Calvo Sotelo. It was small in numbers but had great influence, owing to the wealth of its members and their connections with powerful interests. The party believed in violent means to destroy the Republic – as did the Carlists, who were at the time organising paramilitary militias (*Requetés*) in their Navarrese stronghold. The Monarchists also financed the Falange, the party headed by José Antonio Primo de Rivera, the dictator's son, which was the result of a merger between several small Fascist groups in February 1934. By contrast, the more pragmatic elements of the right viewed the government's success as a direct product of the 1932 coup, which had destroyed overnight all their achievements in stalling reform for months. They instead pursued an 'accidentalist' strategy, or a more legalistic approach, believing that the forms of government were 'accidental' and that the essential issue was the socio-economic content of the regime. Their plan was to play the democratic game, build a mass party with which to win elections and then destroy the Republic from within. Collaboration with more extreme Monarchists never stopped. It was merely a difference over tactics rather than acute political incompatibility which produced the split. Led by the secretary of the CNCA, Jose María Gil Robles, the *accidentalistas* formed (in February 1933) a mass Catholic party: the CEDA or *Confederación Española de Derechas Autónomas* (Spanish Confederation of Right-Wing Autonomous Groups). It was a vast coalition of right-wing Catholic groups whose objective was to gain power by mobilising Catholic and conservative Spain and whose slogan was the defence of religion, fatherland, law, order and property. The CEDA was a right-wing mass force that brought together the professional urban middle classes as well as small property-owners, farmers and big landowners. It included both Christian Democrats and reactionary hardliners. However, its close alliance with the Agrarian Party,[68] its ideological dependence on the Church and the overwhelming financial backing from agrarian associations meant that the overall leaning of the party was towards the reactionary side. Furthermore, the CEDA's refusal to declare its loyalty to the activities of the Republic, its bellicose rhetoric, full of admiration for Hitler and Mussolini, and its uniformed and often violent youth wing, the *Juventudes de Acción Popular* (JAP), made its professed acceptance of the democratic process sound hollow.[69]

With echoes of the August 1932 coup beginning to fade, the other side of the pincer now closed.[70] In January 1933 the FAI launched its second mass uprising. It was rapidly crushed everywhere except in a remote village of Cádiz, Casas Viejas, where the rebels barricaded themselves in the house of the local Anarchist leader and began shooting at the police. They were finally burned out and, together with other arrested villagers, were put against a wall and shot, leaving a final toll of 19 peasants and 3 policemen dead.[71]

### Mission impossible: A republic for Republicans

Nothing was the same after Casas Viejas. Rural repression was hardly new in Andalucía, but this time it had not been perpetrated by the hated Civil Guard but by the assault guards.[72] As a wave of protest swept the nation, Lerroux, in a blatant exercise of hypocrisy, collaborated with the CEDA in accusing the government of representing a barbaric regime that was persecuting innocent peasants and wrecking the national economy. He also appealed to Alcalá Zamora to intervene in the political process, so as to enable the consolidation of a Republic under control of Republicans.[73]

The politically charged climate coincided with the worsening economic crisis. Falling productivity and growing unemployment, aggravated by the lack of a comprehensive social security system, had devastating effects upon the building and mining sectors and, above all, in the countryside, where 72 per cent of the overall jobless were registered.[74] As local authorities were overwhelmed by financial ruin and vainly pleaded to the government for funds, the CNT continued its campaign of violent strikes, while landowners ignored legislation and resorted to lockouts in an attempt to starve workers into defeat. Claiming to be in the vanguard of a 'crusade' to liberate rural Spain from the tyranny of the PSOE, the main land-owning organisation, the *Confederación Española Patronal Agrícola*, demanded the freedom to hire and fire labourers and an end to the Law of Municipal Boundaries. In September some 13,000 farmers and landowners marched against the government along the streets of Madrid.[75]

Amid rising social tensions, frustration began to creep into governmental ranks, particularly in the faction led by Largo Caballero. For them, the Republic had always been not an end in itself but the means to obtain power in the state machinery. So far, the PSOE had been a bulwark of the new regime in cabinet and parliament and the UGT had endeavoured to hold back the rank and file, often confronting Communists and Anarcho-syndicalists in violent clashes. Some of its vital sections – such as the landworkers' federation (FNTT) and the Asturian miners (SOMA) – avoided strikes and relied on negotiation and government legislation. Even as the economic depression deepened in the coal industry, with wage cuts, lay-offs and shutdowns, the SOMA continued to express its total confidence in the Republic. Indeed, the UGT's strike activity took place mostly in order to ensure the fulfilment of existing Republican legislation and contracts negotiated in the arbitration committees.[76] However, after Casas Viejas, accusations of cruelty against poor workers, added to the mounting employers' offensive, began to take its toll. Mixed feelings about bourgeois institutions and about the convenience of remaining in government, thus restraining labour militancy, were in ascendancy. This radicalisation translated into the *Caballeristas* ousting the followers of Besteiro from their dominance in both the PSOE and the UGT.[77] Caballero's growing revolutionary stance was also influenced by the significant inroads of the CNT into Madrid's construction sector, the largest employer in the capital and hitherto a solid UGT stronghold.[78] Furthermore, the unabated rise of Fascism in Europe and growing beliefs that the CEDA was its Spanish variant encouraged even further the hardening of the socialist position.

As 1933 went on, the *Caballeristas*, in somewhat contradictory terms, expressed disenchantment with their experience in government while rejecting altogether being dislodged from office. Feeling that the sacrifices of the previous two years would have been in vain if they lost power, they declared their identification with the Republic as long as the regime stood for the reforms adopted by the Constituent Cortes. In the summer, Largo made it clear that Socialists wanted to enjoy power, if possible along constitutional lines; otherwise they would do so by 'other means'.[79]

Largo's radicalisation was matched by the tightening of the political noose around the government. In April 1933, local elections held in places where the 1931 results had been suspended led to victory for the CEDA and the Radicals. These results in the 'rotten boroughs' of Navarra and Old Castilla could still be dismissed as irrelevant.[80] However, three months later, the Radicals and the CEDA won again in elections for the Tribunal of Constitutional Guarantees, whose members were largely returned by the town halls. To add insult to injury, the PRRS (a key member of the governing coalition) split as one section led by the vehement Gordón Ordás echoed Lerroux's calls for a Republic not dominated by the Socialists and opposed his own leader – the agriculture minister, Marcelino Domingo.[81] The Radicals then tabled a motion of no confidence. Although still won by the government, its narrow margin provided Alcalá Zamora with the excuse to dismiss the administration. His manifestly bad personal relations with Azaña and his unconcealed interest in taking an active part in the political process led to the appointment of a Radical-dominated cabinet which Alcalá believed would be easier to influence.[82] When the new government, lacking a majority in the chamber, was brought down by a vote, Alcalá summoned new general elections for November.

The electoral law had been designed to prevent fragmentation and to ensure the return of strong governments. In a highly complex two-round ballot, the party list in each province with the majority of votes received 80 per cent of the seats; the party that came second received 20. Thus it encouraged electoral coalitions, since a relatively small difference in votes meant huge swings in terms of seats. However, although leaving room for some local arrangements, the *Caballeristas* rejected any nationwide alliance with their former allies. Their frustration with the bourgeois Republic thereby led them to a catastrophic blunder.[83] The PSOE, with 1.6 million votes, only returned 58 deputies. The progressive Republicans dropped to 37 seats (only the Catalan *Esquerra*, with 19, fared well and yet came second to its rival, the *Lliga*, with 24). By contrast, the right-wing parties presented a united front and engaged in a well-funded and aggressive campaign with propaganda techniques modelled on those of the Nazis.[84] The CEDA and the Agrarians (115 and 36 deputies respectively) became the largest group in parliament. The extreme right had 53 seats. Centre and right-wing Republicans returned some 140 deputies (102 of them Radicals). Lerroux's party showed no scruples in entering into tactical alliances which, depending on the region, included the CEDA in the second round.[85] The outcome of the 1933 election was a watershed, marking the crumbling of the ideals of the first years of the Republic. Even Alcalá Zamora was taken aback by what he described as a mind-bogglingly reactionary parliament.[86] Nevertheless, despite this drastic political realignment, the CEDA, even with the support of the extreme right, was short of an overall majority. In December the deadlock was broken when Lerroux was confirmed as prime minister in a Radical-dominated cabinet with the support of CEDA votes in parliament.

Many Radicals, such as Martínez Barrios, the party's deputy leader, were honest politicians. Others, however, including the party leader's inner circle and the Barcelona section, were imbued with a traditional wheeler-dealing view of politics, in which holding office provided the means to enrich themselves through embezzlement and the sale of public contracts. Indeed, Lerroux, much like a dynastic politician, was soon engaged in the distribution of personal favours and appointments.[87] Morally suspicious though some Radicals might have been, they were far from being merely a reactionary group. During the first months in office, for example, they did not attempt to dismantle the reforms of the previous administration. The constitution had, after all, been agreed to and voted for by them. Ignoring the legislation banning the Church from school education was wise for appeasing Catholic public opinion and realistic in terms of the public purse. The education budget was not slashed but increased and that of the IRA remained untouched. Even the pace of resettling peasants on to expropriated land reached an average of 700 families per month in the first nine months of the new government's term in office – twice the figure achieved in the previous year.[88] On the other hand, officials in the arbitration committees were no longer appointed by the Ministry of Labour but came from the legal profession or the civil service. But this rectification, although it dismayed the UGT, was an attempt to make these bodies more independent and was not necessarily a shift against the workers' interests. Actually, many long-standing disputes (such as the construction and waiters' strikes in Madrid, in November and December 1933 respectively) were settled in the workers' favour. The *Patronal* was stunned when the minister of labour, the Radical José Estadella, supported the settlement and had recalcitrant employers arrested in March 1934.[89]

Nevertheless, the 1933 elections demonstrated the impossibility of a Republic governed solely by republicans. As in the previous administration, republicans faced the bitter truth that they were dependent on the support of another mass group, in this case the CEDA. Some have interpreted Lerroux's attempt to reach a working agreement with this Catholic party as a noble attempt to bring it into the regime's fold.[90] However, events in the next two years revealed the naivety of this strategy. Whereas Azaña remained a forceful leader in office, the same cannot be said of Lerroux. A shrewd Gil Robles constantly outmanoeuvred the former fiery revolutionary, who, at 70 years of age, was well past his prime. Having helped to mould the republican order, the Socialists had remained trustworthy members of the previous governing coalition. By contrast, for all its statements of readiness to work within the system, the CEDA never concealed that its objective was to destroy all the original ideals enshrined in the constitution. Being at the mercy of their parliamentary votes, the Radicals were mere pawns in a long-term strategy. This consisted of initial support for Radical cabinets, after which the CEDA would aim to enter office as a partner in a coalition government, until, having achieved a monopoly of power, it would establish a corporate authoritarian state.[91] Thus, Radical administrations became short-lived affairs, continually being held to ransom by CEDA intransigence. By fostering political instability – there were 11 governmental crises in less than two years – the Radicals became a demoralised and split force, with a desperate Lerroux dependent on CEDA goodwill in order to cling on to power. It was a subtle game: one that needed the right amount of pressure to undermine the Radicals but not so much as to disrupt the political process altogether, leading to an early dissolution of parliament and new elections.

Many Radicals expressed their uneasiness about collaborating with a political group that refused openly to declare its adherence to the Republic. The elimination of this liberal sector, led by Martínez Barrios (the head of Spain's Masonry), was the CEDA's primary goal. In February 1934 Gil Robles stated the impossibility of supporting an administration whose interior minister, Martínez Barrios, was unwilling to fight subversion. Consequently, a government crisis ensued in which Barrios and his ally the finance minister, Antonio Lara, were dropped.[92] Rafael Salazar Alonso, a hardliner deputy from Badajoz, occupied the Interior portfolio. It was the beginning of what Alcalá called Lerroux's political capitulation before browbeating tactics.[93] The CEDA then demanded the reversal of some of the anticlerical legislation, including the restoration of state contributions to the clergy and, more tellingly, a full amnesty for the August 1932 insurgents. Lerroux himself, whose part in that event had been less than clear, wanted to comply but he met stern resistance from both his own rank and file and from Alcalá. A new governmental crisis ensued, leading to the establishment of a cabinet (presided over by the Valencian Radical Ricardo Samper) that signed the amnesty. In May, Martínez Barrios abandoned the Radical Party, moved to the opposition benches and created (with 22 other deputies) his own independent group, the Radical Democrats. It merged with that section of the PRRS led by Gordón Ordás in September to form the *Unión Republicana* (UR).[94] In a few months the Radicals had lost 25 per cent of their strength in both the chamber and in the country.

The Socialists had warned that the existence of the Republic would be imperilled if the Radicals managed to hold office. For them, a republic stripped of its social reforms was no longer worthy of support.[95] Moreover, international events fuelled fears that the Radicals were the Trojan horse enabling reactionary forces to gain backdoor access to the state machinery. In February 1934 the Austrian Chancellor Engelbert Dollfuss, leader of a Catholic party ideologically similar to the CEDA, staged a coup and established a dictatorship after the brutal 'cleaning-up of Red Vienna'. In reply, the *Caballeristas* adopted a combination of revolutionary rhetoric and practical reformism. Largo Caballero, although increasingly dubbed 'the Spanish Lenin' by the Socialist Youth, was ideologically miles away from the Russian revolutionary, and his party bore no resemblance to the Bolsheviks (nor did Spain to the Russia of 1917). All the sections within the UGT–PSOE agreed that they would not follow the CNT revolutionary path. In December 1933 the Socialists had rapidly disassociated themselves from the third and, by far, the biggest CNT uprising. Spreading from Aragón to other provinces, it was again a futile exercise in revolutionary gymnastics, the epitome of spontaneous heroism and senseless violence causing some 75 deaths, hundreds of arrests and leaving the libertarian movement badly crippled.[96] In turn, the Socialists remained aloof from these events and stated that only the inclusion of the CEDA in government would force them to abandon legality.[97] Meanwhile, they seemed confident that their revolutionary threats would be enough to deter Lerroux, and ultimately Alcalá, from sharing power with declared enemies of the Republic.

The countryside remained the most conflictive spot. Rural Spain was implicitly recognised as a sphere of primordial interest for the right;

local authorities turned a blind eye to violations of the existing legislation. With Salazar Alonso as interior minister, the rural oligarchy felt confident that the time had arrived to recover much of their lost ground and once more to reduce the peasantry to submissiveness. Socialists were sacked from arbitration committees and replaced by landowners' representatives, salaries were slashed, working contracts unfulfilled and labourers told that if they were hungry they should 'comed república' ('eat the Republic').[98] The growing despair felt by the FNTT, led by the Caballerista Ricardo Zabalza, was of no surprise. The final straw was the repeal of the Law of Municipal Boundaries in May 1934. This meant that now, at harvest time, landowners were able to bring in cheap labour from outside areas to the detriment of local workers. The FNTT decided to launch a general strike in June, affecting 15 southern provinces. In such a crucial conflict, the contrast between the two warring sides was glaring. The Caballerista-dominated UGT failed to support its counterparts in the FNTT, revealing that their radicalism hardly went beyond rhetoric. In contrast, Salazar Alonso was determined to inflict a deadly blow to Socialist power in the countryside. He rapidly declared the harvest to be a national utility and treated the strike as a threat to public order, using ruthless violence to put it down. In fierce clashes with the police, thirteen peasants were killed. Hundreds of Socialist militants, including councillors and even four deputies, were arrested and local trade unions were closed. The tide was turning in favour of the rural oligarchy that began to feel strong enough to restore the relations of dependence which had prevailed before 1931.[99]

Almost immediately thereafter, the centre of contention shifted to Cataluña, the last stronghold of the left. There, in April 1934, the Generalitat presided over by Lluís Companys, introduced the Law of Agricultural Contracts that gave the rabassaires ('tenant vine-growers') the right to purchase their land once they had cultivated it for 18 years.[100] This measure brought the Generalitat into conflict with the central government over legal jurisdiction when the irate Catalan landowners, backed by the Lliga, took their case to Madrid on the grounds of unconstitutionality. Companys agreed to withdraw it but then merely passed the law, in a slightly different form, in the summer. An inexperienced Samper intended to find a compromise. The CEDA, however, had something different in mind. On 9 September it organised a huge rally in Covadonga (Asturias). The chosen spot could not have been more provocative. Covadonga was the place where the mythical Reconquista had begun. In an event reminiscent of fascist parades, a bellicose Gil Robles, cheered by the green-uniformed members of the JAP and hailed as *Jefe* (Chief), launched a rabble-rousing speech against the Republic. Invoking parallels with the legendary past, he threatened to start a new *reconquista* but this time against Reds, separatists and Masons. On 26 September, Gil Robles withdrew his support for the government and demanded ministerial participation in any new administration. On 1 October, Samper duly resigned.

### Turning back the clock

Despite the advice from moderate republicans such as Miguel Maura, on 4 October 1934 Alcalá accepted the formation of a cabinet, presided over by Lerroux and containing three CEDA ministers (Rafael Aizpún in Justice and, more crucially, José Oriol y Anguera de Sojo in Labour and Manuel Giménez Fernández in Agriculture). For the Socialists, the dreaded moment that they had hoped to prevent with their revolutionary threats had arrived.[101] Spain's division into two polarised camps became a dangerous reality. Of course, based on its parliamentary strength, the accidentalist right had a fair claim to be represented in government. Without its collaboration, the legislative process could not proceed. However, influential sectors within the CEDA did not conceal their admiration for Fascism, while Gil Robles insisted on the necessity of carrying out a profound constitutional revision which would drastically alter the original form of the Republic. Besides, Socialist misgivings in the light of contemporary events on the continent were understandable. Examples of how Mussolini and Hitler had accepted a minority of portfolios in coalition governments and then easily destroyed democracy from within gave rise to widespread fear that Spain was heading a similar way. Even more recent and frightening was the Austrian example.

If right-wing forces had attempted to 'rectify' the course the Republic was taking in 1932, it was the turn for the left in 1934. This was the second time that the Socialists had led a massive insurrection against the state. Both times their movement was crushed. If anything, for all the fiery talk of the previous months, they were even less prepared than they had been on the first occasion in 1917. A revolution spurred by squads of militants who mostly existed only on paper and who had few caches of weapons (as most of them had already been seized by the police) was bound to be an utter fiasco.[102] Martial law was declared and the army was given free rein to put down the rebellion. *Cenetistas* remained aloof, proclaiming this to be a political struggle that did not affect them. With the FNTT severely mauled only a few months earlier, the countryside remained relatively quiet. As troops quickly came out in force, thousands of leftist leaders, including Azaña and Caballero, were rounded up. The 'Spanish Lenin's' role in those so crucial moments was telling. In his own words, he stayed at home waiting for the police to arrest him, as he had nothing to do with the course of the events.[103] Despite skirmishes and shootings in some regional capitals, the cities were soon under the control of the authorities. In Barcelona, Companys proclaimed a Catalan state within a Spanish Federal Republic, but had to surrender in less than 24 hours, when the army began bombarding the *Generalitat*. As in 1917, the revolution temporarily succeeded only in Asturias where an alliance of all leftist groups, including the CNT, was established and some 20,000 miners, organised in columns armed with dynamite, held out for a fortnight. The Asturian events foreshadowed the brutality of the civil war. With the declaration of martial law, power passed into the hands of the Radical war minister, Diego Hidalgo. However, it was General Franco, appointed technical adviser to the war minister, who was actually in charge and who ordered, for the first time, the use of colonial troops from Africa on the Spanish mainland: both Moroccan mercenaries under Spanish command and the Foreign Legion were deployed. The operation gained both Franco and the Army of Africa renown and raised their status within right-wing circles. Their decisive role in crushing the revolution also encouraged their own latent messianic mission to restore Spain to its true identity from the barracks of Spanish Morocco, uncontaminated by metropolitan politics.[104] The revolutionaries burnt 58 churches, including the Bishop's Palace in Oviedo, and took hostages amongst businessmen, right-wingers and clergymen. Many of them, including 31 priests, were killed. In turn, the troops resorted to the torture and execution of prisoners to break the resistance of the Asturian workers. The latter offered to surrender – but only on condition that they would be allowed to give themselves up to the regular army and not to the African troops.[105] The total toll of the October events was 1335 killed and 2951 wounded, the majority of them in Asturias.[106]

The aftermath of October 1934 seemed to vindicate the CEDA's legalist strategy and effectively buried the vision of an inclusive republic governed by Republicans. Now a vicious counter-revolution began in earnest. About 40,000 Republicans and Socialists languished in prisons, with many others having to go into hiding or abroad. A special vendetta was pursued against leaders such as Azaña, who, despite his parliamentary immunity, was kept imprisoned until December (when the Supreme Court released him for lack of evidence of his complicity in the October events). Catalan autonomy was suspended and the *Generalitat* replaced by a governor-general appointed by Madrid. All over the country, employers sought revenge for the previous years. There were massive lay-offs, wages were slashed, trade unions were disbanded and arbitration committees were suspended.[107] The traditional order was also restored in the countryside as peasants were evicted and councils were overthrown and replaced by nominees of the local *caciques*. The clock had been turned back to the darkest days of the monarchy.

On the political stage, *Cedistas* and Agrarians abused their parliamentary strength to make and dismiss cabinets, thereby further undermining the Radicals. First, the ministers Samper and Hidalgo (prime minister and war minister in the previous administration) were accused of gross negligence in allowing the insurrection to happen, and they had to go. Then it was the turn of the education minister, Filiberto Villalobos. He was deemed too 'anticlerical'. Equally, the limits of the CEDA's social reformism became evident when its own agriculture minister, Manuel Giménez Fernández, a Christian Democrat who displayed a genuine concern for conciliation in the countryside, came under fierce attacks from members of his own party. Giménez naively believed that landowners could be moved towards a less intransigent position by the appeals of a friendly Catholic minister. Denounced as a 'white bolshevik', his legislation to forbid evictions and favour tenant farmers was torn apart.[108] Increasingly worried by the levels of repression, Alcalá insisted on commuting 21 of the 23 death sentences for the October events. This issue confirmed the strained relations between the head of the state and both Gil Robles and Lerroux.[109]

The price of keeping the CEDA on board was another cabinet reshuffle in May 1935. Still presided over by Lerroux, the CEDA, with five portfolios, for the first time emerged as the strongest party in the governing coalition. Gil Robles seized for himself the crucial post of war minister. In that position, he would transform the army into a counter-revolutionary bulwark. Liberal officers were purged and their places filled by *Africanistas* and hard-liners. General Joaquín Fanjul, a rabid monarchist, became his under-secretary. Franco, for his 'outstanding' role in October, was rewarded with the appointment of chief of the general staff. Martín Baguenas, a former chief of police with the monarchy, became the new director of security and *Africanistas* such as the Generals Goded and Mola were also promoted to key positions.[110] Another of Gil Robles's deeds was his attempt to achieve the destruction of the negative of a Paramount film (*The Devil is a Woman*) starring Marlene Dietrich and directed by Eric von Sternberg, which, in his opinion, denigrated the good name of the Spanish army.[111] At the same time, Giménez Fernández was removed from his post and replaced by the Agrarian Nicasio Velayos. The latter soon introduced the 'Law for Reforming the Agrarian Reform', which meant certain death for any remnant of progressive legislation.[112]

Suddenly, however, in the autumn of 1935, the CEDA–Radical partnership was thrown into disarray when a series of financial scandals surfaced involving leading members of Lerroux's party. With the initial connivance of the CEDA, the Radicals tried to hush the business up, but they ran into the opposition of Alcalá, who, either for reasons of moral probity or in a search for personal revenge, was unwilling to follow suit. Lerroux and his closest cronies had to leave office. A long story of venality and the plundering of public funds had finally caught up with the Radicals, leaving them as a spent force.[113] After two years in power, the most senior republican party left behind a stain of corruption and nepotism. This unexpected turn of events convinced Gil Robles that his opportunity had arrived. In early December the CEDA torpedoed the economic plans of a new coalition government in which they still had the largest representation. The idea was that the president of the Republic would now be compelled to entrust Gil Robles with the premiership of the new cabinet which would then undertake a thorough constitutional revision. To Gil Robles's chagrin, however, Alcalá opted for the other available solution: the dissolution of parliament and the appointment of one of his political allies, Manuel Portela Valladares, to organise new general elections. Gil Robles had overplayed his hand. When Alcalá alleged that his decision had been caused by the impossibility – given the existing composition of the chamber – of finding stable governments, the CEDA's leader could hardly reply that he had engineered that instability in order to speed up his accession to power.[114] In desperation, the CEDA leader tried to lobby Franco and other friendly officers to stage a coup. It was, though, in vain, as the generals felt that they were not ready to act. The CEDA had been frustrated in the final stage of its plan and now had to devote its energies to fighting a new electoral campaign.[115]

## The slippery road to war

It was extremely ironic that, at such a critical stage of the Republic's life, there should be three ex-Monarchist ministers – Alcalá Zamora, Portela Valladares and Santiago Alba – occupying the vital posts of president of the Republic, prime minister and parliamentary speaker. With Spain divided into two strongly opposed political camps, attempts to create a centrist force proved futile. Nobody would join forces with the discredited Radicals, who were now under the leadership of Alba. With the full backing of Alcalá, Portela resorted to old methods of patronage and the appointment of trusted friends as civil governors to secure a sizeable minority in the next parliament.[116] But electoral chicanery was no longer possible in the polarised Spain of 1936.

The electoral campaign was frenzied. Both sides fought the elections as a question of survival. For the left, its cause represented the defence of the Republic of 1931 against the oncoming threat of Fascism. For the right, it was a struggle to uphold Christian traditional values against the peril of disintegrating revolution. However, unlike 1933, this time the right was less successful than the left in building a broad electoral coalition.

The CEDA's attempts to create a grand anti-revolutionary alliance did not bear fruit. The first obstacle was its intransigence towards PNV hopes of Basque self-government. This meant the alienation of the PNV, even though it was a profoundly Catholic party. The PNV, having initially been a rabidly anti-republican party (together with the Carlists, it had formed part of the Vasco–Navarrese minority in parliament), began to adopt a more pragmatic and Christian Democratic stance in 1934, although there still existed hard-line sectors imbued with Arana's racist ideology. In 1936 the PNV nevertheless found their nationalist aspirations pulling them towards an accommodation with their traditional enemies, the Socialists – even though the PNV remained the most important confessional party in the Basque Country.[117] Meanwhile, moderate republicans, such as Miguel Maura, could not share the same platform as other components of the right, who were openly pinning their hopes on a coup. In-fighting between Monarchists and *Cedistas* over positions on the electoral lists also constantly hampered rightist unity, while the Falange refused to accept the candidacies it was allocated and thus went into the elections alone, rather than as part of a coalition.[118]

The construction of the broad left-wing coalition, later known as the 'Popular Front', was an arduous task, accomplished basically by the resilient Manuel Azaña with the support of Indalecio Prieto.[119] Azaña was banking on his personal record as the man who embodied the Republic's original spirit. With his charisma enhanced by months of imprisonment in late 1934, the former prime minister began a frenetic campaign that he termed 'the recovery of the Republic' in 1935. Having already presided over the fusion of left Republican parties in April 1934,[120] he then toured the country holding a series of open-air rallies that culminated, in October 1935, in a monster gathering at Comillas on the outskirts of Madrid. Before a crowd of some 400,000 people, the largest ever in Spanish history, Azaña outlined a pro-gramme encompassing immediate amnesty for the thousands of politi-cal prisoners of October 1934 and the return of the social reformist legislation of 1931 as the basis for an electoral alliance. In November he formally invited the Socialists to join him.[121]

However, the Socialists were anything but united in 1935. With the *Besteirista* faction in open decline, the struggle for control of the Socialist movement – the largest political force in Spain – was between the followers of Prieto and Largo Caballero.[122] Prieto had always con-sidered it a mistake to have broken the alliance with the Republicans in 1933. His opinion was further confirmed by the failure of the October 1934 revolution and its violent aftermath. Certain that the only way to regain power was through a broad electoral coalition, he was eager to co-operate with Azaña. However, he met Largo's obstinate opposition. Largo's governmental experience had been marked by frustration followed by his spell in prison. In 1935 both camps embarked upon a bitter dialectical war. The *Caballeristas* were dominant in the UGT and the Socialist Youth, and the *Prietistas* were dominant in the PSOE, where eventually Caballero resigned his post of president in December 1935. They were also geographically divided. The sections in Madrid and the south were behind Caballero. Ironically, those in the north where its rank and file had been more successful in October, were Prieto's strongholds. Thus, the northern groups were quick to uphold their past record in reminding the *Caballeristas* that their own revolu-tionary rhetoric never went beyond mere posturing and would only serve to hand the Republic to the CEDA.[123]

Largo's uncompromising position was, paradoxically, difficult to sustain, owing to the dramatic about-turn taken by the Communists. With the Fascist tide sweeping over Europe and an attempted coup in February 1934 in France, the French Communist Party offered a tactical alliance to their Socialist counterparts in June 1934 which, in October of that year, led to the establishment of a *vaste rassemblement populaire* that included liberal bourgeois forces which were the equivalent of Spain's republicans.[124] Broad national alliances of progressive forces, the so-called Popular Fronts, were then officially endorsed in the summer of 1935 during the Seventh Congress of the Comintern. Spain, with its own young democratic system on the verge of being overthrown, seemed the perfect place to put this strategy into practice. Even though small in numbers and in strength, the PCE thus became a passionate defender of a pact with Azaña and the liberal bourgeoisie.[125]

In fact, the Communists' ultimate goal was the unification of the country's Marxist forces in the expectation that their small but highly disciplined ranks would assume political control of the Spanish left. The radicalisation of the *Caballeristas* offered them a golden opportunity. The youth of the two organisations merged into the United Socialist Youth (JSU) and the Communists disbanded their trade union, the CGTU, to join the UGT. Ironically, they saw themselves outflanked by the doctrinal intransigence of the *Caballeristas*. Jacques Duclos, the Comintern agent in France, travelled twice to Spain to persuade a stubborn Largo of the need to join the Popular Front. By then, even the most obstinate Socialists could not ignore the popular impression left by Azaña in Comillas.[126] Finally, the Socialists agreed to enter negotiations with the republicans, on the assurance that they would have no ministerial responsibility and that the Communists would be included in any electoral coalition. Last-minute obstacles were removed when the republicans accepted bilateral talks with the Socialists that, in turn, were designated to represent the rest of the working-class forces. The Popular Front's joint manifesto, accepting the moderate goals of the republicans as well as their preponderance in the electoral lists, was agreed on 15 January 1936 and signed by a broad coalition of groups: left-wing Republicans, Socialists, Communists, Angel Pestaña's Syndicalist Party and the POUM (a mostly Catalan-based group of dissident Communists not affiliated to the Comintern). It could also rely on the votes of the CNT–FAI, who were anxious to see thousands of their militants freed from prison.[127]

The electoral results revealed the country's division along political lines. The right obtained 4,503,524 votes, consolidating its grip over both Castillas, Navarra and Galicia. The left, with 4,654,116 votes, dominated in the south, the periphery and the main industrial cities. As a result of the electoral system, the overall narrow margin of the victory meant a huge swing in terms of seats: the right returned 132 deputies (88 of the CEDA) and the Popular Front had 286 seats

(99 of them Socialists). With only 42 deputies, the political centre was practically wiped out (the Radicals had only four seats).[128] Until the last moment, Gil Robles tried to prevent the fait accompli. He persuaded some generals, including Franco, that a victory for the Popular Front meant anarchy. They then tried to cajole the Prime Minister into annulling the results and declaring martial law. However, with such 'bullying' tactics they only hastened Portela Valladares in his transfer of power to Azaña. Finally, right-wing hopes of frustrating the left's return to government were dashed by the position of General Pozas, head of the Civil Guard, who was opposed to any coup and even sent out his forces to surround all the suspect garrisons.[129]

Those who had been at the receiving end of the reactionary backlash following October 1934 greeted the Popular Front victory with enthusiasm. Catalans had seen their autonomy taken away and Basques their nationalist aspirations thwarted. Workers had contemplated with dismay how the social legislation had all but evaporated and how their wages had been slashed and their working contracts disregarded. Peasants had been subjugated again to the dictates of the *caciques*. Thus there could be no return to the elation of 1931. Embittered by the experiences of the preceding months, an avalanche of demands ensued. Cities were brought to a standstill by a wave of industrial strikes, while thousands of landless peasants, encouraged by a revived FNTT, began to occupy landed estates (particularly in Extremadura). The *Generalitat* was immediately re-established, the drafting of a Basque statute began, arbitration committees returned, workers sacked for political reasons regained their jobs and indemnified and land occupations were legitimised *post hoc*. Between March and July 1936, more land was redistributed than in all the previous years of the Republic put together.[130]

Amidst the social commotion of 1936, the Communists were particularly vocal over the need for restraint. In their new role of defenders of a bourgeois regime, the PCE attempted to limit the scale of labour tensions.[131] By contrast, the CNT reaffirmed its commitment to bring about a libertarian society through revolt. Although far from its peak of 1931–32, the CNT, with 559,000 members, still constituted an awesome force. There were mixed signals coming from this camp. In an attempt to recover the lost ground, the CNT was involved in violent disputes in places such as Madrid and Málaga. However, there was no return to the mass uprisings of previous times, and even places such as Barcelona and Zaragoza experienced an almost unprecedented period of social peace.[132]

More threatening to the country's stability was the bitter struggle that continued to tear the Socialists apart. Indeed, during these crucial months the Popular Front's largest organisation seemed bent on self-destruction. The internal feuding acquired, on occasions, unprecedented violence, if not lunacy. In May, Prieto accompanied by the 'heroes' of the Asturian revolution, González Peña and Belarmino Tomás, saw their rally in Ecija (Sevilla), a *Caballerista* stronghold, disrupted by the heckling of the local Socialist youth. Amidst the ensuing havoc they fled to safety, their cars speeding away under a hail of bullets.[133] Caballero's supporters also managed to thwart an initiative that might have provided Spain with a stronger government. It consisted of impeaching Alcalá, whose actions had antagonised every political sector, on the grounds that he had exceeded his authority by dissolving the Cortes twice in one term. The first step of the plan, the elevation of Azaña to the presidency, was rapidly accomplished, but the appointment of Prieto as the new prime minister met with the total opposition of the *Caballeristas* and was dropped.[134] The premiership then went to the Galician Santiago Casares Quiroga, an indecisive man who was sick with tuberculosis and who was far from being the appropriate leader to defend the Republic at its most crucial time of need, when the existence of military plots was an open secret.

Caballero's blocking the PSOE from joining the government could be justified by the frustrations that many Socialists felt during their past experience of ministerial responsibility. Moreover, holding back the masses for the sake of consolidating a bourgeois order for the second time was a tall order in the explosive atmosphere of 1936. For Largo, Prieto's plans were for the PSOE to become Azaña's lackey.[135] However, the *Caballeristas*, poised in a personal vendetta against the executive of their own party, ignored the danger presented by the rightist enemy. In a mixture of idealism and naivety, they believed that power would eventually fall peacefully into their laps. For all their rhetoric, they never envisaged a revolutionary takeover or an alliance with the CNT. On the contrary, in practical examples such as the fisheries strike in Málaga or the building dispute in Madrid (both in June–July 1936), the UGT's traditional conciliatory stance led to clashes with the more radical *Cenetistas* that left several dead on both sides and aggravated the feeling of overall chaos. Prieto argued that a country could withstand the convulsion of a true revolution but it could not resist the constant drip-drip of prolonged public disorder, with the wastage of authority and economic vitality which that entailed.[136] The *Caballeristas'* stance involved the worst of two worlds. Their verbal rhetoric had the effect of terrorising the middle classes and speeding up preparations for an armed insurrection. However, by vetoing Socialist participation in the cabinet, they impeded the formation of a strong government that might have averted armed insurrection.[137] Spanish Socialism had never known such a degree of paralysis as the two rival leaderships effectively cancelled each other out.

At the same time, with the CEDA's legalist tactic shattered by the outcome of the polls, on the political right the initiative passed to the advocates of violence. The Falange found its numbers swelling dramatically as a result of the continuous inflow of disillusioned members of the CEDA's youth wing, the JAP. The CEDA itself began to take a secondary role, allowing *Renovación Española* to take the political lead. On 8 March several leading *Africanistas* gathered at the house of the CEDA's unsuccessful candidate for Madrid, the stockbroker José Delgado, to organise a military coup.[138]

Extremists on both sides succeeded in pushing the country into a whirlpool of violence after February 1936. Right-wing gunmen unleashed a reign of terror, bombing and spraying with bullets the houses of the republican lawyer Eduardo Ortega y Gasset and Largo Caballero respectively. The prominent Socialist jurist Luis Jiménez de Asúa escaped unscathed from an assassination attempt but one of his police escorts was killed. The magistrate who condemned a Falangist to 25 years of prison for that attack was himself shot dead. In turn, left-wing zealots murdered the ex-minister Alfredo Martínez and churches fell prey to arson attacks. There were also numerous incidents of popular anger degenerating into assaults against right-wing political centres.[139] In total there were 269 political killings between February and July. This climate of chaos mainly benefited the right. Its powerful media magnified every small incident in order to incite the army to put an end to this 'lawless' regime. These calls were then echoed in parliament by leading right-wing personalities. They never considered the connection between social upheaval and the starvation wages, endemic hunger for land and high levels of illiteracy endured by the masses. They also forgot to mention in their vehement statements how much of the violence was the responsibility of their own supporters.

The government proved incapable of curbing the military conspiracy, and the imprisonment of José Antonio and other Falangist leaders did not put an end to the cycle of violence. Furthermore, the idea of sending all generals suspected of conspiring against the government to distant outposts only worked in the plotters' favour, as they could now forge a rebel network all over the country. Sanjurjo, from his exile in Portugal, was the visible head of the movement. The real director inside Spain was General Mola, who had been sent to Navarra – a Carlist stronghold and so the ideal place to recruit a popular reactionary mass following. The *Unión Militar Española* (UME), a semi-clandestine organisation that claimed a membership of 3500 officers, played a fundamental part in establishing conspiratorial cells in every province. All the right-wing political groups were aware of preparations for the coup and contributed their contacts, finances and manpower for its successful accomplishment.[140]

In July 1936 everybody in the country except Casares seemed to be conscious of the military threat. With a confidence stretching sometimes to the borders of insanity, the prime minister kept dismissing the worrying news as 'unfounded rumours' and even told Prieto that his warnings were 'menopausal outbursts'.[141] On 12 July, José Castillo, a lieutenant of the Assault Guards, was assassinated by a right-wing hit squad. Previously, other well-known left-wing officers (such as Captain Carlos Faraudo, instructor of the Socialist militia) had also been targeted by rightist terror. Dismayed by the latest outrage and following the pattern of tit-for-tat retaliation, Castillo's companions decided to avenge him by killing a leading right-winger. That night, the Monarchist leader Calvo Sotelo was arrested and then murdered.[142] Two days later, at a hastily assembled *Diputación Permanente* (the standing body of deputies that could be convened when parliament was not in session), right-wing politicians vented their anger. Gil Robles noted that the government, although not to blame for Calvo's execution, was responsible for creating the circumstances which made it possible.[143] Never before had a leader of the parliamentary opposition been kidnapped and assassinated by individuals who were members of the police. Yet, for all their justified exasperation, the right-wing deputies never recalled their level of involvement with the military preparations. Calvo Sotelo's death, however, persuaded dithering officers to participate in the plans for a coup that had been under way since the right had lost the political argument in a democratic ballot.

# 3

## The Distorting Mirror: The International Dimension of the Spanish Civil War

We were born in a distant country
Our soul is burdened with hate
But our fatherland is not yet lost,
Today our fatherland lies before Madrid ...
Comrades, cover the parapets
For life without peace is not life ...[1]

### A reversal of fortune

At no time had the military plotters anticipated the protracted confrontation that the Spanish Civil War was to become. On the contrary, they had assumed that their uprising would meet with success within a matter of days. However, unlike other countries whose constitutional regimes had been overthrown with hardly any struggle, the Spanish Republic fought back and it would take three years of vicious fighting before it was crushed. Spain's fratricidal struggle was to have an immense impact throughout Europe. Indeed, the international appeal of the battling factions, as well as the degree of foreign involvement in the conflict, was a staggering phenomenon that effectively turned an internal affair into a veritable civil war amongst Europeans.

On the afternoon of 17 July, the military insurrection began in Spanish Morocco, where, after a few skirmishes, the local garrisons seized control of the colony. That evening, when meeting the assorted press, the Prime Minister, Casares Quiroga, allegedly joked: 'They are rising? Very well, I shall go and lie down.'[2] His sense of humour was as misplaced as were his defences against the revolt. During the next 72 hours the armed rebellion spread to the mainland.

By 20 July, Spain was effectively divided into two zones that were remarkably similar to the electoral map of February 1936. The military rebels, known to history as the Nationalists, held firmly under their control the traditionally conservative and Catholic areas of Galicia, Old Castilla and Navarra, all the colonies, the Canary Islands and the Balearics (with the exception of Menorca). These regions, covering roughly a third of the country, had voted for the right-wing parties in the elections of February 1936 and now met the insurrection with widespread enthusiasm. The Nationalists could also claim success in capturing some places with a strong working-class presence, such as Zaragoza, Oviedo and a small but vital strip of land in Andalucía that included Seville, Granada, Córdoba and Cádiz. However, in the rest of the country, a combination of the swift action and determination of the trade unions, and the loyalty of police forces (both the assault and the civil guards) and of many senior officers resulted in the crushing of the seditious movement. This territory was the most densely populated and urbanised. It included the main capitals (Madrid, Barcelona and Valencia), all the main industrial areas of northern and eastern Spain, the entire Mediterranean coast as far south as Málaga and all the vast rural areas of Extremadura, Murcia, New Castilla and Eastern Andalucía. Furthermore, Spain's air force (albeit tiny) and the country's huge gold reserves remained in the hands of the government. The Army of Africa, containing the fierce Foreign Legion and the *Regulares* (indigenous Moorish troops commanded by Spanish officers), Spain's most battle-hardened professional military force, was paralysed by the problem of transport across the Straits of Gibraltar after sailors stayed loyal to the Republic, overpowered their officers and retained control of the fleet.

Based on that correlation of forces, it seems reasonable to speculate that the insurrection should have been crushed in a relatively short time. However, as both sides lacked significant modern weaponry and any important armament industry, they rapidly looked abroad for diplomatic and military support. The contrasting response of other countries to the appeals from Spain proved to be crucial. A botched coup d'état soon became a civil war. In turn, Spain became the distorting mirror in which Europe contemplated an exaggerated image of all the tensions, passions and energies of this turbulent era.[3]

Republican hopes of rapidly gaining the upper hand in the exploding conflict rested on the Western democracies, particularly its sister

Popular Front government in France. On 20 July, José Giral, the new prime minister of the Republic, in a confident tone, requested help from the French administration, including 20 Potez aircraft. There was no doubt about the legality of that appeal, since, under international law, a government has the right to purchase arms when confronted with a rebellion. Furthermore, a Franco-Spanish commercial agreement, signed in late 1935, provided for the purchase of weapons in France up to the value of 20 million francs. As expected by the Spanish Republicans, the reaction of the French prime minister, the Socialist Léon Blum, was entirely favourable. With the agreement of key ministers (the Radicals, Yvon Delbos in the Foreign Office, Edouard Daladier in Defence and Pierre Cot in Aviation) steps were then taken to organise the delivery.[4] That decision was not only taken as a result of ideological solidarity but also because it was in France's national interests that a friendly government should remain on its southern border.[5] However, a combination of domestic and foreign pressures was to alter a French stance that, in principle, seemed to be the obvious one for its government to take.

On 23 July, Blum and Delbos travelled on a routine mission to London. There they were left in no doubt of the hostility felt in British governing circles towards possible French involvement in the Spanish struggle. Evidence of this ranged from the personal appeal of the British foreign minister, Anthony Eden, to Blum to be extremely prudent in his dealings with Spain to hints that Britain would not be dragged into a war over events in the peninsula.[6] One day later, the French leaders were faced with an unpleasant welcome home. During their absence, the defection of the Spanish military attaché, Antonio Barroso, and his subsequent leaks to the press of plans to send weapons to Spain, transformed what initially seemed a clear-cut operation into domestic strife.

France had been torn apart in the inter-war years by political polarisation and social upheaval. In February 1934 the French Republic was rocked by financial scandals involving its political elites and a right-wing coup was narrowly averted. As in Spain, with the country divided into two major blocs, a Popular Front coalition of Communists, Socialists and Radicals defeated an alliance of right-wing forces in the spring of 1936. This victory was quickly followed by widespread industrial militancy and rumours of conspiracies. News of intervention in Spain gave the right-wing media, clearly favourable to the insurgents, the required ammunition to mount a devastating campaign against involvement in a foreign adventure. The government was branded as treacherous and unfit for office. Blum himself, a Jewish Socialist, aroused a special hatred amongst right-wing circles.[7] For them, the Third Republic seemed to be in 'enemy' hands. The slogan 'Better Hitler than Blum' summed up feelings that eventually led to Vichy and collaboration with Germany. Additionally, innate hatred of Bolshevism permeated the French officer corps, many of whose members were suspicious of a Popular Front that included Socialists and Communists and that regarded with sympathy the insurrection of their Spanish counterparts. They were, therefore, distraught at the notion of France supplying weapons to the Spanish government and, at the very least, they planned to delay or obstruct such deliveries.[8]

With the country polarised over the Spanish issue, leading elements in the French Radical Party (including the president of the Republic, Albert Lebrun, the speaker of the lower chamber, Edouard Herriot, and the president of the senate, Jules Jeanneney) were firmly against sending military aid to the Republic. They argued that such a move could lead either to the outbreak of a general war on the continent or, at the very least, to the spread of the Spanish conflict to France. After a tumultuous cabinet meeting on 25 July, Blum had to confront the opposition of the majority of his Radical allies. Only Jean Zay, the education minister, and Pierre Cot from that party were staunch friends of the Spanish Republic. The view of the traditionally conservative Quai d'Orsay (French Foreign Office), voiced by Delbos, was crucial in finally tilting the balance. No measure, it insisted, should be taken that could endanger the vital alliance with Britain. Arms shipments by the government were immediately suspended. However, the private sector was not affected and Cot seemed to have already arranged the sale of some weapons to Mexico, a country friendly to the Spanish Republic, which would then hand them over to Madrid.[9] This, however, was not sufficient to save the Republic. Years later, Cot was to stress the significance of the French about-turn: 'I have no doubts that if we could have sent massive aid to Spain, we could have nipped the insurrection in the bud.'[10]

The British government was not taken by surprise by the military rebellion.[11] But, unlike the French administration, British ruling circles were strongly sympathetic to the rebels. For reasons of class and upbringing, they were naturally repelled by what a left-wing Republic stood for and approved of the anti-revolutionary objectives of the insurrection.[12] The national government, led by the Conservative Stanley Baldwin, and the diplomatic corps, an almost exclusive club of the aristocracy and upper echelons of the bourgeoisie educated at

Oxbridge, were steeped in anti-Bolshevik prejudices. The signing of a treaty of friendship between France and the Soviet Union in May 1935, for example, was received with dismay in London. Even more discouraging were the Popular Front victories in Spain and France in 1936. The ambassador in Madrid, the fiercely anti-Republican Sir Henry Chilton, kept stressing the similarities between Republican Spain and the Kerensky administration in 1917 Russia. Alarm bells rang as a wave of strikes paralysed France under its Socialist prime minister. Furthermore, an awareness of the increasingly enfeebled economic and military position of the British Empire led to staunch support of the strategy of appeasement. This policy sought to avoid confrontation with the Fascist dictators and instead to find an accommodation of their revisionist ambitions through diplomatic negotiation. Consequently, the outbreak of war in Spain, and its potential for creating divisions on the continent along ideological lines, constituted a threat for appeasement.

From the first days, diplomatic and intelligence reports confirmed the anti-Republican feelings already dominant in the British government. Indeed, the atrocities committed on both sides were very differently interpreted. Whereas those in the Republican zone were portrayed as the consequence of mob rule, those in Nationalist areas were described as restoring law and order.[13] Additionally, Britain was Spain's most important trading partner (accounting for 25 per cent of Spanish exports and 10 per cent of her imports) and controlled about 40 per cent of total foreign investment (it amounted to 13.3 per cent of Britain's investments in Europe). This capital was largely concentrated in the iron and pyrite industries, followed by the electricity sector, public utilities, citrus fruits and sherry.[14] Thus, ruling economic circles were naturally inclined to favour the victory of a right-wing rebellion, for fear that their huge investments could be seized by the trade unions loyal to the Republic. Consequently, the British administration concluded that, in Spain, the army was combating a virtual Soviet regime under the umbrella of a lifeless government that was unworthy of either direct or indirect support. General Franco was viewed as a good, prudent and conservative officer who had intervened in politics only to fight the spectre of social revolution. His victory would lead to the establishment of 'a liberal dictatorship' very favourable to the interests of the United Kingdom.[15]

The heart of the problem for British diplomacy was that formal legitimacy was in the same camp as the dreaded social revolution, while the counter-revolution remained formally illegitimate.[16] Consequently, since direct intervention in favour of the rebellion was unthinkable, the British government declared, and maintained for the home audience, an image of scrupulous neutrality. However, the imposed arms embargo reduced to the same level the legally recognised government (which retained the sole legal capacity to import this matériel) and the insurgents. This position concealed Britain's real hostility towards a Republic that, in Eden's words, 'we shall be able to avoid supplying, by some means or other'.[17] On 22 July the British administration accepted Franco's requests to refuse the Republican Navy fuel and provisions in the ports of Gibraltar and Tangiers.[18] Two days earlier, the strongly anti-revolutionary feelings that determined British policy-making had been encapsulated by the memo of the cabinet secretary, Sir Maurice Hankey: 'With France and Spain menaced by Bolshevism, it is not inconceivable that soon we will have to throw in our lot with Italy and Germany.'[19] This stance, involving a serious warning to France, was blatantly evident when, on 26 July, Baldwin instructed Eden: 'On no account, French or other, must you bring us into the fight on the side of the Russians!'[20] The Republic was then inflicted a serious blow when, on 13 August, the existing commercial payment agreement between both countries was suspended and trade plummeted. This measure served to block the distribution in London of a considerable quantity of sterling earned by Spanish exports to Britain. Also, a financial transaction of the Republic, via Barclays Bank, to purchase arms in America was impeded, while a simultaneous operation carried out by the rebels through the Westminster Bank was permitted.[21]

While the Republic was being ostracised in the international arena, the Nationalists received an entirely different response. From the start, for example, they could rely on the open support of Portugal. With the sympathy of the dictatorship of Antonio Salazar, the nominal head of the rebellion, General Sanjurjo, and another 15,000 prominent monarchists established the headquarters of the conspiracy there. During the first weeks of the war, moreover, Portugal's proximity to the battleground was of inestimable value. The country became the perfect conduit through which foreign aid could be delivered, and served also to link the divided Nationalist zones. In early August 1936, Franco's brother Nicolás established himself in Lisbon (where he was soon joined by Gil Robles) to procure supplies and organise propaganda and economic assistance. Portugal also arranged the recruitment of about ten thousand Portuguese 'volunteers' (the *Viriatos*) to fight alongside the Nationalists.[22] Believing that a 'Red' victory in Spain would have a devastating impact on the stability of his own regime,

Salazar identified fully with the cause of the Spanish insurgents and played a vital diplomatic role, acting almost as the international spokesman of Nationalist Spain. However, Salazar could offer only minimal concrete military assistance. Much more important contributions came from Germany and Italy. Before July 1936 the Nazis had revealed no interest in Spain's political developments. Germany's economic interests there were very modest, with a relatively small capital investment, and mutual trade plummeting in the 1930s.[23] With expansionist plans focused on Eastern Europe, Spain was a distant land that Hitler had not even cited in any relevant context in *Mein Kampf*. Consequently, a German Foreign Office fearful of international complications promptly rebuffed the first requests for aid from General Mola.[24] However, at this vital junction, with the insurrection floundering, a combination of luck and cunning was to change the fate of the Nationalist camp.

Johannes Bernhardt, a German resident in Morocco and member of the *Auslandorganisation* (AO), the Nazi organisation abroad, offered his services to General Franco, who, showing remarkable foresight, used this opportunity to bypass the bureaucratic web to appeal directly to Hitler. Bernhardt and his immediate superior, Adolf Langenheim, agreed to travel to Germany on 23 July, in a confiscated Lufthansa plane. They flew with Captain Francisco Arraza Monasterio, appointed chief of staff of the non-existent air forces in Africa, with the mission of delivering a personal letter to Hitler pleading for military assistance. However, it was not easy to gain direct access to a *Führer* always surrounded by a circle of courtesans fighting among themselves for his favours and it would take a series of fortuitous events to favour the cause of the Spanish rebels.

Reaching Berlin on 25 July, the Bernhardt mission rapidly met Friedhelm Burbach, formerly the AO's chief in Spain, who then accompanied them to meet Ernst Bohle, the head of the AO. The mission almost floundered when the German Foreign Office confirmed that Germany should avoid being immersed in the internal affairs of another country that could only lead to an international scandal. Yet Burbach convinced Bohle to use the services of Alfred Hess, then Bohle's second in command, to facilitate a meeting with his brother and deputy leader of the party, Rudolf. Understanding the crucial nature of the mission from Morocco, Rudolf Hess telephoned Hitler, who was then on holiday in Bayreuth (Bavaria) attending the Wagner festival, who agreed to receive Franco's emissaries and Burbach that same evening. Once in Bayreuth, they had to wait for Hitler's return from the opera. There and then, after almost three hours mostly dominated by his own monologues, the German dictator convinced himself of the need to support the insurrection.[25]

After summoning Werner von Blomberg and Hermann Göring, heads of the army and the Luftwaffe respectively, and probably still under the influence of Wagner's music, Hitler set into motion 'Operation Magic Fire'. During the next days, ten Junker 52 transport planes flew from Germany to Morocco to initiate the crucial airlift of African troops to mainland Spain. Meanwhile, on the night of 31 July, a German vessel, the *Usaramo*, left Hamburg loaded with 10 Junker 52s, 6 escort fighter Heinkel 51s, anti-aircraft guns, bombs and ammunition, as well as 85 pilots and technicians. On 13 August the *Kamerun* sailed, carrying 3000 tons of fuel, followed the next day by the *Wigbert*, carrying 6 Heinkel 51s, 2 Junkers, 960 50-kg bombs, 10,000 10-kg bombs, and 150,000 machine-gun bullets. All the vessels arrived in Lisbon, from where Salazar allowed the deliveries.[26]

Strategic considerations were paramount in Hitler's decision. After listening to Franco's emissaries and analysing the existing military situation, the German leader concluded that betting on a rapid Nationalist victory was a limited risk that was worth taking. For a small contribution, the rewards to be reaped were immense: namely, the drastic alteration of the continental balance of power, with the creation of a friendly state bordering France, Germany's continental enemy, which then would be surrounded by potentially hostile neighbours.[27] Nazi intervention was consistent with Germany's general and increasingly aggressive policy, pushing and breaking the conditions of the Versailles Treaty. Instances included the withdrawal from the League of Nations in October 1933 and, in 1935, the reincorporation of the Saar, the reintroduction of compulsory military service and the establishment of the Luftwaffe, as well as the reoccupation of the Rhineland in 1936. Nevertheless, Germany was not yet prepared for an armed confrontation and nor did Hitler desire that Spain should be the cause of a wider military conflict. Therefore, German interference in Spanish affairs was predicated upon the expectation of it producing a rapid Nationalist victory and was surrounded by total secrecy.[28] However, if that failed, Hitler thought he could defuse opposition by playing the anti-Communist card and alleging that he was only helping the rebels to rescue Spain from Bolshevism. As the war progressed, other economic and logistical considerations became important. Spain's raw materials were a blessing to a Germany bent on rearming. Furthermore, the Spanish war offered the perfect testing ground for men and equipment, as well as an ideal opportunity to determine the limits of resolution and tolerance of the Allies. It also provided the occasion for Hitler to stir up trouble in Western Europe while he was planning to expand eastwards.[29]

In contrast to Berlin, Rome was, in 1936, a capital better informed about the impending coup. Contacts between the Spanish plotters and the Fascist leaders went way back. For Mussolini's expansionist dreams in the western Mediterranean, it was important to have a friendly Spain. After a period of excellent relations with Primo de Rivera, the establishment of a pro-French Republic was greeted with dismay. Consequently, Italy supported all anti-Republican activities in Spain. For example, the military conspirators of 1932 had met the Italian air minister, Marshall Italo Balbo, who promised them weapons. In March 1934 Mussolini had received a delegation of Monarchists and Carlists who obtained money and training facilities. Also, since June 1935, José Antonio, the Falange leader, was granted a monthly contribution of 50,000 lire. Paradoxically, however, the military uprising of 1936 coincided with the Italian loss of interest in Spanish affairs. After almost a year of warfare, Italy had just emerged victorious from the colonial conquest of Abyssinia. Now militarily and economically exhausted and diplomatically isolated, she was reluctant to become involved so soon in a new enterprise. Hence, in the months prior to the coup, the insurgents' requests for assistance were rebuffed.[30]

Nevertheless, with their plans to seize power in dire straits, the Nationalists turned to Italy for military aid. In an effort to secure Mussolini's assistance, on 19 July Franco sent the journalist Luis Bolín to Italy. At the same time, the general enlisted the support of the Italian consul in Tangiers (Pier Filippo del Rossi del Lion Nero) and the military attaché in Tetuán (Giuseppe Luccardi). They both backed a plea for military aid in which Franco underlined his promise to emulate Italian Fascism in Spain. On 21 July Bolín arrived in Rome, where he obtained a letter of presentation from the exiled King Alfonso XIII. He then met Count Ciano (Italy's foreign minister and Mussolini's son-in-law) who, although seemingly willing to help, also made it clear that the decision was not his. Up to 25 July the negative Italian response stood firm. Nevertheless, all changed dramatically within the following 72 hours. Most scholars have assumed that Mussolini's about-turn was the product of two events: first, the arrival on 25 July of a second delegation, sent this time by General Mola, which included the Monarchist leader Goicoechea who, having already been present in the negotiations of 1934, could confirm the seriousness of the military revolt; secondly, the belief that France, Italy's rival in the Mediterranean, was about to intervene in favour of the Republic.[31] Above all, however, Italy's decision to become involved in Spain was the result of a careful exercise in political opportunism. The *Duce*'s ego was certainly flattered by being the recipient of pleas for help and he was naturally eager to assist the establishment of a potential ally in the Mediterranean.

However, Mussolini's final initiative came as the result of a complex and anything but spontaneous decision-making process based on the evaluation of different sources of information. Between 25 and 27 July the *Duce* received a considerable number of diplomatic and intelligence reports which led him to conclude that, by supporting the rebellion, he held a winning hand. Knowledge of British hostility towards the Spanish government, including its opposition to French involvement, was a good reason for assuming that Britain would not object to discreet intervention in favour of the insurgents. Also, he was aware by then that the divided French cabinet had drawn back from open military support, leaving the Republic badly equipped. It is unclear if he knew of Hitler's recent decision to send aid, but a further consideration was news from the Soviet Union indicating that the Kremlin was deeply disconcerted by the situation and did not intend to do anything. Final confirmation from Italian diplomats in Morocco that once the African troops were in the peninsula the war would be over in a matter of weeks convinced Mussolini that covertly to supply a small amount of equipment was a limited risk for potentially massive rewards. Consequently, on 27 July Ciano informed Bolín that arrangements had been made to fulfil Franco's request. Two days later the Italians dispatched a dozen Savoia-Marchetti S 81 transport and bomber planes, followed by 12 Fiat C.R.32 fighters to Spanish Morocco and the cargo ship *Emilio Morandi* with ammunition. The crews were to join the Spanish Foreign Legion for cover.[32] Then, on 7 August, Rome sent a further 27 fighter planes, 5 tanks, 40 machine-guns and 12 anti-aircraft guns, as well as ammunition, bombs, aviation fuel and lubricant.[33]

However, when, on 30 July, one of the original 12 Italian Savoia-Marchetti planes went down in the sea and two crash-landed in French North African territory, the secrecy surrounding Fascist intervention foundered. The ensuing French investigation left no doubts about the collusion between the Italian government and the rebels.[34] Blum was furious and felt that France should then be free to help the Republic. Yet again the Spanish issue fractured France and left the government divided. Amidst polarised public opinion, a stormy cabinet meeting in

Paris, on 1 August, revealed the fears of several ministers that French intervention could lead to a general war on the continent. Aware of France's possible isolation, due to the British position, the Quai d'Orsay's call for caution prevailed. Masterminded by Alexis Léger, the Quai d'Orsay's general secretary, the French government decided to appeal to all the great powers to refrain from intervention in Spain. This proposal, though, was conditional, as the French still intended to deliver arms unless Italy ceased its own shipments.[35]

In the following days, Britain's attitude ensured that even this half-hearted position had to be abandoned. Indeed, London's stance towards Italian or French intervention could not have been more crucial. Italian diplomats' reports to Mussolini of widespread sympathy for the Spanish insurgents among key figures such as David Margesson (Conservative leader in the Commons) and other senior Tories at the Carlton Club, confirmed the *Duce*'s belief that his adventurism in Spain would face no serious challenge from London.[36] Meanwhile, with a divided country and cabinet, Blum was under increasing pressure on the other side of the Channel to do nothing. On 30 July, Jules Moch, the head of the French premier's general secretariat, visited London, where he became aware of the hostility of British leaders towards the Spanish Republic.[37] On 31 July Winston Churchill wrote to the French ambassador in London, Charles Corbin, that the majority of the Conservative Party sympathised with the cause of the Spanish rebels. He was certain that if both the Fascist powers and France sent aircraft to Spain the British ruling classes would side with Italy and Germany.[38] Nevertheless, Blum persisted in dispatching Admiral Darlan, Chief of the General Staff of the French Navy, to England on 5 August to meet his counterpart, Admiral Chatfield. The idea was to convince the British government, through the Admiralty, of the ominous consequences for its imperial interests of a Fascist-aided rebel victory in Spain. The mission was a failure. Chatfield insisted that Franco was a good Spanish patriot who knew how to fend off German and Italian encroachments.[39]

The British attitude left the French leaders in disarray and the Spanish Republic isolated and unarmed. On 6 August the Spanish Socialist Jiménez de Asúa was told by the French Socialist minister of finance, Vincent Auriol, that 'because of the English' a delivery of arms to take place in Bordeaux had to be suspended. According to Asúa, he met Blum the next morning who, with his eyes full of tears, told him that Baldwin had directly contacted the French president, Lebrun, to warn him that he had learned of the sale of arms to the Republic and that, if this led to war with Germany or Italy, France would be alone.

Blum was close to resigning but was convinced by Spanish diplomats in Paris to stay on.[40]

If any doubts remained about the British position, they were dispelled when, on the following day (7 August), Sir George Clerk, the British ambassador to France, paid a visit to Delbos to state his 'personal' view that French commitment to the Spanish Republic would imperil the close co-operation between London and Paris. The effect of this on the French foreign minister and on other members of the government was critical.[41] Faced with the potential break-up of the Entente with Britain and even the collapse of the Popular Front in France, Delbos carried the day in a rowdy cabinet meeting on 8 August. The next day France prohibited the exportation of all war matériel to Spain, including privately negotiated deals, thereby implementing unilaterally the policy of non-intervention.[42] With Blum's connivance, however, Cot had already ensured the dispatch to Spain of 13 Dewoitine fighters and 6 Potez bombers that had originally been built for Lithuania (although all of them were unarmed). The novelist André Malraux, who had just returned from Madrid and was well aware of the crucial role of aerial warfare, was in charge of the operation. While in France, Malraux also raised a squadron (the *Escuadra España*) of some forty pilots and technicians, most of them mercenaries and adventurers.[43]

### The grand charade

According to Blum, 'non-intervention was essentially an attempt to prevent others from doing what we were incapable of accomplishing'.[44] Nonetheless, he thought that at that moment the introduction of an arms embargo on both sides offered the Republic a good chance of crushing the insurrection.[45] However, all such wishful thinking was soon revealed for what it was: the beginning of an ill-fated retreat that not only confirmed the dominant role of Britain in the Western alliance[46] but also sealed the fate of the Spanish Republic. According to the Spanish foreign minister, the Socialist Julio Alvarez del Vayo, from that time the Quai d'Orsay, at least in relation to Spain, became a branch of the British Foreign Office.[47]

Initially, London only adopted the idea of a Non-Intervention Agreement (NIA) with reluctance, as a means of supporting the Quai d'Orsay in its battles with the interventionists within the French cabinet.[48] Yet, once embraced, Non-Intervention became the foundation of British diplomacy towards the Spanish conflict. Anglo-French concerted efforts soon paid dividends as 27 European nations, including all the major powers, adhered to the agreement by the end of August. The United States, although not formally included, introduced a moral arms embargo on both Spanish parties in August 1936, formalised later in the Spanish Embargo Act and the Neutrality Act of January and May 1937 respectively.[49]

In order to have some kind of common scrutiny, a working committee (NIC) gathered in the magnificent Locarno rooms at the Foreign Office. Presided over by the Earl of Plymouth, one of the largest landowners in Britain as well as parliamentary under-secretary to the Foreign Office, ambassadors in Britain became the representatives of their nations. Plymouth, with his image of a self-confident aristocrat, was the perfect chairman for a committee whose main task was to do very little, while pretending to do much.[50] On 9 September the first meeting was held. Behind all the formalities, the NIA turned out to be one of the most outrageous diplomatic farces ever perpetrated in Europe: a grand charade in which chicanery and hypocrisy became an art. It remained above all an exercise in public opinion, a smoke-screen behind which, to a greater or lesser extent, all the powers intervened in Spain. Rather than a treaty in the formal sense, there were a series of unilateral accords that formed a most unstable foundation for success. The scheme to ensure compliance was full of loopholes: the committee had no power to act and could hear accusations only from its own members, cutting out both Spanish parties and independent accounts of journalists or private citizens. Furthermore, the NIC lacked the means to verify accusations at a local level. Often, when the international press was full of accounts of armament pouring into Spain, the NIC devoted its time to discussing trivial matters. On other occasions, the entire affair descended into theatrical parodies, with flat denials followed by counter-accusations and petty squabbling. Procedure demanded written replies to specific accusations, a protracted process as the charges kept being referred back and forth between the committee and the nations involved. Thus, far from facilitating the presentation of complaints, the NIC was actually discouraging them.[51] The Russian ambassador, Ivan Maiskii, somewhat pejoratively characterised the NIC as the ideal Japanese wife, who sees nothing, hears nothing and says nothing.[52]

The NIA's blatant inefficiency was largely the consequence of being, in reality, a piece of humbug, an instrument of British diplomacy whose objectives were not those portrayed by the official propaganda – that is, the prevention of foreign participation in the war. Rather, based on an initial assumption of the brevity of the conflict, the agreement on non-intervention was the ideal instrument to win time to ensure the demise of the Republic. As the conflict dragged on, the NIA remained in place to ensure the confinement of the Spanish contest, but at the same time formalising the legal anomaly that a democratically elected government was on a par with a rebel military coup. It restrained the French from rushing to help its embattled sister Popular Front, avoiding, as the under-secretary at the Foreign Office, Sir Orme Garton Sargent, noted, 'by hook or crook that France went Bolshevik under the influence of the Spanish Civil War'.[53] This eliminated a potential confrontation with the Fascist powers and the nightmare (for many Conservatives) of Britain having to align itself with the Soviet Union. Finally, the NIA was the perfect façade to conceal hostility towards the Republic, maintaining a semblance of impeccable neutrality for domestic public opinion.[54]

The fraudulence surrounding the entire NIA affair was not missed by the Fascist powers.[55] Joachim Ribbentrop, the future Nazi foreign minister and then German ambassador in London, noted that a better name for the NIC would have been 'the intervention committee'.[56] In London, the Portuguese, German and Italian delegations collaborated to keep the charade going. Meanwhile, as they continued unmolested to aid the Nationalists, the Spanish cockpit brought together Germany and Italy, not long before deeply hostile to each other over conflicting ambitions with regard to Austria.[57] As early as 4 August a secret meeting in Bolzano between the heads of the German and Italian intelligence services, Admiral Wilhelm Canaris and General Mario Roatta respectively, initiated the collusion between the two dictatorships.[58] From then on, high-level summits continued unabated under the pretence of together combating the 'Bolshevik danger' in Spain. In reality, the dictators agreed to recognise and support each other in their respective spheres of influence. On 1 November Mussolini referred for the first time to the 'Rome–Berlin Axis' to describe the growing understanding of the two regimes. The Italians could only be pleased that Germany not only agreed to collaborate in their common anti-Bolshevik crusade in Spain but also confirmed that Italy was the leading partner in the enterprise, as the Mediterranean was their area of control.[59]

Thus, Fascist aid, together with British acquiescence and French paralysis, altered dramatically the course of the civil war. Nationalist desperation, well expressed by Mola's confidence to his secretary on 29 July that he was contemplating suicide, was suddenly transformed by the prospect of a quick victory.[60] By early August the first successful airlift of troops in modern warfare was under way. Under the protection of Italian and German planes which ensured command of the air, in early August thousands of soldiers of the elite Army of Africa initiated their inexorable advance towards Madrid, leaving behind a staggering trail of blood, desolation and carnage. Their offensive followed the south-western route, cutting through the countryside of Andalucía and Extremadura so as to keep close to Portugal, their main conduit for goods and weapons. The ill-armed and inexperienced Republican militias were no match for them in the open field and were either forced to retreat or were massacred. By 10 August the Army of Africa had ended the Republican control of southern Extremadura, permitting, for the first time, the two halves of Nationalist Spain to be joined. Four days later, and after fierce fighting, Badajoz, the major city on the march towards the capital, fell. Thousands of Republican defenders were herded into the bullring and slaughtered. On 3 September Talavera, the last important town before Madrid, was captured. In a month the Army of Africa had completed a successful campaign of 300 miles. Also in early September, the Nationalist forces on the northern front seized Irún, cutting the Basques off from the border with France. Soon thereafter San Sebastián also fell.

Exhausted by weeks of relentless advance and meeting an increasingly dogged resistance, however, the Nationalist offensive now began to slow. Once again, they pleaded to the Fascist powers to step up their aid for what promised to be the final push of the war. Their positive reply, which went further than the initial support in rescuing Franco from Morocco, meant that the dictators were committing themselves until the end of the Spanish adventure. From late August, German and Italian military missions began to provide advice to the Nationalists. On 28 August Hitler authorised his air force to engage in fighting and bombing missions. By late September, aware of the hollowness of the NIC, German intervention was expanded with Operation Otto: the supply of 15 additional fighter planes, 24 tanks, radio equipment and the reconversion of transport aircraft into bombers.[61] Italian commitment was even more substantial, including thousands of hand grenades, small arms, machine-gun cartridges and additional planes that brought the total number of aircraft to 68. Italian planes played a vital role in repelling an attempt to seize Mallorca by a Catalan expeditionary force. In this affair the local Nationalist troops were rallied by a small number of Italians led by an officer of the Fascist militia, Arconovaldo Bonaccorsi (known as *Conte* Rossi), who thereafter ran the island for a few months as almost his private fiefdom.[62]

By late September, Nationalist columns temporarily took a detour to relieve the garrison besieged in the military fortress, the Alcázar, in Toledo. In October, as the offensive to seize Madrid began in earnest, the Fascist dictators awaited the fall of the capital to recognise the Nationalist government. The British did not lag far behind. Ambassador Chilton, who had been instructed to remain in the French border town of Hendaye, was also to grant full diplomatic recognition to the successful Nationalists once the capital fell. French reluctance to follow suit was considered sheer lunacy.[63] The war seemed to be reaching its end.

## The Spanish Verdun

In the autumn of 1936, the fate of the Republic appeared bleak. Apart from a few planes smuggled from France and weapons acquired on the black market, the anticlerical Mexican regime led by President Lázaro Cárdenas constituted the only international source of assistance to the Spanish government. The identification of the heirs of the Mexican revolution with the progressive ideals of the Spanish Republic resulted in the genuine support of this Latin American country throughout the entire conflict. Thus, Mexico sold arms and ammunition to the Republic when every other country denied such aid to the legitimate government of Spain. In addition, Mexico acted as a cover for the purchase of weapons from third countries (that were then reshipped to Spain), sent fuel, food and clothing, and represented Republican diplomatic interests in the many nations where its foreign office personnel had defected to the rebels.[64] Nevertheless, geographical distance and scarcity of resources hampered Mexico's ability to play a major role. However, if foreign intervention had proved vital in turning the course of the war in the Nationalists' favour during its first weeks, it also arrived at a crucial moment to rescue the embattled Republic.

Not only were governments and diplomats sucked into the Spanish tragedy. The volatile atmosphere of the 1930s, marked by economic depression and political polarisation, ensured that at street level, within families and at the workplace, the Spanish Civil War became the leading issue of debate and discussion. All over the world, newsreel footage and daily press editorials brought alive the nightmare consuming a tormented country. For conservative and Catholic opinion, the Nationalists stood for the values of a Christian civilisation threatened by

Communism and anarchy. Within Liberal and Labour circles, the Republic constituted the last-ditch stand in defence of liberty before the inexorable advance of political reaction across the continent. Furthermore, awareness of German and Italian involvement cemented the romantic appeal of a Republic besieged by the international forces of Fascism.

Left-wing organisations and trade unions organised huge rallies, demanding the right of the Spanish Republic freely to purchase weapons for her defence. But calls for 'Arms for Spain' fell on the deaf ears of political leaders. Nevertheless, while governments took cover behind the façade of non-intervention, aid committees began to spring up in cities and villages of the democratic nations, raising money and collecting medicines and clothes to help the beleaguered Spanish people. Nurses, doctors, ambulance drivers and others volunteered to travel to Spain.[65] Also, a small number of foreigners took part in the fighting from the beginning. Many were exiled refugees, mainly German Anarchists, or had arrived to attend the Workers' Olympiad, scheduled to begin in Barcelona on 19 July as an alternative to the Olympic Games in Berlin. Small numbers of foreign volunteers, mostly Italians and French and Jewish Poles, also began to cross the Pyrenees to join the militias in Cataluña or Aragón. Both the French Communist Party and the largest French trade union, the CGT, were engaged in aiding the Republic by all available means.[66] Additionally, an exceptionally large number of intellectuals, writers, and artists poured into the country to express their solidarity with the Republican cause. The likes of Ernest Hemingway, George Orwell, André Malraux, John Dos Passos and many others immortalised the unfolding human catastrophe with their works. This epic struggle also permeated the world of cinema, ensuring the war's romantic and legendary character. Leading scriptwriters, actors and directors in Hollywood expressed their commitment either by attending the numerous pro-Republican evening parties destined to raise money or by transferring the Spanish struggle to the screen. One of Hollywood's most photogenic stalwarts, Errol Flynn, landed in Barcelona in March 1937 to hand over a letter of support to the government, together with a cheque for one and a half million dollars to buy medicines and food.[67]

Popular displays of solidarity with the embattled Republic among Europeans and Americans contrasted starkly with the extreme caution shown by the leaders of the Soviet Union during the first weeks of the conflict. Clearly, priorities under Stalin lay in the consolidation of 'socialism in one country' and not in foreign adventures. Moreover, when the Spanish war broke out the Soviet dictator's mind was occupied with the first show trials in Moscow which heralded the beginnings of the great purges. Nevertheless, the rising threat of Fascism on the continent could not be ignored. Indeed, since 1934 Russian foreign policy had sought to reach an understanding with the Western powers founded on their common fear of German expansionism. Discarding sectarian slogans of class war and world revolution, the support for Popular Fronts, in which the Communist Parties became partners of the liberal bourgeoisie against the Fascist peril, was part of that strategy. Thus the Spanish Civil War presented Stalin with a dilemma. He could not consent to the destruction of the Spanish Popular Front and the subsequent emergence of another Fascist state that would, moreover, seal the encirclement of his ally, France. However, a Republican victory, leading to a social revolution in Spain, could result in driving the Allies to side with Germany against the Soviet Union. Hence an early plea from the Spanish prime minister to the Soviet Union, via the Russian ambassador in France, on 25 July, went unanswered.[68] The Kremlin initially adopted a position of platonic sympathy with the Republicans, a policy restricted to the fierce denunciation of Fascist aggression and the collection of food and money by the official Soviet trade-union movement.[69] Accordingly, the NIA was initially welcomed with relief by Stalin as the best means to localise the conflict and hopefully cut foreign supplies to the Nationalists. This moderate position was underpinned by the optimism still emanating from Comintern sources in Spain that the insurrection was contained and could be put down.[70] However, the continuous flouting of the NIA by Germany and Italy, tilting the military balance in favour of the Nationalists, eventually forced the Soviet Union to act.

On 7 October, the Soviet delegation to the NIC stated that unless violations of the NIA ceased forthwith, the Soviet Union would consider itself freed from its obligations.[71] By then, however, notwithstanding the fairness of the complaint, the Kremlin had already crossed the Rubicon. In late August full diplomatic relations between Spain and the Soviet Union, broken since 1917, were re-established. Marcel Rosenberg and Vladimir Antonov-Ovseenko (ambassador in Madrid and consul in Barcelona respectively) presided over large diplomatic corps that, importantly, included a significant number of military advisers. In turn, the Socialist professor of medicine, Marcelino Pascua, became Spanish ambassador in Moscow.[72] By September caution was finally overcome. The fatherland of socialism could no longer remain aloof to events in Spain without alienating the sympathies of Europe's working classes. Ensuring the survival of the Republic (albeit a Republic in which revolutionary fervour was to be restrained), became central to Russian designs to transform the strategy of domestic Popular Fronts into an alliance between the Western democracies and the Soviet Union against Nazi aggression.[73]

On 14 September Stalin agreed to supply military equipment. Two days later, the so-called 'Section X' was created to co-ordinate this operation in the utmost secrecy and under the supervisory role of the Soviet secret police, the NKVD. On 4 October the first delivery of small weapons arrived on board the Spanish tanker *Campeche* which had left Odessa on 26 September. It initiated the intermittent but steady supply of Soviet equipment. On 15 October the first large-scale shipment of Soviet aid reached Spain when the *Komsomol* docked at Cartagena. Amongst the most important equipment received during the following weeks were T-26 tanks and modern aircraft such as the Polikarpov I-15 (known as '*Chato*' or 'snub-nosed') and Polikarpov I-16 ('*Mosca*' or 'fly') fighters and the SB-2 Tupolev bombers.[74] However, by the time the Russian supplies began to arrive in October, the Italians and Germans had already been supplying the Nationalists with aircraft, all kinds of armament and key personnel for over two months.

Soviet deliveries coincided with the decision to organise the dispatch of foreign volunteers. On 18 September a secret gathering in Moscow of the Comintern leadership became the founding meeting for the recruitment of the so-called International Brigades.[75] Communist parties were instructed to organise the enrolment and transport of individuals. For geographical reasons and because of its influence over the PCE, the French Communist Party played a crucial role. André Marty, a French Catalan and member of the Comintern Secretariat, with a revolutionary pedigree dating back to his participation in the pro-Soviet French sailors' mutiny at Odessa in April 1919, was the man in control. The second in command was the Italian Communist, Luigi Longo.

The International Brigades were not to be aimed only at Communists, however. Rather, they sought to appeal to anyone, regardless of their political leanings, who was willing to take on Fascism directly. Indeed, questioning at the enrolment was not designed to confirm the communist sympathies of the candidates but to establish their military skills and to avoid letting through agents provocateurs.

A besieged Republic, resisting a military insurrection backed by Italy and Germany, proved a resounding appeal for the rallying of the International Brigades. Their success in attracting a staggering number of volunteers from all over the world was unique in modern

European warfare. Intellectuals were significantly represented but the overwhelming majority of volunteers came from working-class backgrounds. For them, Spain constituted the final battle against the apparently triumphal march of reaction in Europe. One of the volunteers, the veteran Italian Socialist leader Pietro Nenni, noted that, like the Greeks in ancient times, the Brigadiers' participation in the war of others was a noble struggle destined to prove their cause back home. For the many political exiles, renewing on foreign soil the war that they had lost at home offered hope that a defeat of Fascism in Spain would accelerate its demise in their own countries.[76] Indeed, the Spanish conflict seemed to provide the chance for a single individual to make a positive stand. Jason Gurney, a Chelsea sculptor who joined the International Brigades, wrote:

> Either you were opposed to the growth of Fascism and went out to fight it, or you acquiesced in its crimes and were guilty of permitting its growth. For myself it was a war of principle, and principles do not have national boundaries. By fighting against Fascism in Spain, we would be fighting against it in our own country, and every other.[77]

A reluctant Spanish government, keener on obtaining weapons than foreign manpower, did not sanction the creation of International Brigades until 22 October. Yet, with great improvisation and hardly any secrecy, the mechanisms for the organisation of foreign combatants had already been set in motion. Volunteers converged on Paris and were easily spotted at the Gare du Nord or the Gare d'Orsay by sympathetic French taxi drivers and then taken to the meeting point, the *Maison des Syndicats* (the CGT's head office). They were then transported to Spain, either by land (crossing the border hardly molested by custom officers until February 1937 when France, complying with the NIC, introduced a formal ban on volunteers) and gathering at the old medieval fortress of Figueras (Girona) or by sea to Alicante from Marseilles. The final destination was Albacete, a small city about a hundred kilometres inland from Valencia, the training ground and headquarters of the International Brigades. The first two contingents of volunteers arrived there almost simultaneously on 13 October: a group of 700 men from Figueras followed closely by another 800 from Alicante.[78]

By early October everybody assumed the imminent fall of Madrid and the subsequent end of the war. As the Nationalist columns kept advancing, General Mola boasted that he would be taking coffee in the

Café Molinero on Madrid's Gran Vía by 12 October, the anniversary of the *Día de la Raza* (the discovery of America by Columbus).[79] A table was kept for him, but he never arrived. World attention was for weeks focused on the assault on Madrid. Throughout October the Nationalists' slow but firm advance towards its objective appeared unstoppable. Bombed relentlessly by heavy artillery and aeroplanes, Madrid enjoyed a foretaste of what was awaiting other European capitals in a few years' time. The situation was so desperate that even the government, led by the Socialist Largo Caballero since September, abandoned the city on 6 November for the safety of Valencia, leaving behind a *Junta de Defensa* headed by General José Miaja and formed with representatives of all the political forces. Colonel Vicente Rojo, Miaja's very able chief of staff and formerly professor of military strategy at the Infantry Academy, was in charge of mounting the armed resistance. The following day Radio Lisbon announced the victorious entry of Franco's army into Madrid. It was not true. Against all odds, the insurgent troops were held at the gates. They were now no longer fighting disorganised local militias but an entire city mobilised behind the war effort. Dolores Ibarruri, the famous Communist heroine known as *La Pasionaria*, used as a rallying cry '*¡No Pasarán!*' ('They Shall Not Pass!'), the successful French slogan from World War I. It was soon to be echoed by André Marty and the Communist newspaper, *El Mundo Obrero*, in their hailing of Madrid as 'the Verdun of democracy'.[80]

Starting in late October, General Franco ordered massive frontal attacks under the command of his fellow *Africanista*, General Varela. It was a strategic error that led not only to even greater slaughter but also rendered useless the superior mobility and quality of his troops. It overlooked the spirited zeal of the people at arms and overrated the fighting value of mercenary troops. The terrain favoured the defenders, as the Army of Africa, hitherto invincible in the open field, was not used to street fighting and barricades.[81] Furthermore, the timely arrival of foreign aid represented a watershed. The Spanish vessel *Magallanes* reached Cartagena with a cargo of 20,000 Remington rifles and 20 million 7-mm cartridges from Veracruz (Mexico).[82] Soviet weapons and the first International Brigades soon followed. Russian planes and tanks proved a match for Italian and German weaponry and put an end to the Nationalists' total command of the air. For the first time, cheering crowds looked up into the sky as Soviet aircraft engaged in combat with Italians and Germans. On 7 November Moorish troops penetrated the Republican defences through the Casa de Campo, the huge forest on the western limits of Madrid, but did not reach the centre of the city. The next morning Varela launched his massive attack. The first four battalions of foreign volunteers were hurriedly merged into the 11th International Brigade and rushed to the front. Although only composed of some 2000 men, its presence was a formidable boost to popular morale. Such scant forces, constituting a mere 5 per cent of the entire Republican army, could not decide the outcome on the battlefield but they had an immense psychological impact. When marching along the main streets of Madrid, they were welcomed with shouts of *'¡Viva los Rusos!'* ('Long live the Russians!'). In fact, there were no Russians but (ironically) mostly Germans. Yet that hardly mattered to a besieged city which was aware of no longer being alone in its plight.[83] By 13 November a second brigade, the 12th, with some 1,500 foreign volunteers, took part in a counter-attack on the southern limits of the city to thwart Nationalist attempts to cut the lines of communication from Madrid. That day, a column of Catalan Anarchists, led by the legendary Buenaventura Durruti, arrived in Madrid. Two days later, Varela's troops launched a new offensive from their positions in the Casa de Campo, crossing the River Manzanares into the University City. Days of hand-to-hand fighting for every floor and lecture theatre followed. Losses were appalling in both camps but the Nationalist offensive petered out. Durruti fell dead, probably killed by the accidental discharge of his own weapon. On 23 November, in a sombre meeting, Franco called off the frontal attack. Madrid had resisted the enemy's onslaught and ensured the prolongation of the war.[84] However, the city remained besieged and the population had to endure constant aerial and artillery bombings. An eerie sensation of fear and mundane impotence was captured by one of the foreign correspondents:

> The beams of light cross and stay still. Near me a voice cries out: There they are! Yes, there they are, five aeroplanes imprisoned in the angles of light from twenty Republican searchlights ... A heavy burst of explosions, the Fascists have dropped their first bombs. The Republican anti-aircraft start shooting with a whistling sound and flames forming multiple points, followed by the clear sound of bursting shrapnel ... The show lasts ten minutes; then all is silent and dark and over. Over? Forty houses destroyed, twenty-eight men, women and children dead, eighty-four wounded. Military aims? The houses were inhabited by harmless citizens, not manufacturers of munitions ... Life and death are at close quarters in Spain.[85]

## The European civil war

Short of manpower and now facing a better-equipped enemy, Nationalist hopes for a swift capture of the capital and the conclusion of the war vanished. In fact, the stalemate in Madrid was a very serious blow for them. With their elite troops bogged down and badly crippled by casualties, the insurgents even contemplated defeat.[86] So far, their paramount strength had been at the front lines with the Army of Africa's ability to knock out their disorganised opponents quickly before they could mount any spirited resistance. To a large extent, the vital but relatively small aid received from the Axis should have ensured this outcome. Yet the successful defence of the Spanish capital brought this plan to a sudden end.

During the following months, the massive increase in foreign support for both sides transformed the Spanish affair into a veritable European civil war, where troops from the same country often found themselves fighting for different camps. This took place while diplomats at the NIC exchanged accusations and denied the blatant reality. Blum himself, aware of the impotence of the NIC, connived in the smuggling of armaments over the Pyrenean frontier, the so-called 'Non-Intervention Relâchée' (relaxed non-intervention).[87] Indeed, the French government presented a paradoxical picture, as part of the cabinet sought to break the arms embargo that other ministers were keen to observe. Thus, Jules Moch collaborated with the future resistance hero Jean Moulin (the assistant of the fiercely pro-Republican Cot) and the head of customs Gaston Cousin (hand-picked for the job by the finance minister Auriol) to supervise the transport of matériel across the border.[88] When Blum resigned in June 1937, he agreed to serve as deputy premier in the new government of the Radical Camille Chautemps, provided that these arrangements would remain in place.[89] Nevertheless, despite all their efforts only a trickle of weapons got through and the Republican war effort continued to depend heavily on the arrival of merchant ships laden with Soviet military equipment. Also the flow of foreign volunteers continued unabated, reaching a peak of some 800 per week during the first months of 1937.

In the light of these new circumstances, Franco once more turned for help to his German and Italian friends. As in the summer of 1936, their positive response proved crucial. In fact, aware of the ineffectiveness of the NIC, Germany and Italy abandoned their previous prudence, officially recognising the insurgents as the legitimate government in Spain on 18 November 1936, and committing enough forces to ensure the ultimate Nationalist victory. The dictators had burnt their bridges, as their prestige was now irrevocably attached to Franco's fortune. Hitler had already agreed, in late October, to dispatch significant reinforcements to counter Soviet aid.[90] Consisting of a permanent squadron of some 5000 German troops and 140 aircraft, the so-called Condor Legion was the finest air force of the period. Subordinated to Spanish command but led in the field by German commanders, it contained anti-aircraft guns, tanks and the most modern bomber and fighter squadrons in the Nazi arsenal. In November the first German reinforcements began to act in the Madrid theatre of operations. They would be crucial in providing the Nationalists with decisive air superiority and in training many of their officers. Their activities also allowed Germany to test its devastating war machine, ready for when a wider conflict broke out in Europe. However, in 1936 Hitler was not yet prepared to frighten the Allies through excessive involvement and thus was happy to let Italy bear the brunt of the military effort in Spain.[91]

On 28 November 1936, Fascist Italy signed a secret agreement with Nationalist Spain, confirming their solidarity in the common struggle against Communism and their collaboration in the Mediterranean. Each side promised the other an attitude of benevolent neutrality if one of them was at war.[92] In early December, Mussolini, in a summit with representatives of the armed forces at which Admiral Canaris was present, announced his decision to increase massively the aid for Nationalist Spain.[93] On 18 December the first 3000 members of the so-called *Corpo di Truppe Volontarie* (CTV) left Italy. By March 1937 nearly 50,000 Italian troops were fighting in Spain; they were organised into mechanised divisions, with a permanent contingent of 300 aircraft (*La Aviazione Legionaria*). Italy's naval activity also grew steadily, with 13 cruisers and 22 destroyers engaged mostly in escorting merchantmen. On two occasions Italian vessels carried out shore bombardments and 42 submarines were active off the Spanish coasts, attacking Republican ships.[94] Franco, however, was not altogether pleased. Fresh troops and, above all, military equipment vital to keep the Nationalist war effort going were obviously welcome. Yet he had to accept the autonomous character of the Italian forces, who had their own companies and officers and were under the command of General Mario Roatta. Impatient with the slow progress of the war, Mussolini wanted to guarantee a rapid victory, at any cost, by pursuing a more energetic strategy of which the Nationalist generals seemed incapable. Besides, the *Duce* felt that he had to make a decisive move at this stage before the NIC could introduce meaningful measures against foreign involvement in Spain.[95]

Following the Battle of Madrid, the significant increase in armament and manpower transformed the previously localised clashes of poorly armed and small forces into greater military confrontations in which planes, artillery and tanks played a leading role. After calling off the frontal offensive against the capital, the Nationalists attempted to encircle and eventually finish off the Republican army during the following three months. In mid-December a new operation began to the north-west of Madrid in the direction of the Coruña road. This operation coincided with another Nationalist advance in the south near Córdoba. They represented the first important clashes in the open field with the participation of significant contingents of foreign manpower and armament on both sides. However, the Nationalists only managed to take a few square kilometres of land and failed to break the military stalemate. The English poets Ralph Fox and John Cornford were amongst the casualties on the southern front.[96]

Even fiercer was the next Nationalist offensive, to the south-east of the capital, destined to sweep across the valley of the Jarama River and cut the vital road to Valencia. The attack opened on 6 February 1937. In the first days, the rebel troops managed to cross the river but soon stiffer Republican resistance slowed their advance. Some 40,000 troops assembled by both camps, reinforced with tanks, planes and artillery, then fought a brutal battle of attrition. Moors and Legionaries, supported by the Condor Legion, spearheaded the Nationalist thrust, while the Republic mobilised its best units (including the already battle-hardened 11th and 12th International Brigades, the French-dominated 14th and the newly formed 15th which contained the US Lincoln and the British battalions). The human toll on both sides was horrifying: there were some 45,000 casualties (25,000 Republicans and 20,000 Nationalists). The British and American volunteers took an extremely bloody battering in holding on to a slope soon known as 'Suicide Hill'. Out of 550 members of the British battalion, nearly 400 fell in the first two days of fighting. The Lincolns lost 127 men and more than 200 were wounded, including their Commander Robert Hale Merriman, in their first major action, the gallant counter-attack on 27 February. The Brigadiers would never forget their heroic deeds and fallen comrades and memorialised the Battle of Jarama in lyrics sung to the mournful tune of 'Red River Valley'.[97] Jason Gurney wrote:

The effect of those brown, ferocious bundles [Moors] suddenly appearing out of the ground at one's feet was utterly demoralizing ... It was a formidable opposition to be faced by a collection of city-bred young men with no experience of war, no idea of how to find cover on an open hillside, and no competence as marksmen. We were frightened by the sheer din of the battle and by the number of casualties ... The horror of seeing close friends and comrades being killed and broken did not really penetrate my mind until later. It was all too fantastic for immediate realisation, like something seen in a nightmare.[98]

The Republic paid a dear price but could consider the Jarama a moral victory, having prevented the Nationalists from reaching the Valencia road and having held ground, for the first time, in a major battle in the open field.[99]

Despite their last offensive stalling, Nationalist plans to capture Madrid and end the war continued unabated. A fresh attack began on 8 March towards Guadalajara, to the north-east of the capital. The objective was to link in a pincer movement with Nationalist forces at Jarama and thereby to encircle Madrid. The Italian CTV units were at the heart of the new operation. Growing steadily in manpower and armament, the Italians had already played a crucial part in capturing the important harbour city of Málaga in early February. Surrounded on three sides, lacking foreign equipment and supplies blocked by flooded roads, Málaga could not withstand the final assault which began in earnest on 3 February. Over 10,000 Italian soldiers participated, in collaboration with the Nationalist Army of the South. The Italian strategy of *guerra celere*, or 'rapid war' based on a mass attack of armoured trucks and tanks covered by air force, easily broke through the Republican lines.[100] Hellish scenes followed the fall of the city on 8 February as masses of refugees attempted to escape while being machine-gunned from the air.

Over-confident from their success at Málaga, the CTV then attempted to repeat its *guerra celere* in central Spain. Mussolini was hopeful that this new offensive would lead to the fall of Madrid and hence to the spectacular conclusion of his Spanish adventure. On 8 March some 35,000 Italians supported by 10,000 Spaniards initiated their thrust towards Guadalajara. But, after three days of steady advances, poor weather began to disrupt the operation and the offensive ran out of steam. The motorised columns were bogged down in icy and muddy roads, while fog grounded aircraft. Roatta was to argue that the Nationalist leadership had sabotaged his operation. Evidently, Franco could not be entirely thrilled with the conclusion of the war courtesy of a stunning Italian victory.[101] In fact, the Nationalists failed to renew their offensive at the other arm of the pincer, the Jarama front. Thus the Republicans could concentrate their reserves in Guadalajara and launch a massive counter-attack supported by Soviet aircraft and tanks. A civil war within the civil war sprang to life when the Italian expeditionary force clashed with the Italian volunteers from the Garibaldi Battalion. The already low morale of the CTV was fatally dented when the Italian Brigadiers resorted to speaking through loudspeakers and asking their counterparts to desert. By 18 March the offensive had concluded with the rout of the CTV.[102] After the setback at Guadalajara, the Nationalists had to shelve the plan to capture Madrid. However, with his prestige now at stake, the always-boastful *Duce* became more committed than ever to the Spanish adventure. He had to recognise that it would be longer and more expensive than he had first anticipated and that, from then on, Franco would run the show, with the Italians being effectively under Nationalist command.[103]

### The final tally

The international response given by the European chancelleries to the pleas of both warring camps proved crucial in determining the course and the outcome of the conflict.[104] The military aid provided by the Fascist dictatorships rescued a botched military coup from potential oblivion and then enabled the Nationalists to regain the initiative, capturing large swathes of territory in their successful march on Madrid. Then the delivery of Soviet equipment and the arrival of foreign volunteers played a vital part in saving the capital and prolonging the war. The subsequent significant increase in the aid received by both sides resulted in the intensification of the combat and produced a military stalemate by the spring of 1937. However, the military deadlock did not last.

The increasingly obvious inability, if not unwillingness, of the NIC to check the blatant involvement in Spain of some its members sealed the fate of the Republic. Emboldened by what they rightly regarded as the weakness of the Western democracies, the dictators decided to throw in their lot with the Nationalists. The Republicans could never match the assistance received by the Nationalists. As Alvarez del Vayo wrote:

Non-Intervention was a deliberate and monstrous farce and the main cause of the collapse of the Republic ... It would be difficult to conceive of a greater violation of the rights of a sovereign state than the NI scheme. It placed the Republican government on an equal footing with the rebel generals ... But the Republic did not refuse to co-operate. We were not crying for the moon. We made no request for armed assistance. We only asked for strict accordance with the policy of NI which Britain and France have forced upon us ... But while Eden stated in the House of Commons that Spain should be left to the Spaniards, the Italian divisions and the German 'technicians' were advancing on Spanish territory and in the rebel ports war material from Hamburg and Genoa was being unloaded by day and night.[105]

Indeed, the embargo imposed by the NIC, and then not enforced, left the Republic at a clear disadvantage. Whereas the Nationalists encountered no difficulty in procuring weapons from the dictatorships, the legally elected government of Spain found international arms markets closed to it and was forced to rely on the black market. Its greatest asset, the gold reserves kept in the vaults of the Bank of Spain, had then to be sent abroad and sold in order to finance the war effort. Without its gold, the Republic would have been doomed. During the first months of the conflict, with the knowledge of the Blum cabinet, the Bank of France purchased at least 26.5 per cent of the total gold reserves, and the Spanish Embassy in France went unmolested as the centre of a huge operation to purchase weapons secretly. In October 1936, facing a desperate situation on the battlefield, the Republican government chose to ship the bulk of the remaining gold from Cartagena (where it had been taken from Madrid for safety) to the Soviet Union. Throughout November, shipments of gold arrived in Odessa, totalling 460.5 tons (or some 518 million dollars). The imminent arrival of significant Russian aid, added to difficulties with Western banks delaying the transfers of funds to Republican agents and diplomats to purchase war *matériel*, persuaded the Republican leaders to make this move. The currency equivalent of gold sold to the USSR State Bank for purposes other than the repayment for Soviet supplies was transferred to *La Banque Commerciale de l'Europe du Nord*, a Soviet Bank in Paris, and used to fund international operations for the acquisition of weapons.[106]

By contrast, the Nationalists obtained their supplies on credit. They relied on oil deliveries from the main Anglo-American companies: Texaco, Shell, Standard Oil and the Atlantic Refining Company. Without them, their campaigns would have ground to a halt in days.[107] As the war dragged on, the mounting debt with the Fascist powers kept increasing. In total, Hitler was to spend $215 million on the Spanish adventure compared to Mussolini's $354 million.[108] Most was to be repaid through commercial agreements in the form of raw materials. In this respect, Italian aid was extremely generous, while Germany sought to take advantage to secure vital economic satisfaction. Two companies, HISMA at the Spanish end and ROWAK as its German counterpart, established in July and October 1936, respectively, monopolised the entire trading relationship between both countries. This arrangement guaranteed an unprecedented penetration of German influence in the Spanish economy. Crucial raw materials (pyrites, iron, copper, zinc, tin and nickel) were thus acquired and then distributed amongst German companies as Hitler's rearmament programme took off. Göring, as the Nazi leader appointed to prepare the economy for war in a Four-Year Plan, was ultimately in charge of the entire operation. Germany's increasingly dominant economic position in Nationalist Spain was then confirmed with the signing of protocols in July 1937 which not only secured the constant supply of raw materials as security and part payment of the debt but also conceded to Germany the right to purchase mining rights on Spanish territory.[109]

Lacking any substantial arms industry, both sides were heavily dependent on foreign military support to maintain their war effort. Consequently, the huge difference between the quantity as well as quality and regularity of international aid was essential in explaining the final outcome of the war. The Republic relied mainly on Soviet supplies, as well as on the even less certain flow of contraband and the black market. Thus, a variety of weaponry came from countries such as Mexico, Czechoslovakia, Poland and Estonia. Merchant ships laden with military equipment left Russia for Spanish ports delivering, in 52 voyages, 623 aircraft, 331 tanks, 60 armoured cars, 302 field-guns, 64 anti-aircraft guns, 427 anti-tank guns, 15,008 machine-guns and 379,645 rifles. France was the second largest provider of aircraft, smuggling 237 planes to Spain. However, only 69 of the planes were military and most of them were not armed.[110]

The Nationalists obtained their armament mainly from the Axis powers. Italy was at war with the Republic in all but name. Her contribution included 759 aircraft, 1801 cannons, 3436 machine guns,

157 tanks, 7400 motor vehicles, 1426 mortars, 7.7 million shells and 320 million small-arms cartridges. Germany sent 737 cannons, 3026 machine-guns and 207,306 rifles. Additionally, the Condor Legion consisted of anti-aircraft guns, 111 Panzer tanks and some 708 aircraft which included the most modern bombers and fighter planes in the German arsenal, such as the Junker 87B '*Stuka*' and the Messerschmitt 109. Hitler, years later, would comment with derision on how the Nationalists spoke of an intervention from Heaven when they should have realised that it was the bombs of the Condor Legion, dropped from heaven, which decided the issue. According to him, 'Franco ought to erect a monument to the glory of the Junker 52. Since it is this aircraft that he has to thank for his victory.'[111]

In terms of manpower, the disparity was also drastically favourable to the Nationalists. Some 35,000 volunteers from 54 different countries joined the International Brigades. Additionally, around 2100 military advisers, pilots, technicians and secret agents from the Soviet Union served in Spain. Allegedly, Stalin, taking no chance of involving the USSR in a general war, instructed his officers to stay out of the range of artillery fire.[112] Eighty thousand Italians of the CTV, some 19,000 Germans in the Condor Legion, the 10,000 Portuguese *Viriatos* and some 70,000 Moors fought with Franco's armies.

In order not to raise major objections in the NIC, the Fascist dictators camouflaged their troops as volunteers who were fighting 'Bolshevism'. But, as the Italian leaders and press kept boasting of the deeds of their nationals, everybody knew the hollowness of that pretence. The number of genuine volunteers joining the Nationalist camp was fairly small, a motley crew of some fifteen hundred Monarchists, Fascists and Catholics from different nations. They included 600 Irish Blueshirts led by Eoin O'Duffy, a few hundred French Monarchists, over a hundred émigré White Russians, and a small number of Englishmen and Fascist Romanians. They mostly served in the Spanish Foreign Legion and played no significant part on the battlefield.[113] The troops coming from Germany were professional soldiers, constantly resupplied and equipped with the best available matériel. The Moors, who with the Foreign Legion constituted the Nationalist crack forces, were mercenaries who flocked to Franco's army to escape misery.[114] In the case of Italy, 43 per cent of its soldiers in Spain were members of the regular army, including some leading generals and officers of the High Command. The others were members of the Black Shirt militia. There were instances of deception being used to lure volunteers. But most of those who went were either genuine

Fascists or were attracted by the high pay, as the large percentage of them coming from the depressed southern regions seems to indicate.[115]

By contrast, the International Brigades were civilians who had to be armed, trained and fed by a besieged Republic. The accusation of them being 'the Comintern's army', a professional force of fanatic Communists and revolutionary professionals, is not borne out by reality. In fact, some of them might have been adventurers but the majority were idealists and common civilians with hardly any knowledge of military fighting. Furthermore, they were not mercenaries but received the paltry sum of ten pesetas a day, the same as any Spanish soldier.[116] Robert Hale Merriman, an agrarian economist and teaching fellow at the University of California who commanded the Lincoln Battalion, called it 'the Pure War' because the volunteers were there out of pure self-motivation, not because they had been forced or paid to fight.[117] Unlike the Italians and Germans, who were equipped with the best available armaments, the memoirs of the brigadiers are full of accounts of jamming rifles and obsolete weapons. Yet their bravery in combat meant that, in nearly every major battle, they were usually to be found in the most dangerous places, playing the role of the shock troops of the Republic. They were given official status in September 1937, becoming the counterpart of the Nationalist Foreign Legion. However, by then the high number of casualties had resulted in the International Brigades being filled with many Spanish volunteers. Most of the officers and political commissars were Communist, and the Comintern controlled the channels of recruitment and mobilisation. But the International Brigades never took part in any of the internal rifts within the Republican camp. Promotion was due to merit on the battlefield and not to ideological loyalty. There were no attempts to woo fighters into the ranks of the Communist Party. On the contrary, political pluralism was encouraged so as to demonstrate that the Brigadiers were the living examples of an international Popular Front army.[118]

Finally, unlike the reliability of the supply routes of the Nationalist camp, which were protected by the German and Italian fleets, the long distance between the Soviet Union and Spain meant irregular and delayed deliveries. Supply from southern Russia grew ever more hazardous as Italian submarines and aviation intervened forcefully, attacking and sinking vessels carrying vital food or military supplies to the Republic through the Mediterranean. After the sinking of the *Komsomol* in December 1936, the already small Russian merchant fleet began to reduce its activities, leaving the transport of goods mostly in the hands of Republican or neutral boats. Eventually, as the

Mediterranean route became too dangerous, Russian weapons had to be dispatched from Murmansk to French Atlantic ports and then smuggled into Spain across the border. Furthermore, unlike the Nationalists who could always obtain their supplies promptly and on request, the diplomatic embargo forced the Republic to operate in the open arms market. To add insult to injury, many of these activities were sabotaged or betrayed by the original Spanish diplomatic corps, which had, for the most part, defected to the rebels.[119] In consequence, purchases from so many sources meant erratic deliveries, different or even incompatible types of armament with the subsequent shortages of accurate supplies and accessories, and overpriced and obsolete equipment from private arms dealers. Indeed, despite an abundance of gold, purchasing agents were faced with a wall of intrigue and deception and were forced to bribe middlemen and adventurers and pay inflated prices for useless equipment wherever they turned. Poland, the second greatest provider of weapons to the Republic, sold 100,000 rifles, 180 million cartridges, 11,123 light machine-guns and 294 artillery pieces but not all were delivered and those that were were little better than junk. Even the Soviet Union participated in this fraudulent practice. Apart from the excellent quality of planes and tanks, and 150 Degtyarev light machine guns, other weapons were old, some even dating from the nineteenth century. Additionally, by fiddling with the exchange rate, the Russians charged some 25 per cent over the normal price for their arms. However, considering the credit and loans never repaid, Stalin did not make any economic profits from the Spanish Civil War.[120]

Viewing this comparative analysis of the crucial international aid received by both camps, the conclusion is that, if anything, it was extraordinary that the Republic, facing such adverse odds, kept fighting for as long as it did.

# 4

# Apocalypse in 1936 Spain

My dear Magnin, we are ... poisoned by two or three very dangerous myths. First the French: The People ... have staged the French
Revolution ... Yet from the fact that a hundred pitchforks can
defeat twenty muskets one cannot infer that ten hunting guns
can beat a plane. The Russian Revolution has complicated matters
even further ... The Tsarists had neither aviation nor tanks and the
revolutionaries had their barricades ... Spain is today covered with
barricades against Franco's aviation ... What one can hear through
the windows, Magnin, is the Apocalypse of fraternity ... It is one of
the most overwhelming things on earth and cannot be seen too often
but it has to be transformed on pain of death ... The danger is that
everyone carries inside an Apocalypse ... and in war this leads to a
certain defeat since the Apocalypse has no future ... Our modest
task, Magnin, is to organise the Apocalypse.[1]

**The subtle art of conspiracy**

The first of the many myths surrounding the Spanish Civil War was
manufactured even before the military insurrection: namely, that
the generals had to rise up to forestall an imminent Communist plot.
Four secret documents, miraculously discovered in the spring of 1936
and curiously labelled, by its supposedly revolutionary authors, the
'subversive movement', exposed the machinations of Moscow and its
allies in Spain. According to them, Comintern and Soviet agents had
organised, in collusion with French and Spanish left-wingers, a coup
to take place sometime between 11 May and 29 June 1936. Counting
on both an armed assault militia and a so-called 'resistance militia' of
150,000 and 100,000 men respectively, according to those sources,

the revolutionaries planned to overthrow the existing Popular Front government and replace it with a Soviet presided over by Largo Caballero.[2] Once dissected, these documents appeared to be no more than a compilation of absurd facts in blatant conflict with the international and domestic political scene.[3] At the very same moment that Moscow was seeking a rapprochement with the Western powers and the Comintern was embracing the Popular Front strategy, they were supposedly plotting a revolutionary putsch against this very type of government in Spain. Far-fetched and even bordering on the absurd was the Spanish part of the conspiracy: namely, the efforts of unlikely allies and the forces they could muster. Thus, Spanish Communists were collaborating with rival Socialist factions, dissident Anarcho-syndicalists (such as Angel Pestaña) and leading members of the FAI (such as García Oliver) to bring Largo Caballero to power. To accomplish this task, the revolutionaries had at their disposal thousands of well-armed and trained militias.

The documents were not even secret. In May they were published and ridiculed in *Claridad*, Largo's Madrid mouthpiece.[4] However, this fantastic subterfuge was believed in many right-wing circles. For them, all Spanish left-wingers, regardless of ideologies and strategies, were merely 'Reds'. With apocalyptic messages hammered home by the right-wing press, it was easy to portray these men as working together, under Largo, to build a Soviet Spain. Hence the documents proved a very valuable weapon. They were produced in the spring of 1936 as a mechanism of psychological warfare to influence the military caste and the timorous bourgeoisie and to prepare them for the acceptance of a counter-revolutionary coup.[5]

Behind the façade of leading a pre-emptive strike against the 'Red threat', the insurgents not only mobilised their frightened constituency but also turned reality upside down.[6] Once martial law was declared, it was those defending Republican legality who were accused of rebellion. The conspiring officers were no longer traitors to the regime to which they had sworn loyalty but knights of a patriotic movement to save the fatherland. This fallacy was spread abroad by foreign apologists and, after 1939, was perpetuated by the propaganda machinery of the new order. Thus, children would be taught at school that the country never went through the cruel experience of a civil war but rather that, after a glorious and epic crusade, Spain was liberated from the fiendish yoke of heretics, Reds and separatists – all of them on Moscow's payroll.

The Red conspiracy was a coarse fabrication. Despite all the revolutionary rhetoric, in 1936 the Socialist faction led by Largo never plotted an uprising against the government. Even the Anarcho-syndicalists, after paying a heavy toll for their 'revolutionary gymnastics' of the previous years, seemed to have abandoned the insurrectionary road. The Communists were not just few in numbers but also had reversed their previously radical strategy for one bent on moderation. If anything remained the same within the Spanish Left it was its deeply-rooted divisions. None of the factions possessed thousands of ready shock troops well-trained and armed. Indeed, it was precisely the lack of weapons which plagued the defenders of the Republic from the first days of the military revolt.

Blatant distortion of reality damaged the Republican cause because vast sectors of public opinion, themselves scared of the 'Red threat', were willing to lend it an ear. Even so, the military's alleged noble purpose of being forced to restore imperilled public order was a fallacy. The wave of violence of the spring of 1936 was smaller than that of the period 1919–23 under the Restoration monarchy. Furthermore, it was not just left-wing groups which engaged in terror activities: right-wing squads were behind many of the atrocities. The symbolic murder of Calvo Sotelo was at the most an excuse to justify the uprising but definitely not the cause of it. At the time of his death, the *Dragon Rapide*, the plane hired by the insurgents' agents in London to carry General Franco to Morocco, had already landed in Casablanca.[7]

In fact, there existed only one conspiracy in 1936, that of elements within the armed forces. The so-called 'glorious national movement' did not seek to pre-empt a revolutionary takeover but to restore the social and political domination of the traditional ruling classes.[8] The coup was carefully planned, following the right's electoral defeat of February 1936, to prevent the new government from introducing wide-ranging social and economic reforms. As the legalist path was barred by the electoral fiasco of the CEDA, the only alternative was to destroy democracy by force.

### The Death of the Third Spain

It would be erroneous to examine the fateful July of 1936 merely as the moment when a polarised country decided to settle its differences by military means. Despite the undeniable levels of radicalism that existed in 1930s Spain, an overwhelming majority of Spaniards hoped that the divisive issues facing the country could be resolved peacefully. Indeed, despite the political divides, only a hardened minority was prepared to impose its views with blood and fire. A huge mass of people who can be defined as 'the Third Spain', often ignored because of their passivity, were pulled into the war with fear or repugnance.[9] For large numbers of them, allegiances to one side or the other in the war were to depend primarily on geography.

However, with their insurrection, the rebel officers opened the gates to innate social hatreds and political antagonisms that had accumulated for generations. As the first blood was being spilt on the streets, die-hards and extremists on both sides were catapulted to the forefront. Long-standing resentments found an opportunity for a violent solution. Spain was embarking upon a long, dark era of death and partisan sectarianism. The country's tragedy was not to end with the three years of fratricidal blood shed on the battlefields. Post-bellum, the victors, headed by General Franco, perpetuated the atmosphere of the civil war, enjoyed the spoils of victory and embarked upon the mythical rewriting of history. For the other half of the country, decades of exile, repression or silence lay ahead. It would be almost forty years before the Third Spain, that of dialogue and compromise, would have the chance to be heard again.

### The die is cast!

At no time had the insurgents envisaged a long civil war. In fact, they were confident that their uprising, in a country with a long tradition of military *pronunciamientos*, would lead to a relatively swift takeover. The passive role initially assigned to the crucial Army of Africa by the director of the rebellion, General Mola, in his secret instructions of May 1936 illustrated the confidence of the Nationalist hierarchy.[10] Thus, the degree of spirited popular resistance came as a shock to them. Yet successful opposition to the coup would have been impossible if a united army had been prepared to break with constitutional legality. In fact, while most colonels and middle-ranking officers backed the uprising, a majority of major-generals and brigadier-generals remained loyal to the government. General Miguel Cabanellas was the only major-general on active command on the mainland who revolted. The significant military support for the Republic, particularly amongst the young officers, was crucial to avoiding outright defeat but not enough to guarantee victory.[11]

As news of the rebellion in Morocco began to filter to the mainland, only the authorities seemed impervious to the events that were about to explode. But for their reluctance to act forcefully, the praetorian revolt might have been nipped in the bud. However, bourgeois politicians and intellectuals of the Republican governing class were as fearful of the unknown consequences of arming the people in order to quell a rebellion as they were of the rebellion itself.[12] Unprepared for a transformation overnight into firebrand Jacobins mobilising the populace in defence of the regime, they were simply overwhelmed and dragged along by the unfolding drama. The Republican President, Manuel Azaña, embodied perfectly the image of a cold and brilliant intellectual falling to pieces when confronted with an impending war between Spaniards. Aware of the horrors and destruction that lay ahead, he remained at his post, but virtually withdrew from public life except in his vain attempts to negotiate peace. Morally broken and politically marginalised, he devoted time to expressing his despair and pessimism in literary works such as La Velada de Benicarló (1939). For him, there could be no winner from a cruel fratricidal struggle.[13]

The hapless Casares Quiroga also refused, during the night of 17 July, to believe the seriousness of the military threat. The following morning he succumbed to panic when awakening to a reality of garrisons revolting and people demanding arms. According to Julián Zugazagoitia, the editor of El Socialista and future minister of the interior, the cabinet resembled a madhouse, and the craziest of the lot was the Prime Minister, who neither ate nor slept and kept howling like one possessed.[14] Amidst widespread confusion, Madrid saw three cabinets succeed each other in one day. A moderate, the ex-Radical Diego Martínez Barrios, took over from Quiroga with the objective of making a last-minute effort to avert a war by negotiating with the rebels. Yet his hopes were rapidly dashed. While Mola spurned Barrios's offers of a political compromise over the telephone, radicalised crowds in the streets of Madrid chanted against such a betrayal. The next prime minister, a left-wing Republican, José Giral, close to President Azaña, finally took the decision to arm the population.[15] By then, however, the Republican state had practically ceased to function. The government lacked any real control and did not actually know what was happening across Spain. The Republicans were caught between their fear of the military and their awareness that the workers' militias, providing the regime's ultimate defence, represented a threat to their own preferred forms of social and political order.

**Seven days that shook Spain**

For over a week there were no clear frontiers between the two camps. In Catholic and Conservative northern and central Spain (Galicia, León, Navarra and Old Castilla), the coup went according to plan. It found little stiff resistance and was even greeted with jubilation by large numbers of the population. A myriad of right-wing and paramilitary forces sprang up. They collaborated with the regular troops in securing the rear and initiating operations towards neighbouring villages. The blue shirts of the Falange and the red berets of the *requetés* were the dominant colours in the pretentiously-known *España Nacional*.[16] Castilian towns, particularly Valladolid, saw an upsurge in the number of young Falangist militants. Catholic Navarra, the Spanish Vendée, experienced, as no other region, an atmosphere of carnival. In this stronghold of counter-revolution, nostalgic stories of past battles in defence of the claims of the Carlist dynasty had circulated for generations. Now, thousands of youngsters wore their Sunday clothes and crucifixes, grabbed the red berets and rifles that their ancestors had carried and joined armed militias (*requetés*). In some cases, this included three generations of the same family and some small Navarrese villages were virtually emptied of men. Under the slogan 'Long Live Christ the King!', they believed that they had embarked upon a glorious campaign to save the fatherland from separatism and Communism. There were even numerous priests carrying rifles as they held confession and gave Holy Communion to ranks of youngsters.[17]

The spectacle was very different on the rest of the mainland. As vividly described by Malraux in the opening of his novel *L'Espoir*, trade-unionists and Popular Front militants in Madrid soon discovered, by telephone or radio, the progress of the military uprising and so assailed their local or regional centres with demands for weapons.[18] Contrary to the absurd claims made in the conspiracy documents, left-wing unions and parties lacked arms to give out to their restless members. Even when the government finally agreed to distribute weapons, it was a far from easy task as most firearms were in the hands of the security forces or deposited in military barracks. Thus, the latter's loyalty to the regime proved essential. Amidst the reigning chaos of these first crucial days, civilian determination and bravery played a large part. But in no major town could the people alone crush the revolt. Unarmed, disorganised and isolated, the masses were in no position to do more than stage a desperate resistance.[19]

The city of Barcelona underwent the most brutal street fighting. Rebel columns, beefed up by Falangist volunteers, began to advance from their garrisons into the centre to assemble in the Plaza de Cataluña. However, the erection of barricades blocked their path, while skirmishes with CNT members (who the previous night had managed to assault some arms depots) and other left-wing militants fighting alongside the local Catalan police (the *Mossos de Esquadra*) and the assault guards harassed their march and undermined their resolve. After bitter hesitations the *Generalitat* opted for arming the people. The balance was finally tilted when the Civil Guard came out on the side of the Republic. Side by side, former enemies, police and workers, surrounded the buildings seized by the insurgents. As workers captured heavy artillery and the loyalist air force entered the action, soldiers deserted their demoralised officers who, in turn, began to surrender. Once arrested, their commander-in-chief, General Goded, who had flown that morning from the Balearic Islands to lead the coup, agreed with the *Generalitat* to broadcast a statement admitting defeat and calling on his supporters to put down their arms. Nevertheless, large numbers of casualties resulted from the mass storming of some garrisons.[20]

Aware that large numbers of military and police units were loyal to the Republic, the seditious officers in Madrid, unlike those in the Catalan capital, decided to fortify themselves in a number of garrisons in the hope of receiving prompt external relief. The local leader of the conspiracy, General Joaquín Fanjul, with sympathisers and some Falangists bided their time in the formidable *La Montaña* barracks on the outskirts of the city. It was soon besieged by scores of civilians as well as assault guards and civil guards. In the fortress were stored the bolts of the rifles that the authorities had distributed earlier. On 20 July the use of heavy artillery and air strikes gained the day for the assailants who stormed the fortress. The fall of *La Montaña* was then followed by the surrender of other military garrisons.[21]

The rebellion also failed utterly in other key cities. In the Basque Country, Vitoria fell into the hands of the insurgents but in the larger capitals of Bilbao and San Sebastián, governmental forces gained the upper hand with relative ease. Hesitations also disrupted the activities of the rebels in Valencia, where tense days of wait-and-see lasted until the end of the month when the garrison was captured without resistance. The outcome was very different in some theoretically working-class strongholds: Oviedo, a Socialist bulwark, Zaragoza, the CNT's second capital after Barcelona, and Seville, with a large Communist and Anarcho-syndicalist following, were all captured by Nationalist guile and audacity. There, the three leaders of the conspiracy, Aranda, Cabanellas and Queipo de Llano respectively, were officers with republican pedigree. They therefore found it relatively easy to proclaim their loyalty and then strike by surprise. Aranda, for instance, waited until a convoy of 5000 armed miners had left Oviedo for Madrid before showing his true colours. They all rapidly declared martial law and achieved the support of most police and Civil Guard forces. The successful rebellion then spread to neighbouring provincial capitals in Aragón and Andalucía. In all cases, the local authorities were taken aback. The fighting became a one-sided affair, as the insurgents' shortage of manpower was compensated for with heavy weaponry. Barely armed, with just a few hunting rifles and pistols between them, government supporters were confronted by cannon and machine-gun fire; uncoordinated working-class attempts to declare a general strike and to seize key buildings were drowned in blood.[22]

With streets and squares of many cities still littered with corpses, the next step was to secure the countryside. Militias of Catalan and Valencian volunteers marched from the capitals to consolidate the grip on the rural areas. From there they crossed into Aragón, with the objective of retaking the three provincial capitals (Zaragoza, Huesca and Teruel) and even organised an abortive expedition to the Balearic Islands.[23] Forces from Madrid gained for the Republic the neighbouring provinces of Guadalajara, Cuenca, Ciudad Real, Albacete, Badajoz and Toledo. In turn, Nationalist troops under General Mola's overall command advanced from the north towards Madrid but, in the key mountain passes of Somosierra and Guadarrama, were held up by forces dispatched from the capital. Depleted and overstretched, the Nationalists had to rely on the thousands of Falangist and Carlist volunteers to shore up the defensive lines in Aragón and the Basque Country.[24] In the rural south, the key urban cities (Seville, Córdoba, Granada, Huelva and Cádiz), seized by Queipo and other officers, were small Nationalist islands in a hugely hostile Republican sea. Consequently, it was common for villages and towns to change hands several times in a few days, as badly armed peasants with wooden pitchforks, weeding hoes and sickles were routed by military expeditions but then quite often returned once the troops moved on. Popular resistance, however, was finally crushed with the arrival of the Army of Africa, courtesy of the Fascist dictators.[25]

## The outbreak of apocalypse

Although it was above all a social and class conflict, the Spanish Civil War also encompassed a variety of crucial issues that had not just divided the country for generations but had even cut across both warring sides. In simple terms, it was not just a matter of right versus left or White fighting Red but a near-Hobbesian struggle of all against all that meant very different things to the combatants: namely, it was a war of Republicans against Monarchists, centralists against devolutionists or regionalists, Catholics against anticlericals, modernists against traditionalists, authoritarians against democrats, industrialists against proletarians, peasants against landowners, farmers against workers, towns against villages. This cruel strife not only awakened the most primal instincts but also produced a foretaste of the technological advances of modern warfare: full-scale battles with tanks and planes, and cities under relentless bombardment.

The immediate consequence of the failure of the military insurrection was widespread chaos and confusion all over the country. There were not two Spains but two thousand.[26] Rather than a clash between two clear-cut camps, the war was an immensely complex combination of disparate, fierce, local, armed clashes. The state, and its control over the nation's public administration, simply collapsed under the impact of either reaction or revolution.[27] In fact, a coherent and unified Nationalist or Republican Spain was something that hardly existed beyond the reports of foreign journalists and diplomats.

Confident in their victory, the Nationalists lacked any proper ideological programme to unify their supporters. Most of the generals at this stage seemed to have preferred some kind of Monarchist restoration, but there were others who wanted a 'rectified' Republic. Even Mola had referred to the constitution of a republican dictatorship.[28] Additionally, the Nationalists were soon without a clear executive leadership. On 20 July the coup's nominal head, General Sanjurjo, died in a plane crash in Portugal before being able to join his fellow conspirators. Two other leading rebel generals, Goded and Fanjul, were executed in Barcelona and Madrid respectively. Simultaneously, the Nationalists were starved of direction on the political front. Gil Robles was discredited after his electoral defeat of 1936. Calvo Sotelo, the most outstanding senior Monarchist, was assassinated a few days before the rebellion. Finally, José Antonio, the Falangist leader, was in prison in Alicante and would be executed in November. If anything, the rebel camp resembled a motley combination of different warlords, separated geographically and assisted in their local endeavours by groups of disparate paramilitary militias. With over 65,000 militants, these right-wing volunteers amounted, as late as October 1936, to over a third of the total Nationalist manpower.[29]

A first step towards unified command was the appointment on 23 July of a Junta of National Defence in Burgos, under the presidency of Miguel Cabanellas, the most senior military commander. His past links with the Masons and the Radical Party served him well: the local authorities believed him to be loyal to the Republic, allowing him to seize the important city of Zaragoza when he was ready to act. On the other hand, this political baggage did little to gain him credibility and support in the zealous atmosphere of Nationalist Spain.

The Junta of National Defence extended martial law throughout Spain and ordered press censorship and the confiscation of vehicles. Its statement to the nation on 24 July was extremely vague, a mere pastiche of reactionary clichés with emphasis on the struggle against communism and separatism and the defence of property and social order. The royal flag was restored on 29 August and crucifixes were reintroduced in schools. However, although Nationalist Spain remained under absolute military control, it was already marked by its polycentrism, ideological confusion and lack of unified military command. While generals such as Queipo and Franco had revolted with shouts of '¡Viva la República!', in the conservative north, other military chiefs did not conceal their Monarchist and Catholic leanings. Additionally, many young officers were attracted to the Falange, while General Queipo de Llano, in Sevilla, was running his area as a private fiefdom. In parts of the north, the Carlists (with the connivance of General Mola) were consolidating their own rump state, whilst Franco was the undisputed head of the crucial Army of Africa. Presiding over them all, the Junta remained a toothless provisional body.[30]

Localism, atomisation and dispersal of authority also crippled Republican Spain. Wherever the insurrection failed, there was a mushrooming of local solutions to the organisation of everyday life: from transport, communications and water supplies to the cooperativisation of food supplies, workshops, restaurants, etc.[31] In fact, the great paradox of the insurrection was that it precipitated the very revolutionary process that the army claimed to be forestalling and consequently produced the collapse of the Republican state.[32] The leading Socialist Zugazagoitia wrote:

Madrid was in dire chaos. Public order was pulverised; it resided in the streets amongst all the citizens incorporated in the struggle against Fascism who then used it as they saw fit ... The government lacked any control. Its previous hesitations had largely contributed to the popular exaltation that was to acquire dramatic proportions and inflict upon us considerable moral damage.[33]

With the people in arms, the authority of the central government hardly reached beyond the ministerial offices. At a formal level, it was challenged by alternative administrations. The Catalan *Generalitat* used the opportunity to enhance its jurisdictional powers. Geographically distant and separated from the bulk of the Republican territory by rebel-held areas, Basque Nationalist loyalty helped secure for the Republic the two provinces of Vizcaya and Guipúzcoa, but tensions with the other left-wing groups persisted. The Anarcho-syndicalist militias advancing in Aragón established there an (in all but name) independent council. There were two rival sources of power in Asturias, the Provincial Committee of the Popular Front in Sama de Langreo and the War Council in Gijón, the first dominated by the Socialists and the second by the CNT. There were also autonomous local councils in Málaga, Valencia and Murcia.[34]

Power fragmentation was the logical consequence of the reality on the ground, the physical separation (total in cases such as Asturias and the Basque Country), distance from the front and the extent of regional consciousness.[35] The traditional state machinery was swept away by the revolutionary tide that followed the defeat of the rebellion in large swathes of the country. The number of armed activists in the streets outgunned and outnumbered the forces of public order. The army, as a standing corps, had melted away. Faced with a military rebellion, the government decreed the demobilisation of the soldiers in regiments whose commanders had revolted. As a consequence, most recruits deserted their companies and either returned home or joined the various militias. Loyal officers found themselves distrusted and with hardly any regular troops to command.[36]

Madrid and the other regions not only often worked at cross-purposes but also conceived of military resistance in local terms and not as a general war effort. Indeed, the central government and its representatives in the provinces were bypassed by a myriad of popular committees, juntas and other bodies that were constituted depending on the local balance of power. A large part of industry, commerce and the public services were taken over by the trade unions. Both the

UGT and the CNT collectivised significant tracts of land. In many cases, peasants responded enthusiastically. However, in places such as Valencia and, above all, Aragón, the Anarchists had to enforce large-scale collectivisation against the resistance of large sectors of small- and middle-scale landholders.[37] Workers' militias took control of re-establishing order in the streets and organised the military operations against the Nationalist-held areas. Naturally, this was a far from uniform process. Where the Socialists were stronger, the collapse of the pre-war social and political structures was much less general than where the Anarchists were dominant (in Cataluña, Aragón and some parts of Andalucía). In the Basque Country, the socially conservative PNV, naturally, ensured minimum structural changes.[38]

Ironically, the existence of other sources of power never constituted a real challenge to the bourgeois government in Madrid. As late as December 1936, George Orwell, one of the many foreigners lured to Spain by the unfolding apocalypse, provided a view of Barcelona in which the triumphant revolution was on the march:

> It was the first time that I had ever been in a town where the working class was in the saddle. Practically every building of any size had been seized by the workers and was draped with red flags or with the red and black flags of the Anarchists. Every wall was scrawled with the hammer and sickle and with the initials of the revolutionary parties. Almost every church had been gutted and its images burnt ... Nobody said 'Señor' or 'Don' or even 'Usted'; everyone called everyone else 'Comrade' and 'Thou', and said 'Salud' instead of 'Buenos Días' ... The revolutionary posters were everywhere, flaming from the walls ... loudspeakers were bellowing revolutionary goals ... In outward appearance [Barcelona] was a town in which the wealthy classes had practically ceased to exist. Except for a small number of women and foreigners there were no 'well-dressed' people at all. Practically everyone wore rough working-class clothes, or blue overalls, or some variant of the militia uniform.[39]

The same pattern of revolutionary enthusiasm could be seen in most of Republican Spain, including Madrid. Women acquired an unprecedented role in a hitherto male-dominated society. Some even joined the militias to fight at the front. Many others looked after the wounded or the children of the combatants, ran collective dining-halls and took up a variety of tasks and jobs now left vacant. Lorries were full of militiamen brandishing their rifles. Seized cars were painted with the graffiti of the different trade unions or parties. Churches were burnt down or occupied. Prisons were emptied and court archives destroyed. Everywhere, people greeted each other with a clenched fist. Places housing leading right-wing personalities or their political quarters were taken over or looted. There was an atmosphere of revolutionary power.[40]

However, this was not Russia in 1917 when the February Revolution had initiated a period of instability marked by the rivalry between the Provisional Government and the Soviets. In Spain there was no Bolshevik party seeking to lead and unify the revolutionary force emanating from the workers' councils to overthrow liberal democracy and impose the dictatorship of the proletariat. The legal centres of power and the ad hoc revolutionary committees, rather than competing, just mixed up their prerogatives with the effect of weakening each other.[41] In the summer of 1936 the destruction of the central state and the parallel growth of trade-union influence determined the scope and limits of the revolution. Workers' organisations took over out of a need to fill the existing void; they did not follow an organised plan.[42] They suddenly acquired immense power in the running of the economy and the upholding of public order, without any apparent check on their ability to carry out takeovers and collectivisation or to patrol the streets. Yet they were unable to construct a centralising revolutionary source of authority. The dispersion of the new workers' power explains why Spain went through a profound social revolution during these months and yet remained so vulnerable at a political level.[43]

Thus, although it had been badly mauled, the legitimacy of the Republican state was never in dispute. The Communists remained outspoken defenders of the inter-class alliance embodied by the Popular Front. The two dominant working-class organisations, the UGT–PSOE and the CNT, saw their pre-war internal tensions increased. Within the Socialist movement, the old guard, best represented by Julián Besteiro, rapidly descended into impotence and fatalism, while the followers of Prieto continued their active collaboration with the Republicans. The left-wing, led by Largo, despite all its radical rhetoric, never even considered taking advantage of the situation to seize control of the Republic.[44]

If anything, the CNT leadership was more baffled than that of the Socialists. The hard-line anarchists of the FAI had no strategy for wielding political power.[45] The leading *Cenetista*, Camil Piñón, graphically expressed the situation in which the Libertarians found

themselves: 'The FAI won a major revolutionary victory and then it
did not know what to do ... The Socialists would seize key positions.
We, with our purism and radicalism that had prevented us in the past
from taking any constructive measure, would have to keep travelling
with a second-class ticket.'[46]
Even in Barcelona, where armed Anarcho-syndicalist forces were
at the peak of their power, revolutionary utopianism ran up against the
political reality. On 20 July the historic meeting of the FAI leaders
with the president of the *Generalitat* revealed their confusion. Still
covered in dust from the fighting, the Anarchist leaders were won over
by Companys, an accomplished politician, with a combination of
flattery and diplomacy. He, and indeed the entire *Generalitat*, could
have been swept away by the revolutionary tide. Yet he was allowed
to remain in office. The following day, at the meeting held by the
CNT local federation, collaboration and not revolution gained the
upper hand. Joan García Oliver found himself isolated even amongst
his close colleagues in one of the most daring action groups of the
FAI, *Nosotros*:

> I believe that the group '*Nosotros*' should lead the organisation
> towards our final objective ... Take advantage of the concentra-
> tion of forces to proceed with the assault on the main centres of
> government, *Generalitat*, and city hall ...
> Durruti spoke: García Oliver's arguments are magnificent ... but,
> in my opinion, this is not the right moment. Firstly, we must liberate
> Zaragoza ...
> Even Durruti was turning his back. None of those present failed
> to notice that we were avoiding taking the march of destiny into our
> hands ... They found a subterfuge, Zaragoza, to avoid openly
> saying no to the revolution.[47]

The abyss between their ultimate ideological tenets and the harsh
realism imposed by war eroded overnight the foundations of Anarchist
faith built up over the years of persecution and clandestinity. Having
lost their strongholds of Eastern Andalucía and Aragón, they could
impose their will in Cataluña and perhaps Valencia, but only by
creating a dictatorship – something which was an anathema to the
libertarian credo and which would, furthermore, have opened up an
internal schism within Republican Spain, thus accelerating defeat in
the Civil War.[48] On a more structural level, the Anarcho-syndicalists,
having failed to establish national industrial federations, lacked a
centralised organism that could have articulated and implemented any

revolutionary initiative across the country. The CNT remained a loose organisation of regional bodies. Confronted with the stark military situation, the old romantic concepts of protest and struggle were redundant. Their temporary hegemony, at least in Cataluña, was sacrificed. Some, like Durruti, left for the front. Those who stayed opted for collaboration. First, they allowed the *Generalitat* to remain in power, alongside a body called the Committee of Anti-Fascist Militias in which all the Republican forces were represented. Two months later, they agreed to dissolve that Committee and even to enter both the Catalan and Spanish administrations.[49]

## Terror unleashed

As the main fighting shifted from the control of towns and villages to the front, the horrors of a fratricidal strife became a glaring reality. Not only was brotherly blood being shed on the battlefields, but also terror sprang up in the rear of both zones. Real power, implying that of life and death over the citizenship, lay with those groups who had conquered the streets. In both camps they included hard-liners and extremists eager to settle old scores and eliminate their adversaries.

The initial victims were the military. The rebel generals rapidly declared martial law, effectively placing total power in their own hands. Those fellow officers who opposed them, or even hesitated to take sides, were themselves accused of rebellion, imprisoned and summarily executed. In the elimination of enemies within the army corps, the Nationalists possessed a clear advantage over the Republicans. Knowing who their comrades were, they could therefore strike at will against those military elements marked by their democratic leanings or reluctance to break their oath of allegiance to the legitimate government. The brutal purge of the armed forces under the new order did not distinguish between ranks or even past friendships. Generals such as Manuel Romerales and Domingo Batet, commanders of Ceuta and Burgos respectively, could not be accused of left-wing leanings. They were just disciplined officers who refused to countenance the insurrection. For this they paid with their lives. The similar fate of others, such as Miguel Campíns (Military Governor of Granada and formerly Franco's deputy in the Military Academy of Zaragoza) and even Franco's own cousin, Ricardo de la Puente Baamonde, illustrated the cruel determination of the insurgents. The Rubicon had been crossed and there was no return.[50]

In Republican Spain, the officers involved in the aborted coup were quickly arrested and in some instances lynched on the spot. The largest bloodbath took place in the *La Montaña* barracks where the crowds, enraged after being shot at while advancing under the lure of white flags, fell upon the defenders, leaving the courtyard strewn with corpses.[51] The leading conspirators in Madrid and Barcelona, Generals Fanjul and Goded respectively, were court-martialled and executed like many others. The bitter betrayal of supposed loyalists such as Queipo de Llano or Aranda, followed by acts of sabotage, fuelled the flames of suspicion. Fears that large numbers of the military were just waiting for their chance to desert or that they were acting as spies led to an all-out purge of the army corps. Many were arrested or assassinated. As a whole, the officer witch-hunt seriously impeded the war effort. In these crucial first weeks, mistrust and embedded left-wing anti-militarism resulted in the loss of the technical services of many military experts and the promotion of officers based not on merit but on their political connections. In a sense, a standing army had ceased to exist.

Terror was not just unleashed against the armed forces. Corpses began to appear in desolate spots and near cemeteries. As violence mounted, innocent words such as *paseo* (ride) and *saca* (removal, but in this instance the extrajudicial execution of prison inmates) acquired dreadful connotations and became common parlance. Social class, profession, friendships or past opinions could mark out anybody.

In Nationalist Spain, members of the Popular Front parties, trade-union activists and anybody with left-wing leanings or simply somehow deemed to be a 'Red' were rounded up and executed without any pretence of formal justice. Not only were the political class and the labour movement decimated, but also intellectuals, bureaucrats and all those associated with spreading the pernicious principles of the Republic were massacred. Their deaths not only served as exemplary punishment but were also an attempt to eradicate their model of society. In this context, teachers who had dared to challenge the prominence of Catholic education and served as the main conductors of democratic principles were particularly targeted. The purge acquired more tragic proportions in rural areas, where old family disputes, class conflicts and closer personal relations, combined with the threat to the vested interests by the labour reforms, fuelled the thirst for revenge.[52]

In turn, right-wingers, landowners, *caciques* and employers were hunted down in Republican Spain. It was, however, the Catholic Church that was particularly singled out for popular hatred. As the 'organic intellectuals' of the ruling elites,[53] the members of the clergy were identified as the cultural bulwark of the status quo. The Church was a class enemy by historically abandoning the gospel of poverty and brotherhood and instead amassing wealth, blessing the glaring social oppression and demanding popular acceptance of the natural domination of the ruling classes. Even more, with its hostility to reform and its loss of privileges, during the Second Republic it became an ideological bulwark of counter-revolution.[54] Thus, from the first moment, except in the Basque Country, religious symbols and buildings became targets of mob fury. Churches, monasteries and convents were pillaged, looted and burnt down or were transformed into shops, hospitals, public canteens and even dance halls. Some 6844 members of the clergy (including 13 bishops) were killed, over a third of them in Cataluña. Priests were the first to be hunted down by militias in most villages, even before landowners or *caciques*. There is the illustrative case of Mosén Josep Puig, the priest of a small Catalan parish. He was actually well-liked by his community, yet one day five men, from a neighbouring town, went to his office and told him that they had come to kill him. When he enquired as to their reasons, they replied that it was simply because he was a priest.[55]

For the Nationalists, the execution of workers meant the restoration of order; for the Republicans, the massacre of priests advanced the revolution.[56] However, although blood was shed in huge quantities in both areas, there existed an essential difference between Republican and Nationalist terror. In the zones where the insurrection had failed, the ensuing orgy of looting and killing was basically the product of the impotence of the central Republican authorities. In rebel Spain, the military leaders could have stopped the actions of the vigilantes at any point. However, they failed to do so because Nationalist terror was a cold, methodical and calculated policy.

With the power of the Madrid government in tatters, bloodletting was largely spontaneous, as popular crowds ran amok, unleashing their anger against both institutions and classes associated with years of oppression and injustice. Terror from below sometimes led to the so-called *sacas* and killing of rightist convicts (normally as a reprisal for devastating air attacks or news of violence in the other zone). All kinds of criminal elements took advantage of the situation to rob, kill and take revenge on their enemies.[57]

However, no Popular Front group could claim innocence in this orgy of mayhem carried out by the so-called '*incontrolados*' (literally, 'the uncontrollable ones'). For example, on 22 July the FAI leader García Oliver concluded a passionate radio speech encouraging

Anarchists to fulfil their duty: 'Do not wait for my words to end. Leave your homes, burn, destroy, and beat fascism', he implored.[58] Indeed, the CNT and FAI took a prominent role in hunting down class enemies in the cities, and their local committees and armed columns left a trail of blood first in Lleida and then in the wake of their advance into Aragón. The Libertarian philosophy of mass spontaneity made it impossible to disavow the large sectors of the lumpenproletariat that now suddenly appeared and overwhelmed the CNT and the FAI.[59] Some Anarchist militias, such as the *Columna de Hierro*, were formed largely by freed prisoners from the *Penal de San Miguel de los Reyes* in Valencia but also contained many right-wingers and agents provocateurs. The ease with which many trapped rightists or leftists sought salvation by joining either Anarchist or Falangist gangs gave way to the term 'Failange'.[60]

Yet the hot terror of the summer of 1936 was not limited to the Anarchists: all the parties and trade unions of the Popular Front were implicated in it. Apart from the criminal newcomers who had joined to act under the cover of political membership, all Popular Front groups contained many *exaltés* who were convinced that inherent to the success of the revolution was the physical liquidation of class enemies and bourgeois parasites. It was necessary for 'public health' to cleanse all those regarded as being exploiters. Consequently, all over Republican Spain, thousands of citizens associated with right-wing parties or social exploitation were rounded up and taken to improvised prisons (*checas*) where they were summarily tried and either promptly released or given their final *paseo*.[61]

Burning churches, night-time arrests, confiscated cars and vans crammed with armed gangs were typical of the capital, Madrid, where the CNT–FAI was not the dominant organisation and, during the first three months of the war, an average of 66 assassinations took place every day. Most of the corpses were abandoned in the huge *Casa de Campo* on the outskirts of the city.[62] The Socialist Arturo Barea (who for much of 1937 was the – unknown – voice of Madrid in his daily radio talks) wrote that some Socialist militiamen proudly boasted of 'selling tickets for the other world at the *Casa de Campo*'.[63]

Red terror was above all the product of passion, revenge and a deeply-rooted sense of undoing historical wrongs. It was not just alien to but also caused by the besieged state in which the Republic found itself. As Barea noted, faced with an all-out manhunt and chaos, the government was powerless.[64] The killings were never condoned, let alone encouraged, by the huge majority of the governing classes or by party or trade-union leaderships. On the contrary, from the start they strived to put an end to this indiscriminate system of mob justice. The CNT leader and future minister Joan Peiró, the Socialist Indalecio Prieto and the Communist Dolores Ibarruri were among the many influential voices who spoke against the existing violence. Others, such as the future prime minister, the Socialist Juan Negrín, even risked their lives leading night patrols that rescued people from their deaths. *El Socialista* and even *Solidaridad Obrera* also condemned the senseless mayhem, while the Catalan *Generalitat* facilitated safe-conducts and helped many of those in peril (such as Cardinal Francesc Vidal i Barraquer and the Bishops of Tortosa and Girona) to flee abroad.[65] In Madrid, the government even permitted over 10,000 right-wing refugees to seek sanctuary in foreign embassies or in private flats which were given diplomatic status under a foreign flag.[66]

With the gradual reconstruction of the Republican state, the terror diminished proportionally and was basically under control by late 1936. Slowly but steadily, traditional channels of order and justice were established. After the *sacas* of 22–3 August in the capital, in which over thirty prominent right-wingers were killed, the government set up Popular Courts, with juries and presided over by career judges, to deal with crimes of treason and sedition in order to prevent mob rule.[67] The Anarchist García Oliver, although a firebrand in the early days of the war, as minister of justice played a crucial part in containing the hitherto uncontrolled violence.[68] Despite these efforts, however, in one of the darkest stains on the Republic, in November and December 1936, over 2400 convicts were executed by their own guards in the villages of Torrejón de Ardoz and Paracuellos del Jarama, just outside the capital. The Anarchist, Melchor Rodríguez, when appointed to organise the prison system, brought to an end the terrible massacres of right-wing prisoners evacuated from Madrid as the fight raged in the city.[69]

Whereas Republican leaders abhorred and sought to eliminate terror, for the Nationalist hierarchy it was a vital instrument for its success and consolidation.[70] Before the coup, General Mola ordered the use of extreme violence in order to crush any possible resistance and warned that hesitations could only lead to failure.[71] Once the insurrection began, wholesale killing started. The surreal and cruel aberration of justice encompassed by the declaration of martial law provided the insurgents with the pretext for an all-out onslaught, liquidating all those who disagreed with the new order for – incredible though it might sound – the crime of rebellion.[72]

Unlike the Republic's hot and spontaneous terror, that which was carried out by the insurgents was cold and calculated.[73] Repression was an intrinsic part of the Nationalist ethos and strategy. The rebel officers, most of them *Africanistas*, conducted the war as if it were a colonial struggle, with the hostile population of Spain playing the part of ignorant and ungodly natives. Their cult of violence and their profound disdain of human rights and liberal values forged in the cruel Moroccan battlefields was now brought to the mainland.[74] There really was very little spontaneity about the bloodbath. Certainly there were abundant cases of paramilitary groups' uncontrolled activities. Yet the military hierarchy not only turned a blind eye but even encouraged large numbers of militia forces to be accomplices in the task. Repression was, from the first moment, the logical result of a deliberate plan of revenge and liquidation in order to eradicate the cycle of reforms begun in 1931.[75]

Nationalist terror had a crucial social component. Mass repression was the perfect tool to terrorise the working classes into acquiescence and to accomplish the necessary *limpieza* (cleaning up) to rid the country of atheists, separatists and Reds. These groups embodied the 'anti-Spain' that had to be purified and destroyed. Violence was in the service of a fundamentally reactionary project whose objective was to re-establish the traditional social order.[76] In fact, constant executions and widespread massacres became the foundation of a new state purged of all its elements of dissent.[77]

The massacres went on for weeks – even in provinces such as Pamplona or Burgos where the left-wing organisations had few followers. Anyone could be killed for holding different thoughts or ideas.[78] The right-wing squads in the rural south, where the slaughter reached near-genocidal levels, were nakedly the instruments of the vested powers.[79] The southern army was, in all but name, the army of the local landowners and *caciques*. Brutal atrocities were carried out not just to defend their properties but also to assert their rightful place in society. A sick joke doing the rounds at the time had it that the rural labourers had finally obtained their 'land reform' – in the form of a burial plot.[80] Knowing their deficiency in numbers, the Nationalists sought from the beginning to paralyse the working class through sheer panic by brutal sorties carried out from the Andalusian cities under their control. But it was with the arrival of the Army of Africa that repression on a massive scale began in earnest. The terror that surrounded its advances was one of Franco's greatest weapons in the drive on Madrid.[81] Colonial officers had long ago learnt the value of systematic 'cleansing' as a means of ensuring order. Thus, a process of selective extermination and torture accompanied the 'liberation' of villages. As a warning to the survivors, unburied corpses were left on display for days. The bloodthirsty Moors were often used as the vanguard troops. Their looting and pillaging and their mutilation of enemies in the captured territory were intended to ensure that those not physically eliminated would be broken by fear and seek survival in submission. In fact, news of advancing Moors was sometimes enough to send the badly-armed and untrained workers' militias fleeing in panic.[82] Memories of the conquest of Badajoz, the first place where the Army of Africa found meaningful resistance, were to remain for generations. There, some 4000 captured prisoners were taken to the bullring to be machine-gunned. Some foreign journalists (such as the Portuguese Mario Neves, the Americans John T. Whitaker and Jay Allen and the French photographer René Brut) were among the first witnesses to report the infernal spectacle: they recorded the smell of death, the piles of corpses and the blood-drenched walls.[83]

Unlike in the Republican zone, where the re-establishment of state power gradually brought popular violence under control, in Nationalist Spain hot terror only gave way – and then very slowly – to institutionalised repression through the use of mass court-martials that were little more than parodies to legitimise the endemic slaughter. Hardly any leading Nationalist voice was raised against the orgy of blood. Even within the Catholic Church, the calls of the Bishop of Pamplona, Marcelino Olaechea, for an end to the slaughter were exceptional and anyway went unheard. In fact, the religious hierarchy did not seek to mitigate the violence but lent it whole-hearted support. The time had arrived, it felt, to crush its heretical enemies and to enjoy the benefits of the new order.[84]

The military commanders encouraged widespread repression. Mola commented that if he found his father on the other side he would not hesitate in having him shot. Queipo de Llano, meanwhile, acquired a sinister reputation as 'the radio general'. In his daily locutions from Sevilla, he insulted and mocked the sexual virility of the Republican leaders, while boasting of the brutal deeds of his men, the tough and macho 'real' Spaniards.[85] Similarly, Colonel Juan Yagüe, who was in charge of the Army of Africa's advance towards Madrid, justified to the US journalist Jay Allen the slaughter at Badajoz: 'Of course, we shot them. What do you expect? Was I supposed to take 4,000 Reds with me as my column advanced, racing against time? Was I expected to turn them loose in my rear and let them make Badajoz red again?'[86]

Indeed, the different responses to widespread terror of the leaders of the two camps was striking. Equally, there was an abyss in the perception of the war by the heads of the two rival states, Azaña and Franco. The Republican president burst into tears when he was told of the *saca* of Madrid prison in August 1936 which left 30 high-ranking right-wingers dead. He was appalled by a violence that he could never understand and thoroughly despised.[87] His sense of despair and outrage was still present in his speech in Barcelona on the second anniversary of the outbreak of the war:

> And when the torch passes to other hands, to other men, to other generations, may they remember, if some day their blood boils with anger and once more the Spanish temper is infuriated with intolerance and with hate and with the appetite for destruction, let them think of the dead and hear their warning; the lesson of those men who fell bravely in the battle, fighting generously for a grandiose ideal and who now, locked in the embrace of mother earth, have no more hatred, no more resentment and who send us ... the message of the eternal fatherland which says to all its children: peace, pity and forgiveness.[88]

While for Azaña a single death was an aberration, Franco, in a characteristically messianic combination of callous determination and cruelty, told the reporter Jay Allen that he was embarked upon redeeming Spain by blood regardless of the human cost.[89] The Nationalist leader embodied the cold and implacable justice of an *Africanista*. His was a message in which there was certainly no room for 'peace, pity and forgiveness'. He began the war giving instructions not to be disturbed while his cousin was being executed and concluded it by signing thousands of death penalties while enjoying an afternoon coffee. In a sickening game of words, Franco's assistants were to comment that every time the general wrote the word '*enterado*' ('noted') in a prisoner's file, it actually amounted to '*enterrado*' ('buried').[90]

## The Republican organisation of the apocalypse[91]

With the battle for the capital looming, the inexorable march of the war made it imperative for both Republicans and Nationalists to harness, centralise and mobilise all the available material and human resources. It was evident that neither the Giral all-Republican administration nor the Junta of National Defence led by Cabanellas could undertake that crucial task effectively. The government in Madrid was impotent before the constellation of revolutionary forces unleashed in July and was struggling to stop the wave of random violence, while the Junta in Burgos had hardly any influence over the commanders in the field.[92] Thus, following parallel processes, both Francisco Largo Caballero and General Francisco Franco were catapulted to power in September 1936. They appeared to be the leaders of the moment; the two crucial personalities who were best suited to rally the disparate forces of their respective camps and thereby deliver victory on the battlefield.

Aged 68 in October, Largo Caballero had a long and distinguished career devoted to the Socialist movement, both in the local politics of his native Madrid and at state level. After serving as minister of labour, he had become increasingly critical of the Second Republic. He headed the left wing of his party and commanded the allegiance of the powerful UGT. By the summer of 1936, Largo was the undisputed master of the capital. On the strength of his revolutionary image, he appeared to be the leader who could channel the existing euphoria into a united war effort. Consequently, on 4 September, amidst scenes of popular enthusiasm, he became prime minister and retained the defence portfolio in a new administration, the so-called 'Government of Victory', which contained six Socialists, two Republicans, one Catalan and one Basque Nationalist and two Communists. In early November two members of the CNT – Joan Peiró (industry) and Juan López (commerce) – and two of the FAI – Joan García Oliver ( justice) and Federica Montseny (health) – also became ministers.[93]

Although hailed, as we have seen, by the Socialist Youth as the 'Spanish Lenin', Largo was no Bolshevik. As many of his rivals in the PSOE had predicted, his fierce radical rhetoric of the previous months was not caused by a sudden conversion to revolutionary principles but by the old Socialist tradition of applying pressure to achieve concessions.[94] Above all, Largo was a trade-union militant whose main concern was the hegemony of the UGT and the solidity of that organisation. As he had proved in October 1934, for him verbal maximalism was one thing but the sacrifice of a lifetime's work for the sake of revolutionary principles was quite another. Indeed, the inveterate reformism that permeated the left wing of the Socialists in general prevented the translation of any revolutionary resolution from the theoretical to the practical plane.[95]

The government, presided over by Largo, reflected the situation on the ground. The balance between representatives of traditional political

parties and of the two trade unions was an indication of the growing influence and power acquired by both UGT and CNT. However, it
was primordially a cabinet of unity, whose main goal was to restore
bourgeois democracy and not to destroy it.[96]

To portray the reconstruction of the Republican state as being solely
a consequence of Largo's reformist attitude would, however, be
misleading. Focusing on the dichotomy between those who gave
priority to the war effort and those who pushed for greater social
revolution is simply to miss the core of the argument. By September
1936 the irresistible advance of Franco's professional troops, well
supplied by the Fascist dictators, had already solved the question in
favour of the former. Indeed, the Nationalists had forced a total war
and the Republic simply had to fight back on those terms. The military
insurrection had certainly triggered off a social revolutionary process in
Republican Spain, and industrial takeovers, agrarian collectivisations
and armed militias were the most glaring manifestations of that. Yet
even during these first weeks of unchallenged working-class power, the
limits of that revolution were glaring. Trade unions and political parties
did not guide but followed the lead of the masses.[97] With real authority
fragmented into local parcels, there was no force – not the Anarcho-
syndicalists, not the Socialists and certainly not the Communists – that
intended to fuse the existing revolutionary euphoria to take over
power. On the contrary, they all initially permitted the survival of the
bourgeois democratic Republic, and later the bitterness of defeat and
retreat made them realise that the main priority had to be to wage an
effective war.[98]

By late August everybody in the Republican camp was aware that
the military situation was becoming desperate. The initial advantage
in terms of material resources and manpower was soon lost owing
to the chaotic fragmentation of power, the absence of a single military
strategy and resistance being focused in merely local terms.[99] The
poorly-armed and ill-disciplined workers' militias, although vital in
crushing the insurrection in street fighting, fared badly in open battle.
Despite their overwhelming superiority in numbers, the Catalan columns advancing into Aragón got bogged down within 20 kilometres
of their objective, Zaragoza, against rebel lines which, although thin,
were, crucially, defended by organised troops led by seasoned officers.
There were more men than arms, more wounded than ambulances,
more shortages than supplies. Yet the main reason for the Republican
failure was the lack of any co-ordinated offensive. Lacking experienced commanders, the government left crucial decisions to random

improvisation, and political rivalries often meant that while one column was fighting, others were watching, or holding a vote before an attack.[100] Even though the militias temporarily halted the Nationalist advance in the mountain passes north of the capital, their lack of martial discipline hindered the prospects of profiting from the initial successes. They mounted an offensive only when and if they wanted. Most militiamen fought on the basis of a working-day schedule. Many of them were bussed back and forth from the front to Madrid, so that by the evening they could be at home with their families or bragging about their heroic deeds of that day in their local bars.[101] The militia's performance was even worse against the professional troops of the Army of Africa, which was marching, without encountering any meaningful resistance, towards Madrid.

Only the effective centralisation, deployment and mobilisation of all human and material resources could stave off the Republic's imminent defeat. There was also widespread agreement that, in the crucial international arena, sweeping away the bourgeois state machinery would have alienated the Western democracies and, as it turned out, even the Soviet Union. Spain, unlike Russia in 1917, possessed a large middle class, largely identified with the Republic, which had to be accommodated if a popular and anti-oligarchic coalition was to be rebuilt. Apart from the socially conservative Basque provinces, Valencia and Cataluña contained large numbers of smallholders who would be alienated by revolutionary excess. The task of appeasing them was imperative because the insurrection itself had meant the loss to the Republic of the bulk of its most radical constituency, the rural landless of the deep south who had fallen victim to the invasion of the Army of Africa.[102] However, the government headed by Largo was not merely a return to 1931. It became the first democratic administration in Europe to contain not only Communists but also and this would have been unthinkable even a few weeks earlier – Anarcho-syndicalists.

Taking the historical decision to join first the Catalan and then the central administration was not quite such an abrupt conversion for the Anarcho-syndicalists as it might, at first, have appeared. Rather, it was for them the logical and final step after accepting the responsibility of running local affairs in collaboration with others and after having joined (in July) the Committee of Anti-Fascist Militias, itself dissolved when three members of the CNT entered the *Generalitat*. Collaboration was not a plot hatched by the Secretary General, Horacio Prieto, and a few high-ranking militants. Ideologically torn since the July days of Barcelona, many members of the CNT and even of the FAI had been gradually dropping all their previous anti-governmental and anti-state concepts.[103] Confronted by the dire military reality, most understood that if the war were lost, there would never be a revolution. Even though a breach developed amongst some of the die-hard extremists, now the slogan accepted by the majority was to fight Fascism above all else. For the Anarcho-syndicalists the question became not whether to collaborate with the others but whether to gain control of the mechanisms of power before others seized them.[104]

The timely arrival of the International Brigades and of Soviet armaments was giving hope to the Republic. However, it would all be for nothing unless, as Malraux vividly expressed it in his fictional account of the civil war, the 'Apocalypse of Fraternity' of the first weeks were organised. Hence, emphasis was placed on creating a strong central government that could run a war economy. Consequently, in October 1936 the Communist minister of agriculture, Vicente Uribe, legalised the expropriation without compensation of all land belonging to those involved in the military revolt. Peasants and agrarian organisations, however, could choose whether to work the lands individually or collectively, according to the decision of the majority. In December, the Ministry then aided the creation of a peasant federation to defend the smallholders' proprietorship.[105] The situation of other competing governments was regularised. In October the PNV's loyalty was rewarded with the concession of Basque home rule and the appointment of its leader José Antonio Aguirre as the Basque Country's first president. The rival sources of authority in Asturias were merged in December into the Council of Asturias y León. Also that month, the Council of Aragón, headed by the Anarchist Joaquín Ascaso and in which all Republican forces were represented, was officially recognised. The establishment of Popular Courts presided over by professional judges and the increase in the number of security and armed police were also manifestations of the intention of regaining control of justice and public order so as to put an end to the period of *paseos*. Finally, steps were taken to create a cohesive military force, the Popular Army. A general staff, manned by loyal officers, was created and military academies were established. On 29 September a decree was introduced, bringing all the militias under central military discipline and under the control of the War Department. The model for the new army was the Communist 5th Regiment, a well-disciplined body which was led by professional officers and incorporated political commissars to train the troops and motivate them ideologically. The basic units of the new popular army were the so-called 'mixed brigades'. They contained some

160 officers and 4000 troops, organised into four battalions of infantry, as well as artillery, engineering, catering and medical services.[106]

By the turn of the year, the Republican forces were being incorporated into mixed brigades that were themselves combined to form divisions and army corps. However, the process was slow and not without difficulties. The shortage of weapons and skilled cadres was a hindrance, while areas distant from the front lines did not share the same sense of urgency with the central zone. The Basque and Catalan executives retained control over their forces and acted almost as independent nations.[107] Additionally, the militarisation of the militias, although finally accepted by the CNT in February 1937, was far from being executed satisfactorily in libertarian strongholds where a lingering mistrust of the state prevailed. Tensions and rivalries remained. Especially in Barcelona, the opposition of some working-class sectors as well as regionalist middle-class constituencies to the central enterprise meant the permanence of bitter, energy-diverting conflicts which undermined the war effort. However, a Republic that was in the process of reconstructing its democratic forms could not, without destroying its own raison d'être, solve this dilemma in the authoritarian fashion of the rebels.[108]

### Caudillo and Cruzada in Nationalist Spain

In Nationalist Spain it was easier to achieve the co-ordination and unification of fragmented forces. This task was facilitated by two significant factors: first, the supremacy of the military and the continuity of its disciplined chains of command; secondly, despite tactical differences and ambitions being nurtured by some to put their own stamp on the future, the fact that there was more that united than actually divided all the diverse political factions among the rebels. Not only had they all collaborated between 1931 and 1936 in the common goal of destroying the Republic but also during this period they had undergone a process of 'fascistisation', sharing a similar anti-democratic, authoritarian, ultra-Catholic and corporativist programme. They then participated in the military conspiracy and readily accepted the subordination of their activities to the military command.[109] More unpredictable but very crucial in the unifying process, however, was the astonishing rise to power of General Francisco Franco.

Born in 1892, Franco's long career was influenced by a combination of his native Galician caution and strong doses of opportunism, ambition and good fortune. After mediocre qualifications in the military academy, in February 1912 he volunteered to serve in Morocco, where by merit on the battlefield he could gain quick promotion and so bypass the bureaucratic, closed scale of an overstaffed officer corps on the mainland. For the next 14 years, the fierce colonial campaigns in North Africa were his great formative experience. Franco would even argue that without Africa he could not have begun to understand himself.[110] In 1926, at the age of 33, he had become a general (he was, indeed, the youngest brigadier general in Europe at that time) and had gained a reputation of bravery and professionalism. However, opportunism and fortunate twists of fate were never absent. Franco was not averse to enhancing his war record and lobbying hard to obtain promotion. His legend was consolidated when he inherited the vital job of head of the fierce Foreign Legion only after José Millán Astray (the Legion's founder and Franco's mentor) was wounded in combat and his substitute, Lieutenant Colonel Rafael Valenzuela, was killed.[111]

Being feted by both monarch and dictator in the late 1920s and enjoying the distinguished post of director of the military academy of Zaragoza, Franco certainly did not greet with enthusiasm the advent of the Second Republic. The new regime introduced military reforms that hindered his career and even closed the military academy. He viewed with extreme suspicion the leftist leanings of the Republican government and was much influenced by the anti-Communist bulletin of the Geneva-based *Entente Internationale Anticommuniste*, to which he, like many other officers, subscribed.[112] However, he stayed clear of the plotters in 1932. Given the task of crushing the revolution of October 1934 by the Radical minister of war Diego Hidalgo brought him back from relative obscurity. With the country under martial law, Franco had no qualms in shipping Moorish troops, for the first time, on to the mainland to put down the revolt in Asturias (ironically, the only part of Spain never conquered by the Muslims). He was hailed in right-wing circles as the saviour from Red evil.[113] Gil Robles rewarded him the following year with the appointment of Chief of the General Staff. Facing relegation again with the dissolution of the chamber in December 1935 and the victory of the Popular Front in February 1936, he toyed with the idea of a coup, but caution prevailed. Banished by the new government to the Canary Islands, Franco was kept informed of the developments of the conspiracy but remained uncommitted. The plotters, annoyed by his vacillations, even nicknamed him 'Miss Canary Islands 1936'. An exasperated Sanjurjo commented that the plans would go ahead 'with or without Franquito'. Yet

Franco's masterpiece of ambiguity came with an extraordinary letter he addressed to the Prime Minister on 23 June 1936, in which he stressed the profound dissatisfaction felt by the armed forces and hinted that a solution could be found if he were reassigned to Madrid. The general's apologists were to argue that this was a last and noble warning to the government. However, the other (and less honourable) possible inference was that, if promoted, Franco was then going to turn against his comrades.[114]

As late as 12 July, Franco refused to join the conspiracy of his fellow *Africanistas*, even though (through the London correspondent of the Monarchist newspaper *El ABC*) they had chartered an English aeroplane, the *Dragon Rapide*, to land in the Canaries and then take him to Morocco. He only changed his mind after hearing of the assassination of Calvo Sotelo.[115] Even so, Franco took a staggeringly long time to arrive. He had by then secured not only the safety of his wife and daughter but also his own safety with a letter guaranteeing his loyalty to the government and, if that failed, a diplomatic passport to flee abroad, where he had been guaranteed a secret bank account.[116]

Paradoxically, the failure of the coup catapulted Franco from hesitant rebel into indisputable leader. Had it succeeded, he would have been awarded the post of high commissioner of Morocco. Yet a series of sinister disasters for the Nationalists cleared his road to absolute power. The most important military men (Sanjurjo, Goded, Fanjul) and the key political figures (José Antonio, Calvo Sotelo) in the rebel ranks had been or soon would be killed. Thus, with the insurrection faltering, Franco found himself without a serious political or military rival to bid for the leadership. In order to prevent the danger of cantonalism, the most important generals gathered in Salamanca on 21 September to choose a single generalissimo. Officially, it had been General Kindelán, a Monarchist officer, who had demanded the meeting. However, it was not a secret that for weeks Franco's brother Nicolás, together with leading personalities such as Millán Astray and the Monarchist José Antonio Sangróniz, had been lobbying hard for Franco to seize control of a unified command. In the generals' gathering, Franco hardly faced any opposition to fill the post. His two potential rivals, Queipo and Mola, could not match his position. Mola, although a strong candidate as director of the rebellion, had lost some clout with his failure to organise a successful coup. Moreover, he was only a brigadier-general, whereas Franco was by now a major-general. Queipo was a major-general of greater seniority but he was widely considered to be an eccentric lunatic and, in any case, was automatically disqualified by his past involvement in conspiracies against the monarchy. By contrast, Franco's claim was unassailable. His lack of clear political leanings made him attractive to all different factions. He had the total support of the Army of Africa, whose successful advances in August had confirmed its primary role in the war effort. Finally, he was the one who had established direct links with Italy and Germany.[117] Before the announcement was made public, the generals returned to the front, after arranging to resume discussions a week later. Franco profited from those days to clinch more military and political power than his fellow officers had in mind. Indeed, he took a polemical but shrewd decision. He decided to divert his northward advance on Madrid in order to relieve the besieged *Alcázar* in Toledo – well to the east of his route but a place that had immense emotional and religious symbolism for the Nationalists.

From the start of the war, a group of rightists in Toledo, led by Colonel José Moscardó, had entrenched themselves with their families (and a number of hostages, a hundred women and children of known leftists) in the old military academy, an ancient fortress or *Alcázar*. By opting to rescue Moscardó's embattled forces, Franco gave Madrid precious time to consolidate its defences. Yet he was aware of the moral and spiritual propaganda at stake. On 27 September the *Alcázar* was saved and became part of the Nationalist legend. Rumours to enhance the events' mythical status claimed that the besiegers had threatened to assassinate Moscardó's son if he did not surrender. As during the *Reconquista* centuries earlier, when the Moors forced the same stark choice upon a Christian knight (Guzmán *el bueno*), Moscardó stubbornly refused to comply and told his son to commend his soul to God and die bravely. Moscardó's son was shot on 23 August, but not because of that threat. Rather, along with other prisoners, he was executed as a reprisal for an air raid on Toledo. Indeed, it is far from certain that the personal threat against Moscardó's son was ever made. In fact, the besiegers even allowed the officers in the *Alcázar* to write to their relatives in Madrid. Yet the myth was of immense propaganda value. Naturally, the legend mentioned neither the fate of the numerous hostages retained against their will in the fortress nor the blood-bath that followed the Nationalists' capture of Toledo.[118]

When the other generals met Franco the following day, they were greeted by a well-orchestrated campaign deifying the 'saviour of the *Alcázar*'. Franco maximised his advantage amidst that frenzied atmosphere and obtained from his companions the ambiguous position of head of the government of the Nationalist state. Significantly, it was agreed that this appointment was only to last for the duration of the war. However, any reference to the provisional nature of Franco's power had mysteriously disappeared when the order was officially published on 1 October.[119] In the emerging Nationalist rump state, the line between myth and reality was already being eroded. Franco was hailed as an invincible military leader and referred to as *Caudillo*, the name of the medieval warrior chieftains. His name was repeated and his portrait plastered in every corner of Nationalist Spain. Patriotic symbols and army uniforms, characteristic of a militarised state, combined with modern Fascist values and arcane religious traditions were the dominant features.[120]

Ironically, except in the northern Carlist strongholds that had always been marked by their fervent zeal, religious allusions were strikingly absent from the generals' initial statements; they were, instead, dominated by anti-Communist and anti-separatist jargon. Indeed, it was not the insurgents who asked for the Church's support but the latter that joined them in body and soul.[121] Soon the alliance between sword and altar was re-created. In this marriage of convenience, the Catholic Church offered its powerful services to the military rebels. The Church's position was not only the result of the persecution carried out in the other zone, but was also consequent to its attempt to regain the privileged position that had come under challenge since 1931.[122] Courtesy of the military authorities, the religious hierarchy embarked upon the enforcement of Christian principles with a combination of zeal and compulsion reminiscent of the Middle Ages. Because the Nationalists lacked intellectuals of any stature, the clergy filled that role for Franco. Despite the Vatican's ambiguous stance, the Catholic network was crucial in mobilising international opinion and, equally, in rallying a large social force in Spain – rural farmers, merchants, traders and religious middle classes who were all scared of the Red spectre. In the absence of any agreed objective other than the seizure of power, Catholicism also played the crucial role of unifying all those who adhered to the insurrection.[123]

The ecclesiastical hierarchy was central in the rewriting of history. The Bishops of Pamplona and Zaragoza and the Archbishop of Santiago already used the terms 'crusade' and 'God's war' to characterise the rebel cause in August. The publication of the pastoral letter 'The Two Cities' on 30 September by the Bishop of Salamanca, Enrique Pla y Deniel, who graciously offered Franco his palace in which to establish the Nationalist headquarters, was the turning-point in this process of lending the civil war a confessional character. According to the prelate, the war was neither a political nor a class conflict but a titanic struggle between two concepts of life. One was represented by an earthly city inhabited by the sons of Cain, those Communists and Anarchists who through jealousy kill their brothers. The other was a heavenly city where the love of God, martyrdom and heroism prevailed. The insurgents were not rebels against their government but blessed as the heroes of a new *Reconquista* – patriots fighting to liberate Spain from the Godless hordes of Moscow and to restore civilisation to the endangered fatherland.[124] From then on, the triumph of the city of God was accompanied by a rhetoric that blended militant Catholicism, patriotism and militarism. Franco's victories were celebrated with *Te Deums*, and the clergy openly endorsed the Fascist salute, harangued the troops and called for the extermination of the Reds. In their characterisation of the Nationalist cause as a patriotic crusade, the Church carefully toned down the role played by Italy and Germany. The ongoing wave of repression, however, obtained its blessing if not open collaboration and thus acquired moral legitimacy.[125] Even more striking was the clergy's apparent ignorance of the vital and murderous part played in this 'Christian crusade' by the thousands of infidel Moors. The Nationalists' assassination of 14 Basque priests who had sided with the also fervently Catholic (but separatist) PNV also seems to have escaped their attention.

The clash between the well-known philosopher and novelist Miguel de Unamuno and the much-mutilated war hero appointed as the Nationalists' chief of press and propaganda, Millán Astray, illustrated vividly the exalted patriotism and brutal fanaticism that permeated the crusade. Despite his anti-Monarchist and polemical past, Unamuno had become disappointed with the Second Republic and sided passively with the rebellion. However, the number of his close academic friends who had disappeared during the first months of the conflict had rattled him. On 12 October, as Rector of the University of Salamanca, he had to preside over the celebrations of the anniversary of Christopher Columbus's discovery of America. The act, attended by personalities including Franco's wife, Carmen Polo, was marked by a stream of clerics, politicians and writers embarking upon a tirade of adulation for the new regime, combined with poisonous rhetoric against the evils of separatism and Communism. No longer able to contain himself, Unamuno declared:

> You know me well and know that I am unable to remain silent ...
> I did not want to speak but I feel it is my duty to do so. It has been

said here that this is an international war in defence of Christian civilisation ... However, our conflict is an uncivil war. *Vencer* [to win] is not *convencer* [to convince] and you must convince above all, but hatred that leaves no room for compassion can never convince ... I will leave aside the offence of calling Basques and Catalans the anti-Spain. Here there is the bishop [that is, Enrique Pla], who, whether he likes it or not, is a Catalan born in Barcelona who teaches you Christian principles. I, born in Bilbao, am Basque and have spent all my life teaching you the Spanish language that you do not know.

In this frenzied atmosphere, Millán Astray interrupted the philosopher with shouts of 'Death to the Intellectuals!' and the Legion's motto of '¡*Viva la Muerte!*' ('Long Live Death!'). Unamuno retorted that Astray lacked the spiritual greatness of that other cripple, Miguel de Cervantes, since nobody could find happiness in seeing the country being filled with more mutilation. All hell broke loose. There were calls to have Unamuno shot, as Astray's bodyguards drew their pistols. Under a hail of insults, he managed to leave the room sheltered by Carmen Polo. Removed from his post and placed under house arrest, Unamuno died, a broken man, three months later.[126]

By the end of 1936 the Nationalists had their crusade and their *Caudillo* and a rhetoric and symbolism largely borrowed from the era of *El Cid* and the Catholic Kings, when Spain had been reconquered from its Muslim invaders. Yet, having failed to seize Madrid and still being officially recognised only by the Fascist powers, their cause remained, in terms of international legality, a seditious revolt against a democratically constituted regime.

# 5

# Breaking the Stalemate
# (December 1936–March 1938)

The real tragedy for Spain was the death of Mola; there was the real
brain, the real leader. Franco came to the top like Pontius in the
Creed.[1]

The *Deutschland* affair ... was foreseeable from the moment that
Italian and German warships, allied to the rebels, were watching our
coasts under the cover of non-intervention ... How could two 'Red'
planes dare to attack a peaceful German warship, resting in a
Spanish harbour, while German troops are at war with the Republic
on the mainland?[2]

### Political vacuum in Nationalist Spain

For the insurgents, the setback at the gates of Madrid proved a blessing
in disguise, as they soon turned a veritable débâcle to their own benefit.
Indeed, the Italians and Germans, with their massive contribution both
in matériel and manpower, not only saved the rebels from the clutches of
defeat but also linked their prestige with the outcome of the Spanish
adventure. The continuity of the war also provided the necessary time
slowly but thoroughly to crush Republican resistance and to consolidate
a powerful myth around the leadership of General Franco.

German, Italian and even some Spanish officers often criticised
Franco's conduct of the campaign. They despaired at what they regarded as excessively cautious advances instead of using the overwhelming material superiority which the Nationalists enjoyed to smash
through the enemy lines and force the Republic to surrender. Yet their
objections were misplaced. Military decisions that appeared baffling to

them were partly a result of the fact that *Africanista* officers manned the Nationalist high command; lethally efficient in small-scale colonial skirmishes, they were far less competent in leading large armies in modern warfare.[3] However, there was also a hidden political agenda. The *Caudillo* was not interested in a quick and conclusive battle, but subordinated military objectives to political goals. As the archetypal *Africanista*, Franco pursued a strategy destined to annihilate the enemy gradually but thoroughly, while always aware that a longer campaign helped cement his own personal prominence.[4]

Whereas Franco achieved supreme military command in October 1936, the political foundations of Nationalist Spain remained extremely vague. The real architect of a state apparatus would be Ramón Serrano Suñer, Franco's brother-in-law. The months of Serrano's life prior to his arrival in Salamanca in February 1937 were worthy of a novel. An intelligent young lawyer, a close friend of José Antonio and a CEDA deputy for Zaragoza, Serrano had been critical of Gil Robles's indecisiveness and was instrumental in bringing over a good number of the JAP members to the Falange in the spring of 1936. Surprised in Madrid by the outbreak of the war, he was soon jailed and narrowly escaped the *sacas* of August, in which many of his colleagues perished. Transferred to a hospital owing to his precarious health, he took advantage of the laxer conditions to organise, in collaboration with the prestigious doctor Gregorio Marañón and some Dutch officials, his escape to that nation's Consulate disguised as a woman. There he heard the news of the murder of his brothers Fernando and José. He then travelled to Alicante by car, accompanied by Captain Fernández Castañeda, General Miaja's assistant, who was also attempting to defect, where, dressed as an Argentinean sailor, he boarded a vessel of that nationality, the *Tucumán*.[5]

Once in Salamanca, Serrano's charisma placed him high above the variety of sycophants who surrounded the *Caudillo*. Handsome, blue-eyed and blonde, he cut a dazzling figure and, when accompanied by his wife Zita, eclipsed the impression made by the pairing of Zita's sister Carmen and the small and chunky Franco. Owing to his meteoric rise, he would be nicknamed '*el cuñadísimo*' ('the supreme brother-in-law') to rhyme with Franco's title of *Generalísimo*. Upon his arrival, he described the Nationalist governmental machinery as being like an army camp (*estado campamental*) dominated by an anachronistic atmosphere of holy war, military values and administrative chaos. Alongside the *Caudillo*'s headquarters in Salamanca were also a powerful Secretariat, controlled by Franco's brother Nicolás, and a press and propaganda apparatus headed by the unsophisticated Millán Astray. A sort of provisional government, known as the *Junta Técnica del Estado* and led first by General Fidel Dávila and then by General Francisco Gómez Jordana was, meanwhile, based in Burgos. In addition, General Mola and General Queipo de Llano, as commanders of the northern and southern armies respectively, ran their zones as private fiefdoms. All sorts of other militias and politicians, all jockeying for influence, could be found between Burgos and Salamanca.[6]

Despite all this, Franco's political supremacy was established in a relatively short time, and discipline was imposed upon the variety of forces that had converged in his camp. Military-dominated and much more expedient in their methods, the Nationalists never experienced the level of squabbling that was to plague the Republic.

The right-wing parties, of course, had established a close collaboration prior to the 1936 coup. In the 1930s they all underwent a process of 'fascistisation', sharing a rabidly anti-liberal and anti-democratic programme. As a result, the genuine Fascist party, the Falange, was peculiarly weak and so, unlike in Italy and Germany, it became subordinated to the other reactionary groups.[7] Grasping the necessity of unity in order to obtain the ultimate prize, victory in the war, all these groups were prepared to back a war leader who, they believed, could deliver that outcome.

After July 1936 there were only two mass political forces in Nationalist Spain: the Carlists and the Falangists. Their ranks were swamped by a massive influx of new recruits and their militias played a vital role at the front and in policing the rear. By contrast, the CEDA entered into terminal decline. Gil Robles, to curry favour with the military command, even decided to wind up his party in November 1936. But in the new and frenzied atmosphere there was to be no central role in Franco's camp for Gil Robles, the embodiment of the legalist right before 1936. In his trips to Salamanca he was often insulted and even physically threatened by Falangists. Semi-exiled in Portugal, his task was to facilitate supplies and economic assistance for the regime.[8] The monarchists, although possessing the best-prepared cadres and crucial links with financial circles and army officers, were few in number, and the idea of a Bourbon Restoration was highly unpopular amongst the Nationalist rank and file – even after the abdication of Alfonso on behalf of his heir, Don Juan.[9] Franco, in a masterful exercise of duplicity, soon curtailed the aspirations of the young royal. Thus, when Don Juan, stressing his experience in the Royal Navy, wrote in December requesting permission to join a Nationalist battleship, the

*Caudillo* promptly declined his offer, citing the need to keep the heir to the throne safe. In fact, Franco was pre-empting a potential rival who might otherwise have rallied a good number of high-ranking officers to his candidacy.[10]

In a way, the messianic spirit that inspired the Carlist *Requetés* made them, after the Foreign Legion and the Moors, the most feared and disciplined troops. However, their medieval populism, combined with their small following outside of Navarra and the Basque Country, hindered their prospects of overall political hegemony. Moreover, Carlist ambitions suffered a severe setback in December 1936, when, after establishing a separate military academy for their own officers without seeking Franco's approval, the Carlist leader, Fal Conde, was presented with the stark alternatives of instant exile or court-martial. The Carlist council, aware of the limits of its strength, avoided a confrontation and replaced him with the more compromising Count Rodezno.[11] To prevent similar incidents, on 21 December Franco decreed the subordination of all the militias to the central army command. Without realising it, the Falangists had lost the first battle.[12]

### April in Salamanca

The Falange's rapid growth, combined with the crucial Axis intervention, appeared to offer Spanish Fascism the opportunity to impose its political agenda. However, the numbers were largely artificial. Unlike the many sincere and fervent Carlists, genuine Spanish Fascists were few. The overwhelming majority of the Falange's new recruits were, rather, reactionaries of all kinds, opportunists and former leftists seeking protection from repression. Furthermore, with most of its leaders killed or captured in the first days of the war, the Falange was decapitated and divided.[13]

The founder, José Antonio, had been imprisoned in Alicante since March 1936. Several plans to engineer his escape were conceived but then aborted. They included commando raids in collaboration with Germany, the bribery of the prison personnel and his exchange for leftist prisoners. Many Republicans believed that his execution on 20 November 1936 was a grave error.[14] But the Alicante authorities, fearing that Madrid would opt for leniency, had him killed before the government could review his sentence. During his imprisonment and trial, José Antonio appeared to have experienced a radical transformation, rejecting the senseless fratricidal violence and asking to be allowed to travel to Salamanca to seek a negotiated end to the conflict. It remains a matter for speculation as to whether he was being sincere in this or was just attempting to fool his incarcerators. Equally, the impact he might then have had cannot be assessed, given the reigning hysterical atmosphere. He was certainly open to the idea of reconciliation in a way that Franco never was. However, his death was a godsend to the *Caudillo*: a charismatic rival became a martyr to the cause, almost to be worshipped as the 'absent', while the Falange could be much more easily assimilated now that its leader was dead.[15] In fact, Franco's support for the several rescue operations was lukewarm and his feelings towards the Falangist leader were far from kind. To Serrano's dismay, the General would denigrate José Antonio's memory in personal conversations. He alleged sometimes that the Falangist leader had not been executed but kidnapped and then castrated by the Russians and at other times that he had died as a coward, needing an injection to stand before the firing squad.[16]

With José Antonio out of the way, Franco and Serrano managed to outmanoeuvre the fragmented Falange with relative ease. The Falange chief of Santander and provisional national leader of the party, Manuel Hedilla, led one faction whose main support came from northern provinces. A mechanic by profession, he represented the idealistic 'left-wing fascism' keen on attracting repentant former leftists and highly critical of the reactionary forces in Nationalist Spain. He was opposed by the so-called 'legitimists', headed by friends and relatives of José Antonio and based in Madrid and the south. According to Serrano, most high-ranking military and political elements were eager to curb the abrasive manners and plebeian populism of the Falangists. They were incensed at being addressed in the informal second person *tú* and as 'comrades' and were perturbed by the Falangists' constant references to a forthcoming National-syndicalist revolution.[17]

As negotiations for the formation of a united national party gained momentum, the internal Falangist feud reached boiling point – not least because the military headquarters were fuelling the flames of discord and playing one side off against the other. For example, Hedilla was encouraged to reaffirm his control, while his rivals were being prompted to remove him. The goal was to facilitate and justify Franco's takeover. By April 1937 both Falangist factions were on a war footing and were gathering their supporters in Salamanca. The 'legitimists' struck first. On the morning of the 16 April, they took over the Falange's central office and deposed Hedilla. The counter-attack took place that night, when armed raids were mounted against the houses of the leading 'legitimists'. In the skirmishes, two Falangists, one from each faction, were killed. With most 'legitimists' arrested by the authorities, and with Hedilla's leadership confirmed by the national council on 18 April, his faction believed that it had won the party struggle. This victory, however, was to be short-lived.[18]

The following day Franco decreed the unification of all the existing Nationalist forces, which necessarily implied the dissolution of the existing party structures. The party's new name, *Falange Española Tradicionalista y de las Jons* (FET), commonly know as 'the movement', clearly stressed the relevance of the two main groups in the Nationalist ranks. Its symbol was the Falangist yoke and arrows but the new uniform involved a combination of the Falangist blue shirt and the Carlist red beret. In fact, the FET represented the birth of a Francoist party and the end of the Falange's hegemonic ambitions. Serrano described it as a *'golpe de estado a la inversa'* (reversed coup d'état). It was not one party that seized state power, but the forceful merger from above of all the political forces.[19] Although allocated an important role, the Falange was just one of the constituents of this new hybrid movement. Hedilla refused the post offered in a new political council manned by lackeys and docile post-July-1936 Falangists. After instructing the old Falange's provincial delegations to resist the enforced merger, he was accused of rebellion, arrested with several other Falangists and sentenced to death. After the intercession of Serrano and some Italian and German diplomats, Hedilla's death sentence was commuted, but he was to remain in prison until 1947.[20] Carlist complaints were even more muted. The Regent, Don Javier, was furious about these developments, but by the end of the year he was ordered to leave Spain. The Carlists felt a certain discomfort at being displaced from key posts. However, they were able to justify their participation in the war and their general acceptance of political unification in the context of the destruction of the atheist Republic, the restoration of social order and Catholic prominence, and the confirmation of their supremacy in Navarra.[21]

## National-Catholicism

Above all, the April coup sealed Franco's personal dictatorship. He was now the Generalissimo of the armed forces, head of state, *Caudillo* of the crusade and chief of the only political party. In less than a year the hesitant rebel had accumulated more power than a medieval monarch. April 1937 was also a considerable victory over genuine Fascism for the 'fascistised' parties. Lacking a mass following, they greeted the opportunity to share control of the administration of the emerging state with the Carlists and Falangists with enthusiasm.[22]

The Falangists faced a stark choice: either they could accept the fait accompli, and so enjoy access to the privileges of power, or they could be left out in the cold and face the possibility of persecution and prison. The docility of most previous die-hards revealed that they were ready to comply. They had never before been so close to the corridors of power and were unwilling to risk that triumph for the sake of excessively rigid doctrinal interpretations.[23] Furthermore, Serrano, who provided a privileged direct link with the *Caudillo*, increasingly represented their aspirations. Falangist symbols, choreography and liturgy were also to some extent being adopted by the Movement, while individual Falangists shared the spoils of office in the administration and in the security services and were given the task of regimenting labour as well as being put in control over most of the burgeoning media. However, Fascist ritual and rhetoric were also being blended with and were sometimes superseded by military and religious values.

By throwing in its lot with the Nationalists, the Church acquired a role in state affairs reminiscent of the sixteenth century. The publication by the Spanish Catholic hierarchy in July 1937 of a collective letter to the bishops of the world was not only the official statement of its partisan attitude but also a vital propaganda coup.[24] The Church confirmed its role as the leading propagandist of the Nationalists' Manichean view of the war and the ideological guarantor of its legitimacy.[25] As in medieval times, religious pomp and magical awe were instrumental parts of the regime. Franco was hailed as the saviour of the persecuted faith. Accordingly, the *Caudillo*, having already established his headquarters at the Episcopal Palace at Salamanca, graciously ceded by Bishop Pla, awarded himself the royal prerogative of entering and leaving religious sites *bajo palio* (under a canopy).[26] In turn, the Church experienced a golden era. It acquired a monopoly of education and a prominent role in social services. It received constant financial aid as well as exemption from taxation. The lay republican legislation was overturned, temples and churches were restored and the clergy became the guardian of people's habits.[27]

The foundations of Franco's Spain were thus a fusion of modernising totalitarian tendencies with medieval and religious–absolutist elements,[28] a marriage that can be defined as National-Catholicism. Thus, constant references to the *Reconquista* and the Golden Age initiated by the Catholic Kings were merged with Fascist rhetoric, as the German 'Ein Volk, ein Reich, ein Führer' became 'Una patria, un estado, un Caudillo'. This blended choreography was clearly present at the swearing-in ceremony of the FET's National Council on 2 December 1937. Modelled on Mussolini's Fascist Grand Council, it gathered at the Monastery of Santa María de la Real de las Huelgas (Burgos). Preceded by drummers and trumpeters in seventeenth-century dress, its members swore loyalty to Franco, who declared himself to be responsible only to God and to history – all this taking place before a gaunt marble figure of Christ and the battle standard of the historic victory against the Moors at the Navas de Tolosa.[29]

Together with the exalted rhetoric and paraphernalia, a highly effective ruling coalition was forged in 1937. Franco's masterstroke was his balancing act between all its components. Bound together by the so-called 'Pact of Blood' (that is, their active complicity in the ongoing brutal repression), all factions shared in the spoils of office, as the national leader safeguarded their particular interests. A clear expression of that reality was the formation of the first Nationalist government on 30 January 1938. Serrano Suñer, as the minister of interior, was the dominant figure in charge of administration, press and propaganda. However, public order was left in the hands of General Martínez Anido, a man with an unequalled reputation for blood-thirstiness. The rest of the portfolios went to a carefully balanced selection of officers, Catholics, Falangists, Carlists and Monarchists.[30]

### Largo's falling star

The war accelerated the Republic's original progressive programme. Criminal records were erased. Women obtained equal civil rights and widow status and the children of unmarried couples were granted legitimacy if the father was killed in combat. In certain circumstances the Catalan government even legalised abortion. Momentum gathered in the fight for cultural enlightenment and literacy. Abandoned manor houses and estates were converted into schools. Workers' institutes were established where two-year study plans including academic and vocational subjects were offered to the non-mobilised aged between 18 and 35. At the front, the so-called 'Militiamen of Culture' used the lulls in fighting to teach fellow combatants and to carry books and films to villages.[31] Simultaneously, the Largo administration undertook measures designed to knit together the Republic's constituent forces.

In the process, however, the government experienced the explosion of its own internal squabbles. As in the enemy camp, the outcome of this confrontation represented a consolidation of the state. But war-weariness and defeatism ensured that these antagonisms remained alive. Eventually they would undermine the Republic's will to resist.

While martial law provided the rebel generals with undisputed control over their territory, mistrust of the loyal officers led to its introduction in Republican Spain only in January 1939, by which time the war was almost over. A regime which, despite all its shortcomings, was still a democracy could not imitate the insurgents' acceptance of a united movement under the supreme authority of a *Caudillo*. Further-more, unlike the past record of collaboration between right-wing forces, the left was marked by a history of fratricidal hatred. Despite the ominous threat posed by the Nationalist advances, those rivalries not only remained but were often exacerbated by the new framework produced by the war.

The ongoing defeats did lead to an overall acceptance of recon-structing a strong state capable of fighting back (although the firmness of that acceptance often depended upon the proximity of a group or individual to the front). However, the apocalypse of the previous months could not easily be overcome. For one thing, the central administration was faced with Catalan and Basque nationalist aspira-tions; for another, the authority of bourgeois Republicans was dwarfed by the rapid growth of the working-class organisations. Socialist and Anarcho-syndicalist internal tensions were also magnified. Additionally, the Communists, an irrelevant force before summer 1936, rapidly increased their influence.

Victory on the Madrid front in the winter of 1936–7 only offered a brief respite for the beleaguered Republic and certainly did not strengthen the position of the so-called 'Government of Victory'. Having fled to Valencia in early November, Largo could hardly take any credit for Madrid's successful resistance. The fall of Málaga, in February 1937, was also a massive blow to his authority. By then, the Prime Minister was almost entirely isolated within the cabinet, and his hitherto concealed shortcomings became troublesome.[32]

Many Socialists and Republicans had not forgotten Largo's pre-vious uncompromising stance, including his blocking of Prieto's access to power in May 1936, which they felt might indirectly have helped to weaken the Popular Front government and facilitate the insurrection. Largo then offended the PSOE's National Executive Committee by accepting the premiership without even consulting them, claiming to be acting in his capacity as the UGT president. To add insult to injury, Largo soon ignored all his revolutionary rhetoric and proceeded as a pragmatic politician, putting all his efforts into reconstructing the bourgeois Republic. This, in turn, infuriated many moderate Socialists, who felt that he was taking over their programme and so revealing that his previous stance had been mere posturing.[33]

To make matters worse, Largo's initial good relations with the PCE soon deteriorated. He resented the Communist seizure of vital posts in the security services, army command and network of political commissars and soon engaged in bitter clashes with the Russian advisers and the Soviet ambassador, Marcel Rosenberg. Still smarting from Communist hegemony in the United Socialist Youth (JSU) and the Catalan United Socialist Party (PSUC), Largo naturally opposed the merger of Socialists and Communists. However, with Republican resistance mostly dependent on Soviet military aid, subtle diplomacy rather than Largo's quick temper was needed. Furthermore, the Prime Minister overlooked the growing importance of the Communists in the war effort. In less than a year, the PCE became, from a relatively minor force of about 20,000 activists, a powerful movement with nearly 400,000 members and effective control over the 350,000 JSU affiliates.

Indisputably, the popularity of the Soviet Union, as the only major power rendering military assistance to the Republic, increased Communist prestige. However, there were further reasons to explain the PCE's astonishing growth. The Communists presented an image of competence and discipline. They also possessed a formidable propaganda machine. With the government's evacuation of Madrid, the Communists filled the vacuum. Their leaders became the heroes of the capital, galvanising the masses with rousing slogans. The Communist Fifth Regiment, with the superior quality of its cadres, political commissars and professional officers, became the role model for the Popular Army. Apart from the prestige gained as a result of its efficiency (unlike the other Republican groups, who were traumatised by the war or plagued by internal tensions), the PCE emerged as the backbone of the Popular Front intra-class alliance. It conserved an important proletarian constituency, whose energies were rekindled with promises of a radical new economic and social deal after the victory. But, at the same time, the moderation of the Communist tactics (championing respect for private property and advocating loyal collaboration between the middle and working classes) appealed to thousands of small tenants, artisans, merchants and white-collar workers, who rushed to join the party. Additionally, the Communists made important inroads into the army and the security organisations. Certainly, their agenda here included an element of targeting control of key posts in the armed services. However, Communist success in this area was not merely based on machiavellian tactics. Police and army officers joined the PCE because it offered them a refuge in which concepts of discipline and command were respected – quite a rarity in those traumatic post-coup times.[34] Nevertheless, the PCE's meteoric growth mirrored that of the Falange. They both gave a largely artificial impression of strength, as many of the thousands of new recruits joined as a result not of ideological convictions but of opportunism and careerism.[35]

Largo's obstinacy in clinging to the post of war minister, despite his obvious limitations, combined with constant displays of pettiness and his refusal to accept advice, confirmed the apprehension of political rivals and alienated potential friends. He lacked the energy to see through the necessary measures of centralisation and mobilisation. In fact, he remained trapped between his verbal radicalism and the moderate course that his political preferences and past practice dictated.[36] When asked by the Russian advisers to instruct militiamen to dig trenches instead of retreat, Largo simply answered that Spaniards were too proud to hide in ditches. His obsession with proper accounting and having receipts for everything – even for cartridges for the desperate defenders of Madrid – led many early supporters to begin to wonder whether he was the 'Spanish Lenin' or an old schoolmaster.[37] Upset by the popularity of General Miaja, he pursued a personal campaign against the hero of Madrid and finally dissolved the capital's Defence Council in April.[38] Following the loss of Málaga, a Communist campaign forced the resignation of General José Asensio, the under-secretary for war. In fact, the real target was the person ultimately in charge of military matters, Largo Caballero.[39]

## May in Barcelona

The disputes within the Republican camp went beyond the dichotomy of the primacy of war versus revolution. They were, above all, the result of the inexorable process of political normalisation. Most Republican forces, overwhelmed by the dynamics imposed by the total war, had concluded that success depended on their ability to pool their resources.[40] However, tensions persisted, owing not so much to the need to reconstruct the state – something grudgingly accepted even by the CNT leaders – as to the struggle to control its agenda. Thus, the retention of local influence translated into a power struggle that, in cases, led to violent tit-for-tat retaliations. Miaja, for example, had to intervene forcefully in Madrid after the killing of the Communist Council member Pablo Yagüe. In Valencia, armed clashes followed the funerals of rival militants.[41] However, it was in Libertarian Barcelona that a massive explosion appeared to be looming.

The Catalan nation's proud capital and Spain's main modern, industrial metropolis, Barcelona had an equally rich tradition of class struggle as well as nationalist aspirations against the central state. Dubbed 'the Chicago of the Mediterranean' due to the high number of killings there during the post-World-War-I class wars, Barcelona had also bred the *Juntas Militares* and then catapulted Primo de Rivera to power. With the proclamation of the Republic, a pragmatic rapprochement had taken place between the *Esquerra* and the CNT. Left-wing Catalan Republicans had often acted as defence lawyers for Anarcho-syndicalists, and a few *Cenetistas* even joined the Catalanist party after 1931. Despite mounting tensions, as the left-wing Catalanists became the 'new party of order', they abided by an unwritten agreement: the *Esquerra* controlled Catalan politics; the CNT controlled the labour movement. However, the military uprising led to uncharted waters as the city became a fiercely contested political space.[42]

The collapse of central power provided a golden opportunity for the *Generalitat* to advance its nationalist agenda. Nevertheless, the Catalan government was itself outgunned and overwhelmed by the CNT's display of street power and popular mobilisation. However, the Libertarians' lack of concerted political action and their inability to articulate the diverse local and provincial committees into a coherent revolutionary force facilitated the survival of the *Generalitat*'s authority.[43] The situation was further exacerbated by the existence of other competing forces. On 23 July 1936 the merger of four small Socialist and Communist groups produced for the first time a strong United Catalan Socialist Party (PSUC) that reached a membership of 60,000 by the spring of 1937. At a formal level, the PSUC affiliated to the Comintern independently from the PCE.[44] Indeed, after July 1936 there was a great influx of members into the PSUC and its trade union, the Catalan branch of the UGT, as people sought a defence against the armed power of the CNT.

Notwithstanding the formidable power they wielded through the local committees and neighbourhoods, the Anarcho-syndicalists could not claim in 1936 to be the only voice of the Catalan labour movement. The CNT had over 400,000 Catalan affiliates in 1919 and still had over

300,000 in 1931. However, weariness following the FAI-imposed strategy of revolutionary gymnastics, and the *Treintista* split halved the membership to some 150,000 by July 1936. The main beneficiary was the UGT which, mirroring the PSUC, in the spring and summer of 1936 brought together most of the trade-union movement outside the CNT, including an important number of *Treintistas*.[45] In the frenzied atmosphere of that year, when a union card was essential, both Socialists and Anarcho-syndicalists saw a membership explosion. However, their constituencies were radically different. The CNT remained the voice of low-skilled workers and the urban poor, while the UGT attracted those sectors afraid of Anarcho-syndicalist power: artisans, urban white-collar workers, liberal professionals, farmers and policemen.[46] Finally, there existed in Cataluña a small revolutionary party of dissident Marxists (POUM) extremely critical of the PCE's moderate political line. Although not merely a Catalan party, it was only in that region that the POUM had a sizeable following. With its most competent leader, Joaquín Maurín, arrested in the Nationalist zone, the more impulsive Andreu Nin took over its direction. Nin's past role as Trotsky's private secretary in the 1920s, combined with his dogmatic attacks upon the Popular Front as an instrument of bourgeois domination and his criticism of the Soviet Union, facilitated the accusations launched by the Communists that the POUM was a Trotskyist party. In fact, Nin had broken with the Russian revolutionary, who often lambasted the POUM in his writings.[47]

The *Generalitat* pursued a subtle and difficult balancing act. It joined forces with the UGT–PSUC in order to contain CNT ascendancy, restore state power and ensure the defence of private property. Nevertheless, there was unease at the centralist tendencies of sectors within the PSUC, as well as the growing inroads of that party into the *Esquerra*'s own social constituency. In fact, the *Generalitat* needed a tamed but still-powerful CNT to serve as a counter-weight to the PSUC.[48] Even before the battle for Madrid, the *Generalitat* saw a temporary solution in the formation in September 1936 of an ample coalition government in which all tendencies were represented. In a surprising surrender of ground, the CNT agreed to participate with ministers and even to dissolve the Committee of Anti-Fascist Militias, a potential embryo of dual power in the city. Yet competing agendas ensured that tensions did not fade away.

In October the Catalan administration passed a decree on collectivisation and workers' control of the economy. It appeared to legalise the gains of the spontaneous revolution of the previous weeks. In fact, though, confirming the *Generalitat*'s overall supervision of the revolutionary process meant a real shift from trade-union to governmental control of the economy.[49] On the other hand, as a result of its control of the Ministry of Supply, the CNT remained in charge of food distribution through its bread committees, and their tight controls clashed with the more free-market measures favourable to the rural Catalan smallholders represented by the PSUC and *Esquerra*. It was, however, to be the POUM's stance that would lead to the first major crisis.

Despite Nin being in government, the POUM's newspaper, *La Batalla*, in analyses which stunningly ignored the military reality, kept talking of the Popular Front as a wicked diversion for the working class, which should have been seeking to accomplish its historical objective independently. Consequently, the newspaper constantly appealed to the CNT–FAI to join forces to destroy the democratic Republic.[50] This only played into the hands of the PSUC which, in turn, in its own publications, began to equate the POUM with internal fifth-columnists who should be eliminated. The POUM could not rely on Libertarian sympathy, as there was a past history of bad blood between them. For the Anarcho-syndicalists, the POUM's advances were a replay of the early 1920s, when a group of Bolshevik-syndicalists led by Maurín and Nin had tried to take control of the CNT.[51] Thus, isolated and under attack by the PSUC, the POUM was left out of the government in the reshuffle of December 1936.[52]

During the first months of 1937 the situation in Cataluña worsened dramatically. The fall of Málaga produced a huge influx of refugees who could scarcely be fed and housed. Tensions increased as the PSUC leader, Joan Comorera, in the governmental reshuffle obtained the post of supply minister, promptly disbanding the bread committees and endorsing free-trade measures which led to higher prices. As the black market flourished, the CNT and POUM orchestrated popular demonstrations and rationing had to be introduced in February.[53] At the same time, for the sake of shared responsibility, Anarcho-syndicalist ministers accepted legislation to normalise public life, including the surrender of all arms held by private individuals. This, however, was ignored at street level, where militants, entrenched in the patrol groups, refused to disarm and abandon the vital parts of the economy seized during the fighting days.[54] As the war's overwhelming practical imperatives saw CNT–FAI leaders increasingly incorporated into the governing machinery, a gap opened with those militants still determined to resist any form of state encroachment.[55] Governmental collaboration came under growing criticism from radical Anarchists such as the so-called 'Friends of Durruti', a group formed in March 1937 by former members of the Durruti column who had abandoned the front after the decree of military control over the militia.[56] Growing tensions led to a proliferation of violence. On 27 April the funeral of Roldán Cortada, a prominent UGT leader who had allegedly been assassinated by Anarchists, turned into a massive display of state strength in the form of a long march of armed troops. A few days later a police raid to wrest control of frontier posts led to several casualties, among them the well-known Anarchist Antonio Martín. For fear of violence, the traditional May Day labour demonstrations were cancelled.[57]

The dispatch of three truckloads of Assault Guards, on 3 May, by the *Esquerra* Interior Minister Artemí Ayguadé (under the command of the PSUC police chief Eusebio Rodríguez Salas) to seize the central telephone exchange held by the CNT was the spark that ignited the fuse. The *Cenetistas* met the police with a volley of shots. Rumours spread across town like wildfire, shops and factories closed and barricades began to be erected. The city was soon on a war footing and was divided between the industrial periphery and the proletarian quarters firmly in the hands of the CNT, and the middle-class city centre, controlled by the *Generalitat*. For four days Barcelona experienced a mini-civil war, as members of the CNT–FAI and POUM fought against the UGT–PSUC, left-wing Catalanists and Republicans.[58] There was widespread concern that the disturbances would spread throughout the region and that the POUM and CNT troops at the front would abandon their posts and descend on Barcelona. This did not happen, but there were several assassinations of Communist and UGT militants (with the connivance of some leading Anarchists of the Aragón Council).[59]

An anxious President Azaña, besieged in his official Catalan residence of the Palacio de las Cortes Catalanas, was a privileged witness to the fighting. As he dispatched messages to the *Generalitat* and to the central government in Valencia, asking to be rescued, his entourage was often fired upon and some of his men were detained (although others were let through the lines and were sometimes even escorted by their captors). Demoralised by the outbreak of the war and then by the *sacas* of August 1936, the May Days in Barcelona produced in Azaña a state of despair from which he never recovered:

> Cataluña is in full disintegration. Nothing remains: Government, parties, authorities, public services, armed forces; nothing exists ...

only revolutionary hysteria ... Clumsiness of the authorities, immorality, cowardice, shootings between rival trade unionists, disloyalty ... Underneath, the peaceful people wishing for a General that could sweep away the existing order, the autonomy and the FAI, all at once.[60]

Absurd conspiracy theories soon circulated and have remained the stock-in-trade of some narrators of these events. The two most extreme versions were those of the Communists and the Anarchists. Communists, endorsing the paranoid jargon of the times, spoke of an 'Anarcho-Trotskyist *putsch*' masterminded by fifth columnists or even directly from the Nationalist headquarters.[61] In turn, Anarchists and *Poumistas* talked of a well-planned operation orchestrated from Moscow, with the complicity of the *Generalitat*. However, to examine the May Days in conspiratorial terms meant to ignore both the historical background of revolutionary Barcelona and the explosive situation at the time. Azaña, a bourgeois Republican from Madrid, lived through and narrated the events without understanding them. Amidst what he described as revolutionary hysteria, he could not grasp this Catalan theatre of the absurd in which he, as the first symbol of the state, was not molested. It was, above all, a spontaneous outburst waiting to happen and yet its unfolding took everybody by surprise. Even George Orwell, another privileged witness (and despite his subjective stance as part of the POUM militia) admitted that the fighting was only planned in the sense that everybody expected it but there were no signs of any definite plan on either side.[62]

For all its mythology, all sides involved in the struggle were pressing for negotiations.[63] Certainly, groups such as the Friends of Durruti were eager to man the barricades. The POUM, after months demanding the abolition of the bourgeois state, assumed the cause of the revolutionaries and even *La Batalla* printed a leaflet drafted by the Friends welcoming the rebellion and calling for the establishment of a revolutionary junta and the shooting of the enemies of the revolution.[64] However, far from organising – let alone leading – any such revolution, they were dragged along by events and backed down as soon as the CNT leadership refused to sanction armed action. In fact, the May events revealed in full the crisis of Anarcho-syndicalism. The CNT and its allies had the upper hand in the contest, possessed the heavy artillery that dominated the city from the heights of Montjuïc and, if necessary, could bring in reinforcements from other parts of Cataluña and Aragón. However, immersed for months in the governmental machinery, the CNT leaders were by now in favour of internal discipline and the greater centralisation of authority in the hands of the national executive. They were very much against uncontrolled outbursts of revolutionary idealism of the sort overwhelming Barcelona. They were also aware that the price of their success would have been further confrontation with the rest of Republican Spain and, inevitably, victory for Franco.[65] Thus, the Anarcho-syndicalist ministers rushed to Barcelona, but only to disown the Friends of Durruti and to agree with the *Generalitat* the broadcast of an appeal to their confused followers to lay down their weapons.

The armed clashes eventually played into the hands of those calling for discipline at the rear, including the Communists. However, although Comintern agents reporting to Moscow described a putsch and saw traitors everywhere, they did not gloat about their success in provoking the confrontation. On the contrary, they were distraught and surprised by an insurrection that they had neither foreseen nor made plans to confront. Naturally, they demanded extreme measures to eliminate the putschists.[66] In fact, the Comintern never offered a clear and centralised direction. Owing to the fast-changing, complex political and military struggle, its operatives had to respond to pressing developments and often took contradictory decisions.[67]

For the *Generalitat*, seizing the telephone exchange on 3 May was just another step in the process of normalisation of public order. The constant interruptions by CNT militants of conversations (even including one on 2 May between Azaña and Companys) compelled the Catalan government to act. If, on the first evening of the disturbances, the *Generalitat* had agreed to the sacking of the two most compromised elements in the raid, Aiguadé and Salas, calm might yet have prevailed. However, it took them longer than that to realise the seriousness of the situation. According to Azaña, despite Companys's bravado of fighting the Anarchists, he was actually an unwilling participant in the confrontation and lacked the means to achieve success in it.[68] The absence of troops and the inability to bring reinforcements demonstrated the *Generalitat*'s lack of foresight and gave the lie to all claims that it was masterminding the May Days. As the conflict escalated, Companys was forced to scale down his nationalist ambitions and kept begging Valencia for aid. But Largo was in no hurry to pay heed to Companys's or even Azaña's constant demands for help.[69] Ironically, after having spent a lifetime combating the CNT, Largo now found that this organisation was his government's most steadfast source of support. Hence, he was reluctant to countenance any move that could result in the loss of political ground by the Anarcho-syndicalists, and hoped that the UGT and the CNT emissaries could end the bloodshed by compromise. He only agreed to dispatch thousands of assault guards to Barcelona when a truce reached after the establishment of an emergency four-man cabinet (representing the UGT, *Esquerra* and the CNT) collapsed when Antonio Sesé, the Secretary of the Catalan UGT, was shot dead on his way to the *Generalitat* to accept his post. But by the time that the Valencia reinforcements arrived, on 7 May, the barricades were already being dismantled and the combatants were returning to work.[70]

### Negrín, the necessary man

Barcelona's May Days had an immense impact across Republican Spain. In particular, the events strengthened the hand of those advocating the centralisation of power and the restoration of order in the rear. The Catalan government lost much of its autonomy, as the central state took over public order, then moved its headquarters to Barcelona in November 1937 and, in August 1938, assumed total economic control in an attempt to improve the performance of the war industry. The CNT, meanwhile, though still a huge force, emerged demoralised from the May Days after what many in its ranks regarded as the capitulation of their leaders. Finally, the May Days sealed the downfall of Largo Caballero and the fate of the POUM.

Largo's ousting was not a consequence of some sinister, Kremlin-orchestrated plot or Communist conspiracy. It was, rather, the settlement of old scores within the PSOE, combined with the growing hostility of most Republican forces towards someone perceived as an inefficient war leader, which led to his fall. The final straw came during the stormy cabinet council of 13 May 1937 when the Communist ministers proposed a political ban on the POUM and the arrest of its leaders. The Prime Minister opposed them and, after a long and very heated dispute, told them that the door was open and they could always use it if they were not happy with his performance. To Largo's chagrin, he was left with only the backing of his UGT comrades and the four Anarcho-syndicalist ministers.[71] The PCE would have been content with Largo's relinquishment of the War Ministry but he was not prepared to let that go. Instead, he proposed a reduced cabinet in which he would conserve an enlarged war portfolio after incorporating control over the air force and the navy, previously held by Prieto. He even incensed the CNT by proposing to halve its participation in the government.[72] Largo's plan for a reduced cabinet was rejected and he was forced to resign.

Days before the cabinet crisis, a delegation of Republican groups, led by Giral, had informed Azaña of their determination to put an end to the rule of the inept and abusive Largo. They claimed that the Prime Minister kept them in the dark about the most important decisions and that he even had the discourteousness to tell them to read the newspapers when they objected.[73] Azaña himself, still furious by what he perceived as Largo's indifference to his pleas for help during the Barcelona fighting, looked forward to his removal. In turn, for the PSOE's leaders the long-awaited occasion to eliminate the influence of the *Caballerista* wing in the party and the union presented itself. Thus, following Largo's resignation as prime minister, the PSOE secretary Ramón Lamoneda led a concerted assault on Largo's remaining power bases: his supporters were purged from key positions, their journals were taken over by force and, finally, in October a new executive seized control of the UGT.[74]

The new prime minister, the Socialist Juan Negrín, has some-times been dismissed as a Communist puppet, 'the Moscow man'. In fact, given the difficulties entailed by his post, he was above all a realist politician whose main endeavour was successfully to lead the beleaguered Republic at war.[75] Born in the Canaries, Negrín completed his medical studies in Germany and crowned an impressive career when, aged 30, he gained the Chair of Physiology at Madrid University. He only joined the PSOE in 1929 and, as a deputy after 1931, remained close to Prieto. In charge of the Treasury during the Largo government, Negrín worked for the centralisation of economic resources, was outspoken against the existing indiscipline and often risked his life in order to put an end to justice by *paseos*.[76]

During the May 1937 crisis, Negrín was above all Azaña's and Prieto's candidate. It was the Republican president who believed that Negrín's energy and determination made him the necessary man to take up the reigns of government. With Negrín replacing Largo as premier, Azaña later wrote, he no longer felt that he was talking to 'a dead man'.[77] Unlike the inept Largo, petty and devoid of fresh ideas, Negrín had a much greater intellectual grasp of international diplomacy and could more effectively and with more conviction plead the Republic's case to the likes of Britain, as he himself was a firm believer in liberal–democratic principles.[78]

The new interior minister, the Socialist Julián Zugazagoitia, himself far from friendly to the Communists, noted that the suggestion that Negrín was a mere front for the PCE was implausible.[79] Indeed, Comintern reports stressed that with Negrín in office the PCE often had to swallow bitter pills and compromise in order to avoid crisis. Communist proposals, although normally accepted, were then put into effect very slowly or not at all.[80]

Negrín was a pragmatist seeking the pursuit of victory. Aware that the war could not be won unless the Western democracies changed their position, in the meantime the Republic's most vital task had to be to concentrate all its efforts on sustaining its long-term defensive capabilities. Thus, excellent relations with the Communists were crucial. Russia remained the main provider of military equipment, the lifeline to a drowning man.[81] Also, with Republican parties in disarray and the PSOE torn apart by its internal divisions, the PCE was the only disciplined force in 1937 which could effectively mobilise all the social components of the Popular Front and would wholeheartedly endorse the reconstruction of the state and the centralisation of authority – prerequisites of the waging of an efficient war. As Negrín eloquently told Western diplomats in October 1938, he would get rid of Communist ministers as soon as the Allies provided the military supplies which so far were only coming from Russia.[82] In fact, it had been Largo who readily accepted the name of 'the Spanish Lenin' and insisted on the presence of Communists in his government. Yet he lacked the diplomatic abilities of Lamoneda and Negrín, who skilfully prevented a merger between the Socialists and the Communists and avoided violent clashes.[83]

Negrín's slogan, 'Resisting is Winning', encapsulated his war strategy. Since victory could not be enjoyed with the existing status quo, it was a question of gaining time and banking on different alternatives: at best, the Spanish conflict could be linked with a European war, or the Allies could be persuaded either to enforce the existing non-intervention policy or to abandon it altogether and give the Republic the military supplies to defend herself; at worst, by mounting an effective war effort the Republic could force Franco to negotiate a compromise peace.[84] The weakness in Negrín's plan was that hopes for a change in the international situation had to be balanced with increasing war-weariness and demoralisation. Furthermore, the task of strengthening state power came with the price of liquidating the revolutionary fervour of the first days, when spirited idealism was the only asset upon which the Republic could realistically rely.

Negrín's rise to power, though, did not mean the triumph of the counter-revolution but represented the culmination of a process of concentration of authority in the hands of the government already begun by the previous administration: the creation of an efficient central machinery in control of the war economy, a unified diplomacy and a concerted military strategy. The CNT leadership had accepted the reconstruction of the state long before Negrín came on the scene.[85] The new government also took control of public order and so firmly put an end to justice by *paseos* and stopped illegal street patrols by militiamen. Regaining control of public order, however, came at a price. Some 3734 anti-Fascists were arrested in Cataluña from April 1937 to January 1939, accused of rebellion, murder or illegal possession of weapons. Repression was partly a settling of scores against the radicals of the first days. However, it was not merely a Communist operation. The police force was far from being a PSUC monolith and its officers' hatred of Anarchists pre-dated some of them acquiring Communist party cards. Above all, the repressive backlash was part of the state recovery of a monopoly of legal violence.[86]

In Cataluña some Anarchists were arrested and assassinated, a number of CNT buildings were occupied and trashed, militants were detained and their union membership cards were torn up and stamped upon.[87] On 11 August 1937 the government decreed the dissolution of the Anarchist-dominated Council of Aragón and appointed a Republican, José Ignacio Mantecón, as governor of the region. The final pretext for the clampdown was the need to reactivate a front which, after the advances of the first weeks of the war, had remained in such a static situation that a foreign comrade of George Orwell claimed that in Spain there was not a war but a 'comic opera with some occasional deaths'.[88] Troops under the Communist Enrique Líster entered the region and imprisoned some high-ranking militants, including the Council of Aragón's President, Joaquín Ascaso, who was accused of jewel-smuggling.[89]

The CNT, still a powerful organisation, was never officially attacked. With the leadership increasingly adopting a pragmatic stance, the Catalan regional committees even threatened to expel all members of the Friends of Durruti, who failed to dissociate themselves from that group.[90] Complaints against the persecution of militants were timid and hardly any reaction followed the dissolution of the Council of Aragón. On the contrary, the CNT regional committees stuck to a legalist view of avoiding any internal conflicts that could damage the broad anti-Fascist front. Ascaso, after being freed in September, was even expelled.[91] Yet the real power shift from trade unions to parties was facilitated by the CNT's self-elimination from power by refusing to endorse any administration not led by Largo. This had little impact on Negrín, who simply formed a cabinet (with half the previous number of ministries) with three Socialists, two Republicans, two Communists, and one Catalan and one Basque Nationalist. By June the CNT was already soliciting representation and promising Negrín total support in the prosecution of the war. In the reshuffle of April 1938 the CNT re-entered the government.

The POUM was targeted for particular punishment after the May Days. Its repression was the result of two parallel but not identical agendas: the internecine wars within the Communist movement and the dynamics of the reconstruction of Republican state authority. After being officially banned, on 15 June 1937, the POUM carried on a semi-legal existence in places such as Valencia and Madrid, but in Cataluña its leadership and hundreds of its militants were arrested on dubious charges of espionage. At the same time, foreign nationals enrolled in that party's militia or suspected of Trotskyist leanings were rounded up and in some instances murdered by Comintern agents.[92] A particularly scandalous incident was the kidnapping and assassination of Andreu Nin, the POUM's leader. The government, for the sake of expediency, avoided any real investigation.[93] Nevertheless, despite all its flaws, Republican legality was not altogether subverted. The show trials enacted in Moscow at the time were not replayed in Spain. The justice minister, the Basque Nationalist Irujo, and the interior minister, the Socialist Zugazagoitia, took decisive steps to uphold judicial and legal channels and made sure that the Communist director of security, Antonio Ortega, resigned. The POUM leaders were eventually brought to trial in October 1938: four of them were sentenced to 15 years' imprisonment and one to 11 years, and two others were acquitted. They were not condemned by the grotesque charges of being Fascist spies, but the full weight of the law was applied to the leadership of a group which had openly supported a rebellion against a state at war.[94]

## War in the north

While both camps were undertaking the reconstruction of their respective states, the military carnage continued unabated at the front. After months of bloody battles around the capital resulting in stalemate, the Nationalists turned their attention towards the hitherto relatively inactive northern front. The capture of this area rich in mineral and industrial resources was an important prize. It contained the crucial coal-mining industry and explosive factories of Asturias and the steel-making plants and shipyards of Vizcaya.

The Nationalist leaders rightly spotted a weak point in the Republic's defensive capabilities there. Cut off from the rest of Republican Spain, the three provinces – Vizcaya, Santander and Asturias – could not be helped by sea, as the bulk of the Republican fleet was engaged in the Mediterranean guarding the supply routes from Russia.[95] Moreover, concepts of unified military command which could have facilitated a co-ordinated defence were absent and the three provinces, in particular Vizcaya, focused their military efforts in terms of local resistance.[96] Within the Basque forces, there were PNV regiments, the so-called *Gudaris*, who attended mass regularly and even had their own chaplains. Professional officers sent from Madrid were ignored and, when the situation deteriorated in May, the Basque President Aguirre himself took military command. Apart from its internal disorganisation, the Republican army was massively outgunned in heavy artillery and air-power.[97] The Nationalists could count both on the mechanised Italian units, eager to delete the memory of Guadalajara, and on the Condor Legion, the decisive element in the campaign.

Under President Aguirre, the overwhelming majority of Basque Nationalists loyally fought on the Republican side. There were, however, cases of defections and rumours of attempts to reach a deal with Franco.[98] In fact, there always existed tensions between the Basques and the other political forces of the Republic. The revolutionary wave unleashed in other regions was practically absent in Vizcaya. The social-conservative and arch-Catholic PNV established its own police force, the *Ertzanza*, ensured respect for private property and the Church, and ignored pleas from the central authorities to apply scorched-earth policies in order to prevent the enemy gaining control of Vizcaya's vast industrial resources.[99]

When the Nationalists' northern offensive began, on 31 March, General Mola demanded prompt and unconditional surrender. Otherwise, he claimed, he possessed the means to raze all Vizcaya to the ground. He was not bluffing. Evacuated Basque children in foster homes in England and France expressed the horror they had had to endure by rushing to cellars or having hysterics whenever an aeroplane appeared in the sky.[100] Despite their overwhelming inferiority in equipment, but helped by the mountainous terrain, the Basques put up a stiff struggle. Mola expected to complete the conquest of Vizcaya in three weeks but it took him three months. The Nationalist offensive was far from brilliant but it did confirm the effectiveness of a strategy of slow but consistent advances based on the systematic and relentless use of superior firepower. Resistance was finally broken by continuous terror-bombing as never previously seen in Europe. Unchallenged in the skies, the Condor Legion tested the technique of mass bombardment of cities. Many places, such as Durango, were devastated by the lethal German air-power, but none had more symbolic meaning than the destruction on 26 April of Guernica, the ancient Basque capital. The operation took over three hours and involved waves of Junker 52 and Heinkel 111 bombers and the modern Messerchmitt 109 fighter. It left a toll of over 1600 dead and 800 injured. The decision to wipe out Guernica was taken in co-ordination with the Nationalist High Command. Crowded with refugees, this small town did not present any military or strategic incentive. The atrocity, which was deliberately timed to coincide with the busiest time of a market day in the city, was a punishment to the treacherous Catholic Basques for choosing to side with the Reds in exchange for autonomy. It was also a clear message, like Badajoz one year earlier, to those who offered resistance to Franco's new order. To add insult to injury, the Nationalists organised a deceptive propaganda campaign alleging that retreating Anarchists had dynamited Guernica in order to fabricate a false story for propaganda purposes.[101] The tragedy of the small Basque town was immortalised, as a symbol of the horrors of war, by the painting by Pablo Picasso displayed later that year at the World Fair in Paris.

General Mola's death in a plane accident on 3 June was not the sign of providence hoped for by the Basques. (The main beneficiary was Franco, who was now rid of his still most serious military rival). With Mola replaced by General Dávila, the campaign resumed in earnest. Under an avalanche of fire and steel, the Basques retreated to Bilbao, expecting to mount a last-ditch stand behind a defensive iron ring. However, through the treachery of the defences' main engineer, Alejandro Goicoechea, the Nationalists knew how to pierce the Basque fortress. On 18 June the city was evacuated and the next day fell into the hands of the besiegers.[102]

On 5 July the Republicans launched a diversionary attack west of Madrid towards the village of Brunete. Masterminded by the Chief of Staff, General Rojo, this offensive was intended to relieve the northern front. In strategic terms, it was an absolute success. Over 50,000 of the Republic's best troops initiated an offensive which forced the Nationalists, who had been taken by surprise, to concentrate on a theatre of operations not of their choosing. In military terms, however, the story was different. After the initial tactical advantage, the Republicans failed in their objective to push back the besiegers of the capital. They had few reserves of equipment, lacked experienced middle-ranking officers to co-ordinate the attack and became bogged down in taking small towns instead of outflanking them. Franco, against the advice of the Axis advisers, picked up the gauntlet and diverted the brunt of his forces there. Thus a Republican breakthrough became a long battle of attrition which favoured Franco's plans to bleed the enemy dry. Fighting in unbearable heat, the battle lasted over twenty days, as the Republicans failed to hold on to their captured enclave and ultimately retreated practically to their starting positions. Both camps suffered an appalling cost in lives and matériel.[103] However, whereas Franco, well-supplied by the dictators, could soon make up the losses, the Republic could barely afford to see the destruction of its elite forces and vital equipment.

The Battle of Brunete only postponed the fall of Santander for five weeks, the city being captured (mostly by Italian troops) on 26 August. Back in April, some sectors within the PNV had begun conversations with the Italians to secure guarantees in exchange for surrender. Aguirre confessed to Azaña that, after the fall of Bilbao, morale plummeted and many Basques felt that, once the homeland was lost, there was nothing else to do.[104] After a deal was finally reached between the Italian Commander Roatta and the PNV leader Juan Ajuariaguerra, several Basque regiments gathered in the small town of Santoña (Santander), where they gave themselves up to the Italians. Yet, to Roatta's chagrin, Franco was not prepared to honour a deal he had not sought. Basque officers already on British ships had to disembark, and face summary trials and the executions that followed.[105]

With the Nationalist armies poised to conquer their last northern objective, the province of Asturias, the Republicans began a new offensive in the hitherto lethargic front of Aragón. In a replay of their earlier enterprise at Brunete, they obtained a crucial tactical surprise over the enemy. However, they fell short of their final objective, the capital, Zaragoza. The best troops of the Popular Army and International Brigades lost vital time as they were held up by the resistance of fortified towns. By late September the offensive had petered out after 12 days spent capturing the village of Belchite. Essential equipment and manpower was thus lost without making any significant impact upon the course of the war.[106] Soon thereafter, the Nationalist conquest of Asturias was completed with the fall of Gijón on 21 October. After their triumphal march across northern Spain, the Nationalists now held more territory than did the Republic. Moreover, the capture of the vital industrial areas of the north confirmed that the military balance was clearly swinging in their favour.

## The turning-point: Teruel

The offensives at Brunete and Belchite revealed that the sheer material superiority of the Nationalists would ultimately prevail over the courage and even the tactical cunning of the Republicans.[107] The Battle of Teruel, a turning-point in the military balance, bore out that fact.

After the conquest of the north, the Nationalists began to prepare a major new operation against Madrid. Yet again they were outwitted and forced to abandon their plans when, on 15 December 1937, the Republic launched its own new offensive against the smallest of Aragón's provincial capitals, Teruel. Following the script of previous battles, the Nationalist High Command was caught by surprise when thousands of Republican troops mounted a massive attack. Franco, obsessed with holding ground and looking forward to a new campaign of attrition, overruled his foreign advisers, temporarily gave up on Madrid and diverted the bulk of his forces towards Teruel.[108]

Freezing temperatures and snow blizzards hindered the Nationalists, as they could not utilise their mechanised transport and planes. On 7 January the Republic celebrated an important moral victory, the capture of a major city. However, outgunned massively in heavy artillery and aircraft, the Republicans at Teruel soon became besieged and cut off from their supply bases. After weeks of exhaustive frontal combats they broke through the encirclement, but with irreparable losses of manpower and equipment. By 22 February 1938 Teruel was back in Nationalist hands.[109]

For once, Franco abandoned his perennial caution and, in mid-March, launched a real blitzkrieg – a tactic that had often been advocated by Axis officers – against the battered Republican troops in Aragón. Under a curtain of fire produced by 1000 Italian and German aircraft, armoured cars and tanks, over 100,000 troops, spearheaded by elite Moorish and Italian forces, crossed the River Ebro. On 15 April they seized Vinaroz (Castellón), reached the Mediterranean and cut the Republican zone in two. Victory seemed imminent.[110]

## The grand charade must go on

The war-weariness which increasingly plagued the Republic was the logical consequence of constant setbacks at the front, and shortages and economic dislocation at the rear. Yet the mounting defeatism which Republican governments had to confront was not so much as a result of their policies but of the strength of international forces arrayed against them. They not only struggled to combat the Axis-equipped Nationalist armies but also wrestled with a crippling embargo which not only prevented the Republic from ever engaging on an equal military footing with its enemy but also in the end undercut the attempts to sustain the physical fabric and morale of the home front – factors crucial to its war of resistance.[111] Indeed, Negrín ultimately lost the war on the diplomatic front. It was Hitler, Mussolini and Chamberlain who were responsible for the Nationalist victory and not Stalin's ambiguous policies and Communist ascendancy. In fact, the PCE, for all its errors, played a major role in keeping Republican resistance alive for much longer than it might otherwise have lasted.[112]

Non-intervention proved fundamental in sealing the Republic's international besiegement. Under respectable ideals of confining the war within the Spanish borders, the NIA contained a crucial element of fraudulence. Assuming the brevity of the conflict, as the Republic seemed close to capitulation, it was initially devised as a diplomatic solution to win time.[113] The unexpected Republican defence of the capital threw this original rationale into disarray. The strategy had to be readjusted on a longer-term basis. From late 1936 the NIA was sold to public opinion as an essential exercise of peaceful diplomacy at work. In reality, the diplomatic community connived in perpetuating for over two years an unparalleled instrument of chicanery. Despite glaring evidence of intervention by many of its leading members, the grand charade went on until the last days of the Spanish Civil War and effectively doomed the Republic.

With countries openly flouting non-intervention, if the NIC had accomplished its work honestly, either the entire scheme would have collapsed or there would have been a frontal collision. Instead, as the German chargé d'affaires in Britain noted in January 1938, a surreal farce went on:

> We have had to follow essentially dilatory tactics in the committee throughout the entire past year ... The entire negotiations have

something unreal about it, since participants see through the game of the other side but only seldom express this openly ... The Non-Intervention policy is so unstable and is such an artificial creation that everyone fears to cause its collapse by a clear 'no' and then have to bear the responsibility.[114]

In order to placate criticism of its inactivity, the NIC began discussions in late October 1936 to establish a supervision scheme of the agreement. It was a flawed and time-consuming process during which the Fascist powers prevaricated in London while meanwhile supplying enough aid to secure a Nationalist victory. Supervision of land frontiers and vigilance of coasts finally commenced on 20 April 1937. This consisted of a corps of international observers on the Spanish borders and at main European harbours which had the right to identify and verify cargo, but only from the NIA-signatory countries. There was never a concerted attempt to make it function. During its short life, the supervision scheme was easily bypassed. The Republican merchant fleet brought in shipments from Russia, while the Germans used ships which flew the Panamanian or Liberian flag and unloaded their supplies in Portugal (with the complicity of the local authorities) and the Italians utilised their own warships. Aircraft went straight to Spanish bases. Unbelievably, the patrolling of the Spanish coasts involved (in addition to the navies of Britain and France) the fleets of Germany and Italy, the main wreckers of the scheme.[115]

The harm inflicted to the Republic by non-intervention and the central role played by Britain in its maintenance was clearly highlighted by President Azaña:

The British government has been so far our greater enemy. All the subterfuges devised by the Non-Intervention have damaged the Republic and favoured the rebels. The hypocrisy is so transparent that it reaches levels of infantile cynicism ... How can their interests be helped by the victory of a side linked to Italy and Germany?[116]

Echoing the Republican president's thoughts, George Orwell wondered whether the British ruling classes were wicked or merely stupid. He found it absolutely baffling that they were acting as accomplices in the victory of a regime propped up by the Axis when it was evident that Europe was heading towards confrontation.[117] Writing in 1943 and with the benefit of hindsight, Orwell overlooked that at the time of the Spanish war the British ruling classes were acting according to their class interests. They perceived that appeasing the dictators was a pragmatic option, as a collision with them would only have benefited the real enemy, the Soviet Union. Additionally, they were convinced that the diplomacy of 'pound sterling' would be enough to safeguard British interests in a future Nationalist Spain. As the NIC Chairman, Lord Plymouth, candidly confided to the Russian ambassador, Britain's vast interests would never be imperilled in an Axis-dominated Spain. After the war, Spain would need money for her reconstruction and the only place to go for that was the City of London.[118]

Thus, for the sake of appeasement, the NIC avoided the real issue – the constant infraction of the agreement by some of its leading members, amounting in the case of Germany and more particularly of Italy to an undeclared war with the Republic. However, even if the objective was to preserve peace in Europe, the dogged maintenance of the NIA actually ultimately increased international tension and made war more likely. The Republic was thrown into the embrace of the only great power willing to help: the Soviet Union. Simultaneously, not only French impotence but also British internal disagreements increased as the dictators, aware of Allied passivity, became gradually bolder and more reckless in their activities.

On 2 January 1937 Britain and Italy signed the eloquently-termed 'Gentlemen's Agreement' which confirmed the existing status quo in the Mediterranean by recognising the compatibility of the interests of both countries in the area.[119] Differences soon emerged within the British cabinet between the foreign minister, Eden, and the majority of his colleagues. Eden had wholeheartedly embraced the NIA as a useful instrument to prevent the Spanish conflict from spreading across Europe. However, confronted by a drawn-out war, he grew increasingly worried by continued foreign intervention. Eden was appalled that, even while conducting negotiations, the Italians kept dispatching massive contingents of troops in open violation of the agreement. He concluded that Mussolini, whom he described as a 'gangster', only understood the value of stern measures. Thus, he concluded, unless the NIA acted forcefully to check the Fascist aggression in Spain, there would soon be trouble in other places. The majority of the British cabinet, however, did not share his concerns and were anxious that the Spanish affair should not hinder appeasement. Additionally, they clearly favoured a Nationalist victory. Sir Samuel Hoare, the First Lord of the Admiralty, claimed that if they were to follow Eden's advice it would appear as if Britain were trying to prevent Franco from winning, while many in the government were anxious that the 'Soviets' should not prevail.[120]

In early 1937 a more resolute attitude would have inhibited Axis intervention. At that stage, Italy and Germany were still testing the determination of the Allies and the validity of the NIA. They were prepared to push the limits of tolerance, hoping to pour enough troops and equipment into Spain to secure a Nationalist victory before the scheme's control came into effect, but still wanted to avoid a rupture and the risk of confrontation with the democracies.[121]

Axis frustration at Franco's sluggish progress forced them to choose between continuing their supply operation and contemplating a humiliating retreat. Yet their hesitations were soon dispelled as the NIC again and again refused to act, despite the blinding evidence of massive shipments of manpower and matériel to Spain. In turn, initial Fascist caution became transformed into boldness and defiance. Indeed, the NIC ignored all the factual evidence of a massive Italian presence in Spain following the capture of prisoners and documents after the battle of Guadalajara in March 1937. There were some threats uttered by the French ambassador Corbin, and Eden wrote in his diary that by then he would prefer a Republican victory. Yet all the countries refused to endorse Maiskii's demands for a full investigation – even after the Italian ambassador seemed to depart from the diplomatic script and claimed that no single Fascist volunteer would leave Spain until Franco was victorious. Ribbentrop wrote that France would do nothing without the approval of England, and the British were keen on reaching a compromise.[122] Nobody was prepared to put an end to a farcical game in which there were many rules and only one possible outcome, the denial of reality.[123]

A similar reception met the shocking destruction of Guernica by the Condor Legion. Official German denials – Berlin, after all, refused to admit that there were any Luftwaffe units in Spain – clashed with the evidence of survivors and journalists such as the reporter from *The Times*, George L. Steer. The British government also had first-hand evidence from their Bilbao consul, Ralph Stevenson, who visited the town 24 hours after the attack. Nevertheless, all embarrassing questions were avoided in the House of Commons, and when the atrocity was discussed in the NIC Lord Plymouth concluded matters with a call to both Spanish sides – deliberately ignoring foreign participation – to refrain from bombing civilian cities.[124]

A grave new incident took place on 29 May 1937 when two Republican planes bombed the German battleship *Deutschland* (anchored in Ibiza), causing 39 dead and 75 wounded. In a reprisal, two days later the German fleet shelled the city of Almería, killing 19 people. The

Republican government then discussed Prieto's proposal to use all
the available aircraft to attack German objectives in order to produce
an international confrontation. It was turned down. Most ministers
believed that the Republic would be abandoned to its fate. Furthermore, the Russians made clear their opposition.[125] In June a new
incident, involving the alleged attacks by 'Bolshevik' submarines on
the Germany battleship *Leipzig*, was the final pretext for the Italians
and Germans to play up their role of victims and to abandon the
NIA control scheme altogether (although they naturally declared their
continuing commitment to the principles of non-intervention).[126]
To the despair of the French government, Britain refused to give any
firm response and welcomed the Axis's decision to remain in the NIC.
According to Winston Churchill, the elimination of the flawed supervision system left the Non-intervention Committee as an irrelevant
body of official deceits, confirmed the subordination of French foreign
policy to British interests and sealed the solution of the Spanish conflict
on the altar of appeasement.[127]

In early August Franco requested Mussolini's help to strangle
the lifeline provided to the Republic by the convoys of Soviet supplies in the Mediterranean.[128] His compliance resulted in an exceptional and short-lived display of resolve by the Allies. For over a
month Italian submarines and aircraft attacked some thirty vessels,
including Spanish, Russian, French, British and other neutral ships.
On 27 August Fascist participation in Spain was echoed by the Italian
press's publication of Mussolini's boast of the conquest of Santander
by his troops in a telegram of congratulations to Franco.[129] The press
began to use the euphemism of mysterious 'pirate actions' in the
Mediterranean. In fact, even the Italians, informed by the Germans,
were aware that British intelligence had broken their naval codes and
therefore knew that Italian submarines were responsible for all the
mayhem in the Mediterranean. However, as Ciano noted, they were
confident that Britain would not risk a clash.[130]

In fact, since the rise to power in May 1937 of Neville Chamberlain,
the isolation of Eden and other anti-appeasers had become more acute.
The French, on the other hand, whose patience appeared to have
reached its limits, threatened the abandonment of the NIC. Finally, an
international conference, to be held in the Swiss city of Nyon in mid-
September, was agreed upon to discuss the mysterious sinkings in the
Mediterranean. France insisted on Russian attendance and even that of
Republican Spain, but the British imposed the view that no Spanish
side should be present and duly extended the invitation to the Italians,

who refused it after feigning offence at Soviet accusations of their having torpedoed two Russian vessels.[131]

With the Fascist powers absent from the conference at Nyon, those present agreed to divide the Mediterranean between zones of patrol and to intercept and destroy all pirate activity. Eden noted that Fascist aggression could be stopped if matched by force.[132] However, his was an isolated voice in a British cabinet dominated by appeasers. The spirit of Nyon hardly lasted. Furthermore, the Russians were furious when the British again invited the Italians, the real villains of the story, to participate in the patrols.[133] Ciano could boast that the 'pirates had been turned into policemen'. In mid-October, in his diary, he described the French climb-down, when faced with British opposition to the enforcement of compliance with non-intervention, as marking the decline of the Western democracies.[134]

Even though the piratical attacks stopped, the Mediterranean route was effectively interrupted. France's so-called 'relaxed non-intervention' now became vital for the survival of the Republic. Negrín had travelled to Paris in July 1937 and obtained guarantees from the new French prime minister, Chautemps, that he would continue the policy of his predecessor. Blum, now deputy premier, claimed he was in a better position to help now that he was no longer under the spotlight.[135] Indeed, the French seemed to respond more positively to Republican pleas. International controls on her border were suspended and ideas raised by the Fascist powers in the NIC to give belligerent rights to both sides were promptly rejected.[136] *France-Navigation*, a company created in April 1937, run by members of the French Communist Party, manned by reliable crews from the CGT maritime trade union and financed by the Soviet bank sited in Paris, *La Banque Commerciale de l'Europe du Nord*, undertook the bulk of voyages from Mursmank in northern Russia to the French Atlantic harbours. With the complicity of elements within the French administration, convoys of armoured trucks, accompanied by hand-picked customs agents, smuggled the equipment across the border.[137] However, as the French Radical minister Jean Zay claimed, his country intervened enough to be under constant criticism and yet not enough to give the Republic efficient support.[138]

The Nationalists had definitely gained the upper hand on the battlefield by early 1938, but there were glimmers of hope for the Republic. Negrín's strategy of resistance to gain time appeared justified as Nazi aggression in central Europe appeared to be about to plunge the continent into an all-out confrontation.

# 6

## The Republic's Defeat (March 1938–March 1939): Chronicle of a Death Foretold?

On January 26th Barcelona had fallen to Franco. The exodus from all the towns and villages along the coast had begun. Women, children, men, beasts, struggling along the roads, through frozen fields, in the deadly snows of the mountains. Pitiless planes overhead, a blood-drunk army pressing from the back, and a small band of soldiers checking its advance, pushed back inexorably and still fighting on, face to the enemy. Poor people with pitiful bundles, fortunate people in overloaded cars cleaving their way through the packed highways, and at the gates of France an endless queue of exhausted fugitives waiting for admission into safety.[1]

### Keeping resistance alive

In the spring of 1938 the Republic appeared to be on the verge of imminent defeat. The year could not have begun better: the capture, for the first time, of a provincial capital (Teruel). However, optimism had soon turned into demoralisation. Unable to hold on to that victory, the Republican army had been forced to retreat in disarray as the Nationalist troops marched eastwards through Aragón and Cataluña, reached the Mediterranean and cut the Republican zone in two. Despair pervaded the Republican camp. Every defeat furthered the pressure on its already badly overstretched human and material resources. Together with the constant loss of valuable matériel and thousands of soldiers (who were often recycled and joined the Nationalists), the Republic had to provide for an avalanche of refugees. In turn, aerial bombardments, grim news from the front, and painful shortages of basic goods took a heavy toll. The rear started to crumble as the increasingly war-weary population, whose meagre rations consisted mostly of rice and lentils – referred to as Dr Negrín's pills – began to long for Franco's white bread and wonder when the tragedy befalling Spain would end.[2]

Defeatism and gloom also spread amongst those holding high political office. President Azaña's willpower, like that of many other bourgeois Republicans, sank progressively as a vicious struggle that he could neither understand nor stomach dragged on. Never having recovered from his close experience of the street-fighting during the May Days, Azaña began to hope for a negotiated end to the conflict. In May 1937 the coronation of King George VI had appeared to him as an opportunity to explore the possibility of British mediation in ending the hostilities. For that sensitive mission, he enlisted Julián Besteiro to represent Spain at the ceremony.[3] Deeply dismayed at the radicalisation undergone by the PSOE between 1931 and 1936, Besteiro, like Azaña, had been seriously affected by the ongoing orgy of blood and mayhem. He therefore accepted his assignment with enthusiasm and was left disheartened by its poor results. Besteiro's meeting on 11 May with Eden had been encouraging and the British Foreign Office had even raised the question of international mediation with the other great powers. France and the Soviet Union accepted in principle but the Axis powers procrastinated. Britain then dropped the initiative.[4] To Besteiro's chagrin, a peace proposal also clashed with Spain's domestic reality. It was not only that Franco was against any negotiations short of unconditional surrender but, more painfully for Besteiro, any deal was also in open contradiction to the commitment to fight to the end of the new Negrín administration – a government that had come to power during his mission to Britain. Deeply wounded by having his efforts ignored, Besteiro from then on held a fierce grudge against the new prime minister.[5]

Following the debacle at Teruel, the gap between the supporters of continued resistance and those willing to find a negotiated solution to the conflict widened. Azaña was a leading member in a growing camp of Republicans increasingly affected by war-weariness but unable to present a coherent alternative. As a whole, they had reached the conclusion that the struggle had been lost. Given the existing international isolation and the glaring Republican military inferiority on the battlefield, Azaña and his colleagues felt that the emphasis should be put on finding a satisfactory way to end the war. In contrast, Negrín and his allies believed that nothing had changed. For them a policy of staunch resistance remained the priority. Even if victory was ultimately un-achievable, only by mounting an effective war effort could the Republic extract fair conditions from the Nationalists. Resistance was imperative to gain time since, they argued, Fascist aggression, sooner or later, would reveal the chimera of appeasement. The most likely outcome would then be a major European conflict in which the Spanish Civil War would be just one battleground.[6]

Nevertheless, in the spring of 1938 the Republic seemed to be about to collapse. After the Republican front was smashed in Aragón, town after town fell to the Nationalist juggernaut, Barcelona was subjected to relentless bombardment and the rear was paralysed by fear and gloom. In these crucial moments Zugazagoitia singled out Negrín's iron will as vital to keeping resistance alive. Seemingly impervious to the ongoing military débâcle, he continued to offer an image of con-fidence and optimism.[7] However, the Prime Minister was on the brink of falling out with his formerly close friend, Indalecio Prieto.

The previously warm relations between Prieto and the PCE had deteriorated beyond repair by the spring of 1938. As war minister, Prieto had passed measures that had, incidentally, received Negrín's full backing and were clearly aimed at limiting Communist influence in the commissariat and armed forces. He banned political propaganda in the army, sought to strengthen the authority of career officers vis-à-vis the political commissars, and placed his own man, Crescenciano Bilbao, in charge of the commissariat.[8] However, the Communists' open criticism of Prieto only mounted in the aftermath of the Teruel disaster. By then, sunk in the blackest despair, the War Minister had become an embarrassing source of defeatism.[9] On 29 March 1938 Prieto offered such a devastating picture of pessimism in a cabinet meeting that Negrín confided to a friend that upon his departure he had not been sure whether to tell his driver to take him home or straight to the border![10]

On 16 March 1938 there was a massive demonstration in Barcelona demanding the removal of the 'treasonous' ministers. Its main pro-moters were the Communists – and the target was clearly Prieto – but all the Popular Front organisations were represented. Despite growing war-weariness, they were aware that the only alternative to the policy preached by Negrín was capitulation. They therefore sought to apply pressure to Azaña to allow Negrín to carry out a cabinet reshuffle. They believed that otherwise, if Azaña gave power to a defeatist-dominated cabinet, the outcome would be surrender and the extermination of thousands of Republicans.[11] As proof of their determination to carry on the fight with undaunted vigour, the UGT and the CNT signed a unity of action pact on 18 March. To the dismay of many Anarchists, the CNT's national executive had long before retreated from the revolutionary ideals of the early days and pursued a 'realist' strategy, the logical conclusion of which was the CNT's endorsement (together with the UGT) of the authority of the state, its full support for central economic planning and the establishment of an efficient popular army.[12] On 6 April 1938 Negrín formed a new government of *union sacrée* in which all the members of the Popular Front were represented. Its most outstanding innovations were the Prime Minister's own assumption of the War Ministry, the return to the Foreign Office of the Socialist Alvarez del Vayo and (as a reward for their unions' backing) the inclusion in the cabinet of the veteran UGT leader from Asturias, Ramón González Peña, as justice minister and the *Cenetista* Segundo Blanco as minister of health and education.[13]

From then on, owing largely to his bruised ego and personal rancour, Indalecio Prieto became one of the most formidable of Negrín's detractors. Anger at losing his cabinet post festered into the full-blown hatred of his former friend. After the war Prieto would claim that, as in the case of Largo Caballero, he had become the victim of a Communist witchhunt: he had been thrown out by Negrín following Moscow's orders![14] It seems he had forgotten his own central role in Largo's ousting. In fact, the 'Russians' had nothing to do with Prieto's dismissal. Weeks earlier Stalin had suggested that the Communists should take the opportunity of any governmental crisis to leave the government, thereby making it more palatable to the Western powers. His advice was not heeded by the PCE. The Spanish Communists who counted upon the support of the Comintern's delegate, the Italian Palmiro Togliatti,[15] argued that their abandonment of ministerial office would not be understood by the fighting masses and would turn the balance of power against Negrín.[16] Moreover, the Prime Minister had tried to retain Prieto in the cabinet, as minister for public works, but he declined that offer. Prieto's sabotaging pessimism had therefore barred him from remaining at the helm of the Republic's war effort.[17]

By July 1938 the Republic had managed to survive despite the overwhelming odds of the previous months. Even Azaña had to concede that the Prime Minister had maintained morale and had transformed the government into a real fighting body.[18] Negrín was helped in his endeavours to stabilise the political and military situation by two crucial factors: Franco's military strategy and the obvious deterioration of the international context.

The Nationalist advance to the Mediterranean had left the Republican army in tatters and its defensive capabilities badly dented. Holding the military initiative, Franco's forces seemed poised to seize the rest of Cataluña. Taking control of the Republic's main industrial centre and crucial harbour, as well as sealing the French border for good, might have dramatically accelerated the end of the war. However, instead of turning north, Franco directed the bulk of his troops south, towards Valencia. This not only gave the Republican forces a necessary breathing spell to rest and regroup but also brought an end to the Nationalist momentum. With the mountainous terrain favouring the defender, the advance was now painfully slow and very costly in terms of casualties. On 14 June 1938 Franco's forces seized Castellón after two months of fighting but soon thereafter the Nationalist offensive stalled, 40 km short of Valencia. Given the demoralisation of a few months earlier, the successful containment of the Nationalist attack turned out to be one of the most impressive Republican defensive victories.[19]

Although some leading generals, such as Kindelán and Vigón, could not conceal their bafflement, several explanations (or most likely a combination of them) can be put forward for the strategy pursued by the Nationalist high command. It has been argued that halting the advance towards Barcelona might have been the result of the poor tactical quality of the *Africanista* generals. Choosing Valencia as the Nationalists' next objective could also be regarded as part of Franco's desire to prolong the war to consolidate his personal power and slowly bleed the enemy to death. However, a crucial consideration in postponing the invasion of Cataluña was certainly the need to avoid unnecessarily alarming France. At a time of growing international tension, it would clearly have been diplomatically unwise to have the Condor Legion and the Italian divisions moving towards the French frontier.[20]

### The infernal frontier

Confronted by the undisguised ambitions of the Axis, Western appeasement, throughout 1938, began to reveal its utter hollowness. By the beginning of that year the disagreements within the British administration could no longer be reconciled. In November 1937 Italy's decision to join the Anti-Comintern Pact with Germany and Japan and, one month later, its departure from the League of Nations confirmed

Eden's view that a tough stand should be taken and that Spain should
become the test of Mussolini's sincerity. For Neville Chamberlain and
the majority of his ministers, however, Spain was 'the great stumbling-
block' in the way of Britain improving its relations with Italy.[21]
Furthermore, Chamberlain believed that his government should take
steps to secure the goodwill of the winner of the civil war, which was
clearly going to be the Nationalists. Thus, on 12 November 1937, the
Duke of Alba was recognised as General Franco's official agent in
London (a post that he had filled since the outbreak of the war without
having official status), and a retired diplomat, Sir Robert Hodgson, was
appointed official British agent in Nationalist Spain. Although this still
fell far short of legal recognition, it was a clear diplomatic coup for the
Francoist authorities.[22]

Eden's position as head of British diplomacy was becoming
increasingly untenable. In September 1937 his support for the proposal
by the French foreign minister, Delbos, for the mutual collaboration of
both governments to give teeth to the Non-Intervention Agreement in
order to end Italy's flouting of its principles left him isolated in the
British cabinet. Most ministers, bent on achieving good relations
with Italy, were actually determined to restrain French 'firmness'.
Subsequently, Eden was dismayed when Lord Halifax, the deputy
prime minister, visited Berlin in November 1937 and informed Hitler
that the British government would not oppose any 'reasonable territorial adjustments' in Europe, as long as they were pursued through
diplomatic means. The irreconcilability of the two opposing views
about how to proceed in the negotiations with Fascist Italy finally
exploded. While the foreign minister wanted Italian compliance with
non-intervention in Spain as an implicit condition before any agreement was signed, Chamberlain was prepared to continue to turn a blind
eye to Mussolini's involvement in the Spanish adventure. The Italians
were fully informed of the divisions within the British cabinet by their
ambassador in London, Dino Grandi. On 19 February 1938, when
the Italian diplomat was confronted by Eden (in a conversation at
which Chamberlain was also present and during which he often showed
visible annoyance with his foreign minister) with evidence of Italy's
constant flouting of the Non-Intervention Agreement, Grandi had the
cheek to reply that Italy was on the side of General Franco for the same
reasons that had led the British to send troops to Spain to defeat
Napoleon in 1808! Grandi concluded from his experience that day that
Chamberlain and Eden were enemies confronting each other, like 'two
cocks in true fighting posture'. On 20 February 1938, isolated in the

British cabinet, Eden resigned and was replaced by the arch-appeaser Lord Halifax.[23]

Eden's demise had a devastating effect in France and was a personal blow to Delbos.[24] Simultaneously it sent a clear signal to the Axis capitals: London would not object to their military adventure in Spain. As Ciano noted, when the news of Eden's resignation arrived at a party he was attending, the public applauded and cheered.[25] During his negotiations with the Italians in March 1938, Halifax suggested that a symbolic gesture such as a partial retreat of their 'volunteers' would favourably impress British public opinion. Mussolini's air force did indeed then proceed to impress the world – but with the intensification of its devastating bombardment of Barcelona.[26]

The farce of non-intervention could reach no greater height. In late February 1938 Hans George von Mackensen, state secretary at the German Foreign Office, wrote that Franco could not achieve military victory without constant supplies of matériel and this depended not on German goodwill alone but on the developments at the NIC in London.[27] Nevertheless, Franco had nothing to worry about. Non-intervention continued to ensure that the international embargo and isolation affected the Republic alone. The British government was perfectly aware of Italy's devastating participation in Spain. However, in March 1938 London did not demand that Mussolini should stop his open involvement in that war, as required by the NIA, but instead begged Ciano to order the end of the bombing of Spanish cities because the situation could be 'delicate' for Chamberlain. Ciano's reply was telling: he would do what he could but Barcelona was the government site and not an open city![28]

Regardless of Italy's adventurism, on 16 April 1938 an Anglo-Italian treaty, 'the Easter Agreement', which recognized *de jure* Italy's conquest of Abyssinia, was signed in Rome. The agreement's full implementation was still hampered by Chamberlain's pledge to parliament, during the debate following Eden's resignation, that it would not come into force until there was substantial evidence of the withdrawal of Italian troops from Spain. However, Halifax left no doubt about what that meant. In his diary he wrote that Franco's victory should take place within one or two months.[29]

Nevertheless, the escalation of German expansionism gave the Republic a glimmer of hope. On 12 March 1938 Germany annexed Austria (the *Anschluss*) and laid plans for grasping the next prize: the Sudetenland in Czechoslovakia. Alarm bells rang in Paris, where a second Blum cabinet was formed. Negrín did not let this opportunity pass and travelled to France to obtain weapons (planes in particular) from the new French administration.[30] The Spanish plea did not fall upon deaf ears. Blum was no longer the hesitant premier of 1936 and was determined to stand up to Fascist aggression. As the public outcry mounted after the indiscriminate Italian bombing of Barcelona, the French Premier convened a gathering of the Permanent National Defence Committee. Blum wanted to send an ultimatum to Franco demanding the withdrawal of foreign troops and also suggested the dispatch of arms to the Republic. Yet Blum's suggestions were met with reluctance and ultimately collided, once again, with the same rock that had wrecked his plans during his first cabinet: Britain's undisguised hostility towards any French intervention in the Spanish arena (a fact that had been conveyed by the British ambassador, Sir Eric Phipps, to the French foreign minister, Joseph-Paul Boncour, before the crucial meeting). French generals and diplomats opposed any measures that could endanger peace in Europe. If anything, with the international scene becoming more dangerous by the day, most French politicians and officers felt that they could not risk a breach with Britain. The officers also stated that in the current climate France could not spare any military equipment. Having been summoned to Paris for consultations, the French military attaché in Spain, Lieutenant-Colonel Henri Morel, told his prime minister: '*Monsieur le président du Conseil, je n'ai qu'un mot à vous dire, un roi de France ferait la guerre*' ('Mr Prime Minister, I can say only one thing, a French king would go to war'). But Blum was no king and, in the end, he had to settle for a half-hearted formula: the total opening of the French border to the delivery of Russian weapons to Spain.[31] The most that France seemed able to do for the Republic was to allow others (the Soviet Union) to help. Nevertheless, between March and June 1938, with Franco concentrated in Valencia, the Republican army enjoyed a few valuable months to rearm itself with the 18,219 tons of war matériel that crossed the border.[32]

London's reaction to the *Anschluss* was diametrically opposed to that in Paris. The British government accelerated its negotiations with Mussolini and, consequently, was dismayed by Blum's undisguised sympathies for Republican Spain. Indeed, the French administration's 'reckless' behaviour was said to have jeopardised the appeasing efforts and instead of the couple of months to Franco's victory predicted by Halifax, Blum's 'lunacy' was criticised as threatening to prolong the 'Spanish distraction'. Thus, it was not surprising that the British welcomed the demise of the existing French cabinet after barely one month in office. More importantly, the new government in Paris included only members of the Radical Party and, although it was presided over by the hesitant Edouard Daladier, the 'sensible' Georges Bonnet, a staunch supporter of appeasement, was now at the Quai d'Orsay.[33]

Since April, Chamberlain and Halifax impressed upon their French counterparts two crucial points: their concern about France's firm assurances to the Czechs in the case of German aggression and the urgency of sealing the border with Spain.[34] For the British government, bent on a passionate adherence to appeasement, it was the French attitude, not the blatant Axis display of force in Spain (or elsewhere), which flouted the principles of non-intervention and was leading Europe to the verge of war. In the summer of 1936 the British had forced the French Popular Front to stay away from Spain while turning a blind eye to the flagrant intervention of the Italians and Germans. Two years later the collapse of 'Red Spain' was still clearly deemed to be a worthwhile sacrifice for the sake of appeasing the dictators.

British pressure mounted on their French allies to seal the border, the last and only safe channel of arms to the beleaguered Republic now that the Mediterranean supply route was practically closed by Italian activities. Indeed, the Chamberlain administration was furious that Republican resistance was an impediment to the implementation of the Easter Agreement with Italy. On 5 June 1938 Lord Halifax's secretary wrote: 'the government is praying for Franco's victory and pressing France to stop supplies reaching the Republic'.[35] In the case of Bonnet, they were preaching to the converted. A doubtful Daladier finally gave way and the border was closed on 13 June.[36]

Incidentally, the British government's crucial support for the Nationalists seemed undeterred by an ongoing aerial campaign carried out by Franco's air force against the neutral merchant ships (70 per cent of them British) in Republican waters. Only after ten British ships had been sunk and another thirty-seven damaged in May and June 1938 alone, did Chamberlain heed the outcry of public opinion. A blunt message was conveyed to Franco's headquarters to stop the attacks. The *Caudillo* complied, although bombing continued at a far more sporadic tempo.[37] On 29 June, Bonnet asked the British ambassador for help to ensure that Daladier would not be influenced by a similar massive movement of sympathy caused by the Francoist bombardments. Sir Eric Phipps wrote that day to Halifax:

> I am going to see Daladier tomorrow morning and shall impress upon him the absolutely vital importance that His Majesty's

government attach to the continued closure of the Pyrenees frontier, for I feel it is very important to support Bonnet in every possible way in what I now believe to be his genuine fight to keep that *infernal frontier* closed.[38]

## Between the Ebro and Munich

In the early spring of 1938 most foes and many friends of Franco believed that his victory parade was fast approaching. However, out of the ashes, the Republic managed to mount an astonishing comeback. Undeterred by growing demoralisation and military disappointments, Negrín launched an unprecedented parallel diplomatic and military offensive. It represented the high point of his leadership and the most ambitious Republican attempt to find a favourable outcome to the conflict: either by holding on until the Spanish conflict was subsumed within the European war that increasingly seemed more imminent or by forcing a compromise peace with honourable terms. The offensive was a valiant effort, but proved also to be the Republic's swan song.

On 1 May, Negrín published a 13-point declaration. This was a liberal and moderate programme, stating the Republic's war aims but leaving the door open for a negotiated peace.[39] The Prime Minister sought to show the domestic as well as the international audience that his administration was not blind to the possibility of compromise. The moderate character of Negrín's aims came as a shock to Anarchists such as García Oliver, who wrote that he did not know whether to laugh or cry. However, after having renounced all their ideological tenets, many die-hard revolutionaries were prepared to go along with Negrín's plans, as talk of 'the revolution' was no longer a requisite in the CNT official discourse. The emphasis was now on winning the war.[40]

Negrín's vision of a liberal and democratic post-war Spain was aimed at gaining support in his own camp while also impressing the Allies. The 13 points stipulated that post-war Spain would be a democracy, independent from foreign interference, with free elections and full civil rights including freedom of thought and worship. There would be a popular plebiscite to determine the social and political structure of the state. Regional peculiarities would be respected in a united Spain. Private property would be guaranteed within the limits dictated by the national interest, foreign companies affected financially by the war would be compensated, an agrarian reform would be carried out, workers' rights guaranteed and Spain would embrace the League of Nations' collective security. Finally, there would be a generous amnesty for all Spaniards willing to participate in the national reconstruction.[41] It goes without saying that Negrín's points had no chance of winning Franco's approval.

At the same time, in the early hours of 25 July 1938, in order to show that the Republic was far from beaten, a daring offensive, masterminded by the Republic's leading strategist and Chief of the General Staff, General Vicente Rojo, was launched. The new so-called Army of the Ebro had been created in April specially to carry out the attack. Being the descendant of the fifth regiment, it contained the elite of the Republican forces and was overwhelmingly led by Communist commanders: notably Juan Modesto, Manuel Tagueña and Enrique Lister.[42] Profiting from the military reserves accumulated before the closing of the French border, the Army of the Ebro crossed the river of that name with the objective of relieving the pressure on Valencia. Their ultimate aim was to gain time, as war in Europe seemed ever closer.

Initially the operation was a brilliant success, taking the Nationalists by surprise, breaking their lines and establishing a bridgehead 40 km from its starting point. In the first week the attackers had gained 800 sq km of ground. Nevertheless, the Nationalists rapidly rushed fresh troops and equipment from other fronts, and their air force acted with devastating accuracy. The offensive became bogged down, certainly not helped by the late use of its scarce air force, at the gates of the key town of Gandesa. By early August the Republicans had dug deeply in and had adopted defensive positions. Despite immensely adverse material odds and having to fight with a river at its rear, the Army of the Ebro proved a formidable opponent, a far cry from the ragged militiamen of earlier days. Entrenched on the high peaks of a mountainous terrain, they withstood a hail of fire produced by seven major Nationalist offensives. The Battle of the Ebro turned out to be the longest and bloodiest of the entire war – four months of constant slaughter in which positions were often taken and retaken. Once again, the *Caudillo* shocked many generals of his entourage (as well as the Axis officers) with his tactics. Once the Republican attack had been contained, the Nationalists could have resumed their operation against Valencia or turned against Barcelona. Instead, Franco chose to pursue a frontal battle of annihilation, taking advantage of his aerial and artillery pre-eminence to bleed the enemy, regardless of the human cost to his own side.[43]

However, as the battle raged on, the eyes of the combatants were focused on events on the rest of the continent. Rather than on the blood-soaked sierras of eastern Spain, the fate of the war appeared inextricably linked with decisions taken in the European chancelleries. For a good part of the 'hot summer' of 1938, Franco's hopes of a crushing victory began to unravel. Not only had the Republic mounted a surprise attack, bogging the Nationalist troops down on the Ebro, but the international arena also seemed to be moving against the *Caudillo*. After months of triumphs, there existed for the first time doubts in the Nationalist camp and low morale in its headquarters.[44] At the same time, the Axis powers could not conceal their dismay. Having been practically written off, the Republic was still fighting back and with a certain success. They could not understand Franco's anaemic conduct of the war and his inability to put his immensely superior firepower to decisive use. The German ambassador, Eberhard von Stohrer, expressed frustration with the lack of progress at the front and noted the emergence of war-weariness in Nationalist Spain. The Italians were even more blunt. On 22 August General Mario Berti, the CTV's commander, passed to Franco Mussolini's instructions that the campaign should be prosecuted with more vigour. A week later an upset *Duce* told Ciano to record in his diary: 'Today, 29 August 1938, I predict Franco's defeat. This man does not know how, or does not want, to make war. The Reds are fighters, Franco is not!'[45]

For a brief time the Republicans were jubilant. German intransigence regarding its claim to the Sudetenland threatened to plunge Europe into war. The Republic believed that at last the tide was turning. In order to keep the momentum going, on 21 September Negrín travelled to the League of Nations in Geneva to announce the unilateral withdrawal of foreign soldiers. From now on, the Republican war reports, not unjustifiably, would refer to their troops as 'Spanish forces'.[46] The loss of the remaining 12,000 foreign members of the International Brigades was not of any serious military consequence. It was, rather, a symbolic but extremely cunning act. Negrín sought to impress upon his interlocutors the determination of his government to abide by the principles of non-intervention. This would, hopefully, bring about international pressure to force the Nationalists to follow suit.[47] And, of course, Franco, bereft of Axis aid, could not have pursued the war.

The farewell parade of the International Brigades was celebrated in Barcelona on 29 October 1938. They marched past the Republic's leaders while military bands played, thousands cheered, flowers were thrown and girls rushed to kiss them goodbye. Negrín and others expressed their gratitude but the Communist leader, 'La Pasionaria', uttered the most moving words:

Political reasons, reasons of state ... are sending you back, some to your own countries and others to forced exile. You can go proudly. You are history. You are legend. You are the heroic example of democracy's solidarity and universality. We shall not forget you, and when the olive tree of peace puts forth its leaves again, mingled with the laurels of the Spanish Republic's victory – come back![48]

In September 1938, as Republican expectations appeared to surge, the other camp was plagued by gloom. Franco was horrified and perplexed. Suffering from extreme stress, for the first time in years he became unwell and was confined to his headquarters for days.[49] On 27 September, after agonising hesitations, he reassured the Allies of his commitment to remain neutral in the case of a European war. Having been previously informed of that decision, Germany, focusing on the Czech question, appeared to understand Franco's dilemma and only asked for benevolent neutrality. The Italians, however, were incensed. Ciano described Franco's initiative as sickening and added that those soldiers who had died in Spain must be turning in their graves.[50]

Despite their pleas of neutrality, the Nationalists were aware that they could not control the international agenda. Franco's declaration had serious flaws in terms of credibility and application. After all, there existed in Spain significant contingents of Axis matériel and troops that the Allies could not ignore and that the Nationalists could not do without. Francoist headquarters could only dread that, as soon as hostilities broke out on the continent, the Republic would declare war on Germany and link its fortune to that of the Western democracies. With the Republicans still resisting on the Ebro, the rebels would find themselves geographically isolated from their friends and facing great difficulties in obtaining military supplies. Furthermore, as soon as the war began, the French military strategy included sending troops to Cataluña and Morocco.[51] The Nationalist ambassador in Berlin, Count Magaz, revealed the anxiety experienced by his side in those days: 'A European war was a nightmare since regardless of our actions, the Republic would automatically declare war on the Axis and thus become allies of those whose neutrality we wished to preserve.'[52]

In the event, the international situation could not have evolved more favourably for Franco. Although pushed to its furthest limits by the Czech crisis, Western appeasement still prevailed. On 29 September, rather than risk war, Chamberlain and Daladier met Hitler in Munich, with Mussolini acting as mediator. Tellingly, the Soviet Union and Czechoslovakia were not invited to attend. The Western leaders, bent on conserving peace *à outrance*, agreed to go along with Hitler's plans, and the Czechs were browbeaten into surrendering the territory the Germans wanted. Some, such as Bonnet and Chamberlain, thought that peace had been preserved. In fact, war had only been postponed. A new western retreat emboldened the insatiable Fascist appetite and, thereafter, a powerful and greater Reich would be even less inclined towards peace. Nevertheless, relieved British and French crowds enthusiastically welcomed back their leaders. There were, however, no celebrations at Negrín's headquarters. In all but name, the death sentence of the Republic had been sealed in Munich.

## Curtains

On 16 November 1938 the last Republican fighters retreated back across the River Ebro, putting an end to the battle. It had taken the Nationalists almost four months to expel them from the territory captured in July. They could feel proud that they had for so long withstood all the offensives of an army which outgunned them so massively. In the end, moreover, they had not been routed and the final withdrawal had been a tidy operation.[53] And yet the outcome could not have been more favourable to Franco. The Ebro campaign had been the sort of war of annihilation that he had always pursued. The human toll was the heaviest of the entire war: the Republicans had some 70,000 casualties and the Nationalists 60,000.[54] However, it was the solution of the Czech crisis, rather than the human slaughter, which accelerated the end of the war. All at once, the Republic's hopes of being rescued by the Western democracies – or, at the very least, of the implementation of genuine non-intervention – had been shattered. In turn, Franco knew that total victory was within his grasp. In early October a triumphal Duke of Alba cabled from London confirming that Franco's declaration of neutrality the previous month had been welcomed by the British government. On a personal level, one of the leading members of the Chamberlain administration, Lord Hailsham, had confided to Alba that the British cabinet was looking forward to a Nationalist victory, which he described as 'the final act of an European peace'.[55]

In late 1938 the two Spanish zones could not have presented more contrasting images. Whereas in Nationalist Spain there was an abundance of food, fuel and basic goods, war-weariness and material privations ravaged the Republic. The humanitarian situation in the Republican zone was reaching alarming proportions. Severe rationing and shortages caused despair in the rear where the civilian population had to endure long queues, poor diets and constant bombardment. At night, gangs of women in places such as Valencia foraged the countryside and the docks in search of food. Simultaneously, fifth columnists, emboldened by the course of the war, began to operate with increasing audacity in the streets and garrisons, encouraging defeatism and fuelling the mood against continued resistance.[56] The future also appeared bleak in military terms. Both armies were exhausted after the gruelling Battle of the Ebro. However, whereas the Republic had used up some of its best troops and matériel, which could never be replaced, Franco could afford the appalling losses.

Still undeterred by the dire military and diplomatic scene, once again Negrín resorted to the Soviet Union. In early December he sent the Chief of the Republican Air Force, General Ignacio Hidalgo Cisneros, to Moscow with a personal letter (dated 11 November) for Stalin, requesting a new dispatch of weapons. In the warmest terms, Negrín described the Soviet leader as the Republic's last chance to hold on. He stressed that Spain was the last bulwark of democracy before the outbreak of a major war between democratic and totalitarian powers which he considered imminent 'unless there were new sickening capitulations'. The Prime Minister recognised that the Republic's worst enemy had been Chamberlain. In turn, he said, the feeble Daladier had allowed British interests to dictate French foreign policy.[57]

Stalin did not need to be lectured on the current international situation. He had already drawn crucial conclusions from Munich. Indeed, dismayed by the outcome of the Czech crisis, he was already beginning to test the possibility of a rapprochement with Germany which, in August 1939, would finally lead to the conclusion of the non-aggression pact between the Soviet Union and Germany. The Allies were perplexed. However, the Soviets were simply showing that they could also play the appeasement game. That, though, was in the future. In late 1938 the Fascist danger was still a reality and Stalin had not yet written off the Republic. Despite the exhaustion of Spanish gold reserves in Moscow, the Soviet Union attended to Negrín's petition and dispatched massive military supplies (40 T-26 tanks, 134 planes, 359 artillery cannon with over a million shells, 3000 machine-guns, 40,000 rifles with 1 million cartridges, etc.) worth 55 million dollars. However, this matériel arrived in France only in January 1939, by when it was too late to alter the course of the war. Moreover, most of the equipment never even reached its destination.[58]

In contrast, Franco, although not without his own problems, could rapidly restore his depleted stocks of matériel. After more than two years as the Nationalists' main source of armament, Italy was exhausted. Furthermore, on 15 October 1938, still incensed by the 'betrayal' of September, Mussolini even withdrew 10,000 troops. It was the symbolic gesture of 'goodwill' that enabled Chamberlain to implement the agreement of the previous Easter on 16 November (the day in which the Battle of the Ebro ended).[59] Far from placating their ambitions, the emboldened Italians saw this as proof of a Western decline. On 30 November black-shirted deputies interrupted Ciano's speech to the Fascist Grand Council with demands for the return of Italy's historical territories now in French hands (Nice, Corsica, Tunisia, etc.).[60] However, the *Duce* was not prepared to abandon his Spanish adventure. When Franco wrote to him in October 1938 with his usual flattery, explaining the circumstances that had forced him to take a neutral stance, Mussolini reassured him that Italy intended to see their common crusade through to its successful conclusion. Some 30,000 Italian 'volunteers' remained on Spanish soil and, more crucially for the Nationalists, their mechanised divisions and air force were resupplied.[61]

In fact, it was Hitler, already preparing his new coup in Eastern Europe (in Poland), who was most anxious to see the end of the Spanish adventure. However, unlike the *Duce*, the German dictator would, first, extract massive economic gains. For months the Nationalist authorities had successfully staved off Hermann Göring's 'Montana project', the code-name for the purchase and control of substantial mining rights in Spain. But now, in the autumn of 1938, the Nazis made the replenishment of the Condor Legion and the delivery of new important military supplies (50,000 rifles, 1500 light and 500 heavy machine-guns, 100 75-mm guns, etc.) conditional upon the acceptance of their economic demands. Aware of the dire situation of their matériel reserves, the Nationalists complied, and Franco's foreign minister, General Jordana, confirmed the granting of exploitation rights in over two hundred mines.[62]

The rapid re-equipment of their troops in the autumn of 1938 enabled the Nationalists to break the military stalemate at the Ebro. Then, on 23 December, Franco initiated the final push into Cataluña. For that operation he assembled the largest military concentration seen in the war: 300,000 soldiers, 300 tanks, 500 planes and 1000 pieces of artillery. Starved of supplies and heavily outgunned, the Republican defences collapsed after three weeks of dogged resistance. By mid-January 1939 the Nationalist troops had broken the front lines and were advancing towards Barcelona.[63] In a desperate attempt to divert the Nationalists from completing their conquest of Cataluña, in early January the Republic launched a new offensive in Extremadura. It had no effect on the march of the war. After some initial inroads, the attack fizzled out in a few days and, after two weeks of heavy fighting, the Republican army was pushed back to its initial positions.[64] On the verge of total defeat, Negrín pleaded to France for aid. The Republican Prime Minister argued that the French government, by helping to defend Cataluña, would be protecting its own country. On 15 January, after agonising hesitations, Daladier agreed to reopen the frontier so that trains loaded with the recently dispatched Soviet weapons could arrive in Cataluña.[65] It was too little and too late. By then the Republican army had been routed and was no longer an effective fighting force. Nothing short of fully-fledged French intervention could prevent the Republic's military débâcle. And this was not an option. The British, who were always ready to stop French 'adventurism', informed Daladier that Ciano had warned that any last-minute intervention in Spain would risk a European war. Mussolini was boasting of being ready to send Italian divisions to Spain, regardless of the consequences.[66] Appeasement was coming full circle. After two years of shameless surrenders, it was not the advance of Axis forces towards the Franco-Spanish frontier but the potential French reaction which imperilled peace! By then, however, while Daladier hesitated but still retained a certain sympathy for the Republic's cause, Bonnet was beginning to impose his line and to explore ways of gaining the favour of the Nationalist victors.[67]

In early 1939 the popular heroism and stubbornness which had saved Madrid two years earlier was absent in Barcelona. There was no timely arrival of Soviet weapons and foreign volunteers. Not only was the Catalan capital starved of food, packed with refugees and constantly blasted by bombs, but also the Munich agreement had crushed any hopes of international sympathy and sparked widespread demoralisation. Once the front was broken, in mid-January 1939, the bulk of the Republican army simply disintegrated. Large numbers of the badly armed soldiers, in many cases just recently called up, took advantage of the fast retreat to desert throughout the Catalan countryside, hiding in haystacks or the houses of sympathetic villagers.[68] On 26 January Barcelona fell without resistance. Finally there was rejoicing for the thousands of secret Francoist supporters who had been constantly in fear of their lives. Many Catalans, exhausted by privations and war-weariness, welcomed with resignation what they hoped was an end to the nightmare. However, for the hundreds of thousands identified with the Republic, the nightmare had just begun. The Catalan language, together with any manifestation of Catalan culture and traditions, was immediately banned. The new authorities ordered everybody to speak Castilian, 'the language of the empire'. By early February the frontier was a scene of tragedy. The remnants of the Republic's army in Cataluña, Republican politicians, government workers and a vast number of civilian refugees (in total half a million people) fled towards the border. People of all ages, with the few possessions that they had been able to salvage, continued their odyssey along frozen roads, spurred on by the fear that the Moors and the Fascists were close behind.[69]

On 1 February the rump of the Republican parliament (64 deputies) reconvened in the castle of Figueras (Girona) for its last meeting on Spanish soil. Negrín gave a lengthy speech in which he underlined his three conditions for peace: a guarantee of Spanish independence from foreign interference; a popular plebiscite on the structure of the regime; and a guarantee of no reprisals or persecutions after the war.[70] During the next few days the Republican potentates crossed the Pyrenees. On 10 February the Nationalists reached the border.

The Republican military débâcle was soon accompanied by a diplomatic death-blow. On 27 February 1939 Britain and France officially recognised Franco's Spain. Under pressure from their British counterparts, lingering French doubts had been dispelled by the outcome of the secret mission of the right-wing senator Léon Bérard in Burgos. France agreed to return to Franco's Spain whatever part of the Spanish patrimony (arms, treasures, money, etc.) remained on its territory and to prevent the mounting of any Republican military operation from French soil. In return, the Nationalists promised to establish friendly relations and to practice a policy of loyal collaboration in Morocco.[71] More or less at the same time, almost without notice, the NIC was being dismantled. It had achieved its objective of marginalising the Spanish problem but had also ensured the Republic's isolation and defeat. On 16 January 1939 Sir Robert Vansittart, chief diplomatic officer at the British Foreign Office, noted:

> The whole course of our policy on non-intervention has in reality, as we all know, worked in an entirely one-sided manner, and has been putting a premium on Franco's victory … It was only a question of time … pressing the French to close their frontier while consenting the Italians to do as they pleased.[72]

Indeed, without the asphyxiating arms embargo imposed by the NIA while simultaneously turning a blind eye to the flagrant military and economic assistance provided by the Axis to the Nationalists, the outcome of the conflict would have been very different and certainly far from the total victory that Franco contemplated in February 1939.[73] Alvarez del Vayo could not have been more accurate when he compared the browbeating of the Czechs by the Western powers to surrender the Sudetenland in September 1938 to their unwillingness to stop the adventurism of the Axis powers in Spain:

> The London [Non-Intervention] Committee was the equivalent of Munich. It was the finest example of the art of handing victims over to the aggressor States, while preserving the perfect manners of a gentleman and at the same time giving the impression that peace is the one objective and consideration.[74]

On 28 February a despairing Azaña resigned from office. As president of parliament, Diego Martínez Barrios agreed to occupy temporarily the post of president of the Republic, although not without some hesitation.[75] Neither of them was prepared to join Negrín who, refusing to accept defeat, had gone back to Spain on 10 February. His justification was simple: 'How could the government, after preaching resistance for so long, abandon to their fate those still under arms?'[76]

Negrín was not a fool. He was aware that the Republicans could not dream of mounting a victorious offensive. Nevertheless, the Republic still controlled the central–south-eastern zone. This Republican redoubt encompassed one-third of the country, included the cities of Madrid and Valencia, and had a population of 10 million people and an army of half a million men. At best, Negrín planned to make a last-ditch stand between Madrid and Valencia and, hopefully, to hold out there until a general war broke out in Europe. If this did not materialise, then at least by prolonging the resistance he might force the Nationalists not to take their victory for granted and to accept negotiations, while creating the time and space to structure a staged Republican retreat.[77] Meeting Negrín before his return to Spain, Zugazagoitia was certain that the Prime Minister's main objective was, at the very least, before conceding defeat, to force the enemy to provide guarantees for the safe evacuation of those Republicans whose lives could be in danger.[78]

Negrín's stature as a statesman was confirmed by the fact that he could see beyond the despair, complexity and uncertainty of the moment to the near certainty that, without previous guarantees or international mediation, the civilian population in the remaining Republican territory was destined to enjoy a peace based only on the cruel vengeance of the victor.[79] He knew that there was no alternative. The rhetoric and the deeds of the Nationalist leadership left little room for doubt about what it had in mind if the Republic were crushed militarily. Franco had emphasised often enough that he sought the extermination of his enemies.[80] On 13 February 1939, with victory within his grasp, the *Caudillo* made it starkly clear that there could be no thought of amnesty or reconciliation for the defeated Republicans, whom he referred to as 'criminals'. On the same day he introduced the Law of Political Responsibilities, which declared supporters of the Republic guilty of siding with an 'illegitimate' political system. The law was retroactive to October 1934 and declared membership of Popular Front parties to be a crime. It was a foretaste of the kind of peace that Franco had in mind: draconian repression in which mass executions, labour camps and persecution would be the fate of the vanquished.[81]

Negrín's efforts to rekindle resistance were futile. In early 1939 all the Popular Front parties were thoroughly divided. The executives of both the PSOE and the UGT, led by Ramón Lamoneda and Ramón González Peña respectively, were in the hands of supporters of the Prime Minister, and the Anarcho-syndicalist national committee under its secretary general, Mariano Vázquez, followed a loyalist course. With greater or lesser reluctance, they backed the government well up to the Catalan débâcle. However, they were based in Barcelona and, after crossing the border, most of them chose exile. Meanwhile, within all the political forces, shell-shocked and demoralised by the course of the war, there were growing voices of dissent against their executives, deep resentment against the Communists' aggressive proselytism and calls in favour of seeking a rapid end to the tragedy. Only the PCE remained united behind the official policy of continued resistance, and its political and military leaders followed the government back to Spain. The cabinet finally established its headquarters in the small town of Elda (Alicante). Negrín would later be accused of surrounding himself with Communists; in fact, they were practically the only people prepared to return with him.[82]

After 30 months of combat, the central–south-eastern zone was plagued by defeatism and low morale. Surrounded by the enemy, this territory had been cut off from the Republican leadership since the spring of 1938 and had been spared the major military operations. Nevertheless, material privations, physical exhaustion and the blow suffered at Munich had fatally undermined civilian expectations.

Nowhere was this situation more desperate than in Madrid. By early 1939 this city was no longer the bulwark of courage and resistance that it had once been. Under siege since November 1936, the morale of the population had plummeted under constant bombardment and growing misery. Orphaned of political leadership during all this time, the city was a natural terrain for the activities of a fifth column that was well infiltrated into the administration and armed forces. During these long months, growing food and fuel shortages had intensified feelings of isolation and despair. It was this increasing hardship and hunger which finally undermined the Republic's legitimacy on the home front.[83]

On 16 February the Prime Minister met the Republican army commanders in the aerodrome of Los Llanos (Albacete). All, with the exception of General Miaja, painted a bleak picture of shortages, low morale and widespread defeatism. They all agreed that there was no point in attempting further resistance. Nevertheless, Negrín tried to explain that he was not opposed to seeking peace on honourable terms through mediation. Indeed, in the autumn of 1938 he had for that purpose met secretly with the German ambassador in Paris, Count Johannes von Welczeck. The disappointing results of that liaison, however, had only strengthened his belief that Franco was bent on the complete annihilation of his enemies. He concluded that the only alternative to continuing the war was unconditional surrender. It was imperative to keep on fighting, therefore, since only from a position of strength and mass resistance might the Republic extract concessions. Channels with the enemy should remain open but secret. Otherwise, it would lead to the final disintegration of the Republican army as a standing force and, in turn, to a catastrophic defeat.[84]

In fact, by the time of the meeting at Los Llanos, a coup was in progress against the Republican leader. The political intrigues and hostility of the previous year between Azaña and Negrín now gave way to a fully-fledged plot to oust the government, by force if necessary, and to seek an end to the war. The rebellion represented the collusion between army officers and some increasingly disenchanted sectors from the political forces – Republicans, Socialists and Anarcho-syndicalists among them. After the Munich agreement and the loss of Cataluña, they all believed that continued resistance was close to lunacy. Furthermore, they were united by their hostility towards the government and the Communist Party. Having reached the conclusion that the war was already lost and that the slaughter should be halted, they all ranged together against a PCE that was perceived as excessively influential in the military cadres and administrative bodies.[85] For two years army officers and political parties had tolerated the Communists' aggressive recruitment and coercive practices for the sake of winning the war. Now, however, the PCE was blamed for the recent defeats, and the myth that the Prime Minister was a puppet in its hands gained widespread credence.[86] Consequently, Negrín and the PCE, once accepted as vital to the Republic's survival, were now considered the stumbling-block to a negotiated settlement. They represented the party of a futile war. The calls for 'resistance to the death' from some Communist leaders in Madrid only increased their isolation, as the party became a target for the anti-war feelings of growing sectors of the political parties and the war-weary population.[87]

Colonel Segismundo Casado, commander of the Republican army of the centre, was the architect of the conspiracy. Like many other army officers, Casado had concluded, at least since the end of the Battle of the Ebro, that the Republic was fighting a lost cause. Additionally imbued with profound anti-Communist feelings, he believed that overthrowing the government and destroying the PCE's influence would ingratiate him with his brother officers in the Nationalist camp. However, while Casado naively dreamt of finding a compromise solution to the conflict, Franco only believed in a total victory and thus in the unconditional surrender of his enemies.[88]

Aware of Casado's defeatist mood, in November 1938 members of Madrid's fifth column had approached his brother, César, a lieutenant-colonel in the cavalry. By February 1939 Casado was in permanent contact with leading fifth columnists (shockingly, they included one of his assistants, Colonel José Centaño, and his personal doctor, Diego Medina) who kept Franco's headquarters fully briefed of the conspiracy. Either expressing his own feelings or attempting to endear himself to the enemy, Centaño noted that Casado stressed his own hatred of Masons (such as Azaña), Reds and Jews, the usual bêtes noires of the Nationalist discourse.[89] Meanwhile, Casado gradually obtained the support of many professional officers as well as leading members of the political parties in Madrid. Most importantly, he secured the backing of the Anarchist leader, Cipriano Mera, the commander of the 4th army corps.[90]

The most prominent of all the politicians to lend his support was Julián Besteiro, the veteran Socialist leader, who had remained in Madrid throughout the war, refusing numerous opportunities to seek safe exile, and who had become a fierce exponent of defeatism and anti-Communism. He did not need much convincing to subscribe to the thesis that the government was under the thumb of the Communists and was leading Spain to catastrophe. Despite all his differences with Negrín and his mistrust of the PCE, on 19 November 1938 Azaña showed concern in his diary at Besteiro's rabid anti-Communism and at his opinion that Negrín was a mere stooge of Moscow, acting as a Trojan horse in the PSOE. But of course, as Azaña's brother-in-law Cipriano Rivas Cheriff noted, the Republican president would never act like Besteiro and offer legitimacy to a military coup against the constitutional legality that was reminiscent of nothing so much as the uprising of July 1936.[91]

It seems difficult to believe that Casado, Besteiro and their fellow conspirators were unaware of the scale of Nationalist repression. However, physical exhaustion and despair might explain their unprecedented levels of naivety and the irresponsibility that caused them to underestimate the horrific reality in the other zone. They easily fell prey to all kinds of delusions. In particular, they fooled themselves into believing that they could reach an 'honourable peace' with Franco, once Negrín and the Communists were deposed. In his naive belief that he had been called for the higher purpose of stopping the bloodshed, Besteiro had been in touch with the fifth column since the spring of 1938 – meetings facilitated by the fact that some secret Nationalist agents were members of the university. Besteiro seems even to have imagined that Franco's regime would be similar to the paternalist dictatorship of Primo de Rivera and, thus, that a reformed UGT, purged of revolutionaries, would be allowed to function.[92]

In turn, the Battle of the Ebro and the subsequent retreat of a mostly Communist-led army tilted the balance against the government for many professional officers. The same opportunism which in the past had allowed some of them even to accept PCE membership now turned into resentment.[93] Spurred on by the fifth-column agents, Casado and other officers deluded themselves in the hope that, unlike Negrín, they could obtain a *paz digna* (honourable peace). Nationalist headquarters had expressed their intention to show magnanimity to those prepared to render 'good services to the cause of Spain'. And what better service could be rendered, the rebel Republican officers might have thought, than that of crushing Communism![94] They even began to think that the fratricidal strife could end in a similar fashion to that other cruel civil war of the previous century, the first Carlist War. Then, in 1839, the commanders of both armies had put aside political differences and terminated the slaughter with an embrace (the '*abrazo de Vergara*'). The Carlist officers had even conserved their ranks and commissions in the new post-war army.[95] Delusions were also kept alive by contacts with British intelligence agents such as Denys Cowan, who had been aboard the British cruiser HMS *Devonshire* on 7 February 1939 as negotiations were taking place in order to obtain the surrender of Menorca. Two days later the Nationalists seized control of the Balearic island while the Republican governor and some six hundred combatants left for exile on the *Devonshire*. The example of Menorca might have encouraged Casado to believe that a similar process would then be applied to the rest of the Republican zone.[96] By then, however, Casado was determined to ignore or to play down all proof of the Nationalist plans for the vanquished. Indeed, if anything, Franco was consistent in his reiteration that he wanted only the total and unconditional defeat of the enemy. With victory within his grasp, Menorca was an isolated case and far away from the central battleground; 30 per cent of mainland Spain was an altogether different affair.

Events gathered momentum following the publication on 3 March 1939 of a series of promotions in the armed forces. The plotters would later cultivate the myth that Negrín was effectively handing the army over to the Communists. In fact, nothing could have been further from the truth. In order to keep resistance alive, the Prime Minister would have been fully justified in relieving of their posts those defeatist officers of Los Llanos and replacing them with determined and courageous men, and at that stage he could mainly rely only on Communists. However, within the list of new appointments, Communists were only promoted to take command of Cartagena, Murcia, Albacete and Alicante – all places near the Mediterranean coast. The conclusion was evident: trustworthy officers would be in charge of holding on to key positions when there was a general evacuation. Nevertheless, it rang alarm bells amongst those who had already decided that Negrín was a Communist puppet. The plotters might have also been worried by the fact that some of them had been promoted but only to positions on the general staff without effective command. It was déjà vu: as in July 1936, the military could now distort the reality in order to claim that their coup against the constitutional legality was only a gallant effort to pre-empt a Communist take-over.[97]

On 4 March, Republican officers revolted in Cartagena in order to prevent the Communist Colonel Francisco Galán from taking control of that vital naval base. In the bizarre unfolding of events, to their embarrassment, the conspirators soon realised that their initiative had given a number of fifth columnists in the military the opportunity to mount their own coup and to take control of key positions in the city. After more than twenty-four hours of heavy fighting, Republican reinforcements rushed to Cartagena and regained control for the government. However, amidst the reigning confusion, the fleet (in order to avoid capture) departed from its base and eventually surrendered to the French authorities in Bizerta (Tunisia). With one stroke, the Republic had been deprived of the means to carry out a potential evacuation. Ironically, the Cartagena affair also ended with a minor disaster for the Nationalists. Confident that their supporters were on the point of seizing control of the city, they sent two warships with landing troops. Hence they were surprised when the coastal batteries opened fire. *El Castillo de Olite* was sunk and 1270 soldiers perished and another 700 were captured. *El Castillo de Peñafiel* was hit but managed to escape with 4 dead and 25 wounded.[98]

On the evening of 5 March, with the battle still raging in Cartagena, Casado made his move. In the cellars of the old treasury ministry he established the Council of National Defence, with representatives of all the major parties in Madrid except the PCE. In the middle of having supper in Elda, the government was surprised by a radio transmission from Madrid. The leading speaker was Julián Besteiro, who had accepted the post of foreign minister in the Council. The veteran Socialist made clear the objectives of the conspirators. He claimed that the existing cabinet no longer enjoyed moral authority or political legality, which now rested only with the military. The Council had, therefore, seized power in order to initiate a dialogue with the enemy to put an end to the ongoing slaughter. During the next frenzied hours Negrín talked to Casado on the telephone while the ministers engaged with their own political counterparts. However, there was no turning back.[99] Having failed to dissuade the plotters, Negrín understood that the game was up. Only after a bitter struggle which the government was unlikely to win could the rebellion be crushed. However, by then the war would have been lost. On 6 March, Negrín and his ministers fled by plane. They would never return. Communist leaders and agents of the Comintern followed suit.

Counting on the sympathy of most professional officers, Casado's coup went smoothly in most of what was left of Republican Spain. Ironically, the prompt success of the rebellion deflated the myth that the army had been under Communist control. Many officers who had joined the PCE immediately deserted it, demonstrating that they carried the party card merely for opportunistic reasons (career advancement, political protection against the early days revolutionary excesses, etc.).[100] In fact, there was hardly any resistance against the rebellion, since, by then, the Communists' priority was to save as many of their cadres as possible and let Casado proceed with his plan. Thus, in most places Communists sought an accommodation with the Council. The exception was Madrid, where the isolation of the local Communists from their fleeing leadership, combined with Casado's stringent measures against them as a means of establishing a set of credentials acceptable to Franco, sparked a mini-civil war when some army contingents sought to crush the Council.[101] For over a week Communist troops fought supporters of Casado for control of the capital. Again, in a new ironic twist, those who had been the protagonists of a revolt accused those fighting on behalf of the legal government of rebellion. In fact, after three days of combat, Casado's forces were on the verge of defeat. By then, however, news of the departure of the government and the Communist leaders left the loyalist side immersed in doubts and without clear objectives or direction. Tellingly, the Council asked the Nationalist headquarters for help. Franco only complied half-heartedly, mounting some attacks against the positions manned by the enemies of Casado. Indeed, the *Caudillo* was not thinking – at least not yet – of seizing the capital. He was, in fact, delighted to observe Republican forces tearing each other apart and, in the process, destroying any possibility of mounting any meaningful resistance thereafter. Eventually, the intervention of the 4th army corps, led by the Anarchist Mera, tilted the balance in favour of the Council. The battle for Madrid had resulted in thousands of casualties but, more importantly, it signalled the end of the Republican army as a fighting force.[102]

On 12 March the triumphant Council attempted to initiate negotiations with the Nationalist headquarters. It was not long before its euphoria evaporated. In fact, during the next two weeks the bankruptcy of Casado's plans was brutally exposed. All demands for time to organise the evacuation and for assurances of no reprisals – conditions that echoed those of Negrín – were dismissed. Franco simply reiterated what had always been his goal: unconditional surrender. The *Caudillo* was bent on humiliating the enemy and would not even let the Council mask its embarrassment with a meaningless treaty.[103] In a few days Casado had ruined the possibility of further resistance and had rendered pointless the bloodshed and sacrifices of the previous three years.

On 26 March the Nationalists resumed the offensive virtually unopposed. Republican troops deserted en masse, while many others escaped towards the coast in a final – and in most cases futile – attempt to escape abroad.[104] When the capital was occupied two days later,

Ciano noted that Fascism had won its most formidable victory to date.[105] On 1 April 1939 the *Caudillo* announced the end of the war: 'Today, with the Red Army captive and disarmed, our victorious troops had achieved their final military objectives. The war is over', he boasted.[106]

# 7

# Epilogue: The Legacy of the Spanish Civil War

I believe there are or might be in Spain as many Fascists as you want. Yet there will be no Fascist regime ... We will fall back on a military or ecclesiastical dictatorship of a traditional type. No matter how many slogans they might put forward ... this country can only produce swords, cassocks, military parades and homages to the Virgin of the Pilar.[1]

## The death of history

In July 1936 hardly anyone in Spain could have predicted that the military rebellion would develop into such a cruel and protracted fratricidal struggle. Even less could it have been imagined that General Franco would preside over a dictatorship that would last nearly 40 years. Largo Caballero wrote that, based on the evidence of the Spanish Civil War, Franco could not go down in history as a great army leader. Despite thousands of Moorish mercenaries, massive Axis aid and even the farce of non-intervention, it had taken the Nationalists almost three years to defeat badly armed militiamen.[2] Though Largo's verdict might have been accurate, he was missing the point.

Truth was the first casualty of the new order. Franco's Spain set out to accomplish massive cultural revisionism. Teachers, academics and writers – the liberal intelligentsia, in general, were purged from their positions. Instead, a huge propaganda apparatus was established to offer a Manichean view of the past. Reminiscent of medieval times, the Catholic Church enthusiastically lent its might and influence to legitimise the mythical foundations of the new regime. History was rewritten and, for 40 years the population (and particularly children) learnt that there had been not a fratricidal strife but a war of national liberation against the Moscow hordes. Nationalist Spain was praised as the successor of the grandiose and imperial Castilla of the *Reconquista*, the Catholic Kings (Ferdinand of Aragón and Isabella of Castilla) and Philip II, all of which had suffered a long period of decline with the arrival of the foreign ideas of enlightenment and liberalism introduced by the weak Bourbons. Franco himself was portrayed as the '*Caudillo invicto*' ('undefeated chieftain') who had led a glorious crusade to overthrow the Reds, the Masons, the Jews and the separatists who had been leading the nation to catastrophe. Of course, the role played by the Axis powers and the Moorish mercenaries was minimised. Instead, the Nationalist victory acquired an epic dimension: the 'modern crusaders' had fought and defeated the barbaric Muscovite hordes who had invaded Spain.[3]

Other blatant manipulations of events also became fundamental canons of the new order. For instance, the Spanish dictator would be hailed as the cunning and zealous leader who had outwitted Hitler and thus spared Spain the ordeals of the Second World War.[4] In fact, Franco's non-belligerence could not have been more removed from real neutrality. The wartime Spanish media was saturated with propaganda which acclaimed every Nazi victory, German submarines received unrestricted aid, the Gestapo collaborated with the Spanish police and Nazi intelligence services operated at will in Spain. The *Caudillo* saw himself as a comrade in arms of Hitler and Mussolini and despised the Western democracies. He wished for a German victory, helped the Axis as much as he could and even pushed for Spain's entry into the war. The British ambassador, Sir Samuel Hoare, who incidentally had been a supporter of the Nationalists when a member of the Chamberlain government, recounted in his memoirs how he had had to endure constant discourtesies: the pro-Axis speeches of ministers, the constant harassment of his staff, the hostility of Falangist mobs and, finally, meeting the *Caudillo*, whose desk was flanked by signed photographs of Mussolini and Hitler.[5] Spain's final non-involvement in the war was not due to the immense skill and vision of the Spanish dictator but to a combination of circumstances in which luck as well as external factors beyond Franco's control were crucial: the dire economic reality that did not permit new military adventures, the unexpected resistance of Britain and, above all, the disinterest of Hitler in seeing Spain on the battlefield. Had the German dictator exerted pressure or show a willingness to satisfy Franco's imperialist demands (encompassing large chunks of the territory in North Africa under Vichy France), Spain would have joined the Axis. However, following disastrous Italian campaigns in the Balkans and Libya in late 1940, Hitler, by then planning his next big enterprise (the invasion of the Soviet Union), had concluded that it was better to have a benevolent friend than another costly and inefficient ally.[6] Nevertheless, Nationalist Spain sent a contingent of 47,000 volunteers ('the Blue Division') to fight on the eastern front so that, in Franco's words, 'they can join the battle for which Christianity has for so many years longed and in which the blood of our youth will now mingle with that of the Axis as a living expression of our solidarity'.[7]

After the Second World War, the Francoist regime was the only state in Europe whose origins and nature were closely associated with the defeated Axis. However, in relation to other urgent political questions, its fate was perceived by the great powers as a marginal issue in the troubled post-war period.[8] Thus, international pressure never went beyond the withdrawal of ambassadors and symbolic acts of ostracism and never developed into a sustained and vigorous campaign to unseat the Spanish dictator. Soon thereafter the outbreak of the Cold War guaranteed the survival and even consolidation of Franco's regime. In September 1953 the signing of a treaty of mutual defence assistance and other accords with the United States ensured the return of Spain to the fold of the international community. Official propaganda spared no effort in demonstrating that the world had finally recognised the legitimacy of Nationalist Spain. If, in 1941, the Spanish Civil War had been hailed as the first battle against the decadent plutocracies, now it was described as the first victory against Soviet aggression. The *Caudillo*, the successful warrior against the Communist threat, was lauded as the 'Sentry of the West'.[9]

Nonetheless, the most pervasive and cynical of all the myths of this era was the insistence that Franco's victory had initiated a golden era of peace in Spain.

### The pact of blood

Modern scholars have often been bogged down in a debate, in my opinion largely sterile, on the extent to which Franco's political order was Fascist. The label given to a regime is a secondary matter. Fascist or not, the record of internal repression in Nationalist Spain, if anything, surpassed that of Hitler's Germany and Mussolini's Italy.

The Francoist order counted on a base of genuine mass support: the Catholic smallholders and farmers of northern Spain, the large landowners of the south, the urban industrial and propertied classes and, in general, the many who had been alarmed by the revolutionary upheaval of the previous years. The National Movement itself was a bloated bureaucracy that guaranteed career advancement and job safety to hundreds of thousands. The *Caudillo* was the head of a very pragmatic governing coalition of different forces ('families', in the regime's later rhetoric) brought together during the war years. This coalition represented the same anti-democratic and counter-revolutionary alliance which had emerged to seize state power in Italy and Germany. Franco's Spain was also based on a single party, resorted to a widespread use of terror and copied its leadership principles, economic autarky and even a large part of its choreography, legislation and rhetoric from Fascism. Nevertheless, the correlation of forces in Spain was not exactly favourable to the Fascist party itself. On the contrary, the original Falange had been a relative loser vis-à-vis the other conservative and indeed 'fascistised' groups. Furthermore, the regime never pursued the popular mobilisation and aggressive foreign policy of Germany and Italy. Neither did the *Caudillo* base his authority on the strength of the party; rather, he held power as Generalissimo of the army and 'by the grace of God'.[10] Azaña was, thus, correct in suggesting that no 'pure' Fascist order would be created in Spain but instead one in which the habitual forces of reaction – 'cassocks and swords' – would play a dominant role. However, the Republican president was wrong in believing that it would be a traditional type of dictatorship.

For all the propaganda, the Nationalist victory did not usher in a period of peace. On the contrary, under Franco there would never be any forgiving – only the perpetuation of the climate of the civil war and the institutionalisation of full-scale vengeance. All the Francoist families were inextricably linked by the so-called 'Pact of Blood': that is, their active complicity in the ongoing savage repression and their shared authoritarian values.[11] Franco's Spain never saw the *abrazo de Vergara* that Casado and Besteiro had naively expected. For 40 years society was divided between the patriots of 'Real Spain' and the 'Communist scum' who had supported 'Godless anti-Spain'. For the latter, the only possible peace was that of prison, exile or the cemeteries.[12] Unlike the paternalism that had characterised the regime of Primo de Rivera in the 1920s, the dictatorship of General Franco was one of the cruellest in twentieth-century Europe. The weakness of the Spanish Fascist Party did not make Nationalist Spain less repressive or vindictive. If anything, the opposite was true. The brutal persecution of its own domestic population went much further than that of Nazi Germany and far surpassed that of Mussolini's Italy. Unlike the Fascist states, with public order in the hands of *Africanistas*, energies were not to be spent in attempts to integrate and mobilise the labouring classes. The enemy had to be vanquished, imprisoned or terrorised into submission as the colonial natives had previously been. In turn, a crusading Church blessed the reigning terror, as it had during the *Reconquista*.[13]

In recent years the meticulous research carried out by Spanish scholars on the Francoist repression in different provinces indicates that at least 150,000 people were killed. However, the exact figures will probably never be known. The Nationalist authorities had nearly forty years to hide all traces of their 'justice'. Thousands of Spaniards went 'missing' and their deaths were not registered, and there were many others listed as having died from all sorts of mysterious diseases and accidents.[14]

### *Vae Victis!*

For all those who had fought for the Republic, 1 April 1939 meant the beginning of a long nightmarish journey. For the hundreds of thousands of Spaniards who fled into exile, it was the beginning of a long diaspora. Scattered and divided until the early 1970s, bitter recriminations marked the history of the Republican political leadership. In August 1945 a semblance of government in exile (excluding the Communists) appeared under the leadership of José Giral in Mexico. Recognised only by the Mexicans, Republican politicians remained there in their insular world, totally disconnected from events in Spain, while other rival political groups established themselves in France or in the Soviet Union.

For the many who did not manage to reach the safety of Mexico, years of persecution and misery awaited them in Europe. Unprepared for such a human avalanche, the French administration interned a population of nearly half a million exhausted fugitives in camps where food was scarce and shelter and proper sanitation were lacking. The appalling living conditions were a deliberate invitation for them to escape and return to Spain.[15] Many former soldiers of the Republican army in Cataluña, such as my own grandfather, his two brothers and his brother-in-law, did so. Travelling in small groups, they lived off the compassion of sympathetic French Catalans who gave them food and shelter. They were among the fortunate; many never reached home but perished while crossing the Pyrenees on foot.

The outbreak of World War Two surprised the thousands of Spanish Republicans who, fearing for their lives, had decided to stay in France. Many joined the French Foreign Legion or the labour battalions who helped build the Maginot Line and other fortifications. However, the Nazi occupation of France marked the beginning of a new ordeal for them. Stateless and regarded as politically undesirable, they were not only an obvious target of the Third Reich but also a leading element in the resistance against it. Some, such as the last Catalan president, Lluís Companys, and the ex-ministers Joan Peiró and Julián Zugazagoitia, were rounded up by the Gestapo and delivered to the Spanish authorities. They would be executed. Thousands of Spaniards became slave labourers for the new masters of Europe. Nearly 30,000 were deported to work in Germany. Some 4000 were sent to the Channel Islands to build underground constructions; only 59 of them survived. Over 15,000 Republicans ended up in Nazi concentration camps. Nearly 7000 were exterminated in Mauthausen alone. Largo Caballero was a broken man after the long-drawn-out agony of Sachsenhausen.[16]

After the war a monument was erected in the Père Lachaise cemetery in Paris in homage to the many Spaniards who had lost their lives in the liberation of France. With nowhere to go, thousands of Republicans had no choice but to fight the Nazi occupation. Furthermore, they perceived the war against the Third Reich in France as part of the struggle against Fascism which, of course, included Hitler's comrade in arms, Franco. Thus, they played a central role in the resistance, their recent military experience proving a vital asset when they joined the *maquisards*. Others, like Miralles, the fictional protagonist of the Spanish bestseller, *Soldados de Salamina*, joined the French Free Forces who fought all the way from Africa to Europe.[17] As a reward for their bravery in combat, General Leclerc allowed the Spaniards to be among the first contingent to enter Paris in August 1944. By then they had been fighting, almost without interruption, for over eight years, but their war was far from over. From the summer of 1944, thousands of Republicans crossed the Pyrenees and launched a guerrilla campaign against the Francoist regime. However, let down yet again by the Western democracies, their dream to overthrow the Spanish dictatorship would not be achieved. Lacking heavy weapons and the support of the military might of the Allies, they were no match for the better-armed and organised Francoist forces. The Civil Guard's effective repressive tactics, as well as the impossibility of rousing an exhausted countryside, ensured their isolation and eventual liquidation. By 1951 the Communists, recognising the futility of this strategy, abandoned the armed struggle, although some Anarchists continued fighting until the early 1960s.[18] Paradoxically, the intensification of the guerrilla war after 1945 was a godsend for the regime. With the country ravaged by economic dislocation and ostracised in the international arena, it allowed the perpetuation of the state of emergency and the closing of ranks of the different Nationalist factions.

Franco's peace was as fraudulent as his neutrality in the Second World War. After almost three years of fratricidal strife, the economy was in tatters, the transport system had collapsed and there were critical shortages of food and fuel. These appalling conditions did not deter the triumphant Nationalists from embarking upon an unprecedented programme of repression. For large sectors of the population, the period until the early 1950s was known as *los años de hambre* (the years of hunger); worsening living standards, widespread misery and the rationing of basic staples were the norm. However, the protection of the interests of the social elites whose privileges had been threatened by the Republic's reforms was a priority: wages were slashed, strikes were treated as sabotage (and made punishable by long prison sentences) and the labour movement was regimented under Falangist control.

The war did not finish on 1 April 1939; in fact, it lasted until the dictator's death in 1975. Indeed, the Nationalist victory ushered in years not only of hunger but also of silence and persecution. In 1939 Spain resembled an enormous concentration camp. The Francoist jails had a clear social function: to purge, cleanse and exterminate all the enemies of the motherland, the 'anti-Spain'.[19] Some half a million people whose political reliability was suspect were rounded up and crammed into overcrowded prisons. Military courts worked flat out delivering vindictive sentences. Those who escaped execution had to survive deplorable conditions, including a scarcity of food, poor hygiene and constant humiliations, beatings and torture. Their mail not only underwent strict military censorship but the prisoners also had to write slogans such as 'Vivas to the *Caudillo* and the new regime!' in the margins of their letters.[20] In the best Nazi tradition, those with long sentences were given the chance to redeem their crimes through work. Thus, thousands of Republican prisoners had to join labour battalions who were employed by private companies or by the state. The biggest aberration and insult of all was the construction, between 1940 and

1959, by 20,000 political prisoners, many of whom died or were badly injured in the process, of the so-called '*Valle de los Caidos*' ('Valley of the Fallen'), a gigantic mausoleum to the north-east of Madrid to commemorate those who had died for 'God's cause' and which was to become the burial place of the *Caudillo*.[21]

The climate of collective psychological terror went far beyond the prison walls. Of course, the working class became the main target of state control and repression, but discrimination affected every aspect of people's lives. In order to obtain such vital things as a ration card or a job, it was necessary to provide evidence of loyalty to the new system by means of an official certificate signed by a person who was accredited by the regime (a priest, an army officer or a local heavyweight of the Falange).[22] One has to look back to the Middle Ages to find a time when the clergy possessed similar might and influence. Now, all but in name, the priests became officials of a regime that was rightly described as 'National-Catholic'. The Church controlled the education of children as well as the censorship of the habits of the community, ensuring in the process the eradication of any sign of modernity and dissent. Indeed, the priests were not only propagandists of the state but also acted as policemen who played a leading role in the denunciation of those deemed to be part of the anti-Spain.[23] Thousands were prepared to volunteer information that would almost certainly lead to the imprisonment and even the execution of their neighbours. Ancestral hatreds, the settlement of old scores, the willingness to prove loyalty to the new regime and the expectation of filling the posts and jobs of those denounced were all powerful motivations in these times of persecution.[24] A life of fear, alienation, shortages and depressed salaries did the rest. Those who did not share the principles of the regime were condemned to renounce their past and identity and to seek survival in their silent submission.[25]

**Towards a new Spain**

With the opposition physically eliminated or in exile and Spain back in the international fold, the dictatorship entered a period of normalisation in the 1950s in which the repressive measures of the previous decade were no longer necessary. The *Caudillo* retained all his posts and remained the ultimate arbiter when situations demanded his personal intervention. However, Franco gradually withdrew from the daily

business of politics, began to assume the distant air of a royal person-
age and was regularly portrayed by official propaganda as the tireless
leader, receiving foreign dignitaries, opening dams or factories and
ensuring the welfare and peace of his people. In the late 1950s the
accumulation of native capital and the flood of foreign investment
initiated a massive and sustained economic boom in Spain.

Ironically, it was the rapid economic modernisation on which the
regime prided itself which led to the collapse of the dictatorship. The
opening of frontiers and markets meant the arrival of modern ideas and
values through cinema, literature and tourism. Spaniards learned from,
imitated and identified with the people of Western Europe, their
institutions and their way of life. In the late 1960s and early 1970s the
gap between a modern consumer society and an obsolete state still
anchored on the principles of the crusade widened to the point of no
return. Increasingly, the emergence of a modern, more complex and
plural civil society meant that sectors from without and even within the
regime coincided in regarding the dictatorship as an anachronism and a
hindrance to progress.[26]

Following the death of the *Caudillo* in November 1975, the dismantlement of the dictatorship was successfully accomplished in less
than two years by a cross-class and cross-party consensus between
elements of the old order and the opposition. The new political elites,
heir of those who had fought 40 years earlier, sought to leave the past
behind, to abandon old passions and to start from scratch through an
exercise of collective amnesia that would be known as the *Pacto del
Olvido* (Pact of Forgetfulness).[27]

Drawing a curtain over the past might have been logical for the
political class, but it threatened to enshrine the blatant distortions and
manipulations of the previous regime. It ensured that Spain never had
to undergo the bitter process of self-examination undertaken by many
European countries after 1945. The new democratic climate, however,
has permitted a new generation of scholars since the mid-1980s to
have access for the first time to original sources with which gradually
to undermine the Francoist myths and re-create history as it really
was. At a more popular level, their ground-breaking task has been
aided by a flood of novels, films, television documentaries and
journalistic articles. The new generations of Spaniards certainly do
not want to hold on to the demons of their elders. However, the
fratricidal tragedy and the post-war repression are a vital part of their
collective memory and identity. Like their counterparts in Europe,
they must live in the present and plan for the future but they have

the right to know the truth about a dark age of hatred, violence and terror. Only after having learnt from the passions and errors of their ancestors will they be able to understand and embrace Azaña's message of peace, pity and forgiveness.

# Notes

## 1 The Painful Road to Modernity

1. *España*, no. 203 (27 February 1919).
2. These were a combination of dynastic and social disputes. The Carlists took their name from the pretender Don Carlos, brother of Fernando VII, who rose up against his niece, Isabel II, who was supported by the Liberals. His largest following was in the rural areas of Navarra, the Basque Country, Cataluña and Valencia, where relatively well-off Catholic peasants were opposed to the centralising and anticlerical principles of the new regime. The urban centres, as well as the majority of the landed nobility, sided with the Liberals. The first Carlist war lasted from 1833 to 1840; the second, from 1846 to 1849, was confined to Cataluña; the third and final of them took place between 1872 and 1876.
3. H. Graham and P. Preston (eds), *The Popular Front in Europe* (London: Macmillan, 1987), p. 1.
4. The term 'Generation of 98' was coined by the writer Antonio Azorín in 1913. The diverse ideological leanings of these intellectuals make it difficult to apply the concept of a generation, yet their common call for self-examination and regeneration had a vital influence on subsequent thinking. Leading figures were the novelists Pío Baroja and Antonio Azorín; the essayist Ramiro de Maeztu; the novelist and philosopher Miguel de Unamuno; the philosopher José Ortega y Gasset; and the essayist Joaquín Costa.
5. At the deathbed of Alfonso XII in 1885, the agreement between both parties was formally sealed in the 'Pact of El Pardo'.
6. For instance, the parliament elected in April 1916, packed with family members of all the main dynastic politicians, was dubbed 'the Cortes of Relatives'. See F. Soldevilla, *El año político de 1916* (Madrid: Julio Cosano, 1917), pp. 91–5.
7. Obviously, the state could not be reduced to being simply the instrument of a well-defined and unified 'capitalist' class. It was, rather, an arena in which conflicts between competing factions of the bourgeoisie were regulated. The links between Span's ruling economic classes and governing parties, the so-called Power Bloc (*Bloque de Poder*) has

been documented by M. Tuñón de Lara in *Poder y sociedad en España, 1900–1931* (Madrid: Espasa-Calpe, 1992), pp. 112–17, 210–11. Emphasis on the complex nature of the ties between the economic and political oligarchies is discussed in F. del Rey, *Propietarios y patronos: La política de las organizaciones económicas en la España de la Restauración, 1914–1923* (Madrid: Ministerio del Trabajo y Seguridad Social, 1992), pp. 689–95, and M. Cabrera and F. del Rey, *El poder de los empresarios: Política y economía en la España contemporánea, 1875–2000* (Madrid: Taurus, 2002), pp. 74–5. *El Socialista* (22 April 1916) produced a list of dynastic politicians who were members of the administration boards of banks, railway companies and other leading firms. This editorial ironically commented that the Spanish case could not have adhered more rigidly to the words of Marx and Engels in *The Communist Manifesto* that governments were little more than committees to safeguard the interests of the bourgeoisie.

8.  P. Carasa, 'La Restauración Monárquica (1875–1902)', in A. Bahamonde (ed.), *Historia de España. Siglo XX, 1875–1939* (Madrid: Cátedra, 2000), pp. 45–9.

9.  M. Ballbé, *Orden público y militarismo en la España constitucional, 1812–1983* (Madrid: Alianza, 1985), pp. 247–8.

10. J. Berruezo, *Por el sendero de mis recuerdos* (Santa Coloma: Fernando, 1987), pp. 20–1.

11. The name originally came from the native American chieftains through whose control of certain territory the Spanish had managed to secure vast areas of that continent. S. Cruz Artacho, 'Clientes, clientelas y política en la España de la Restauración (1875–1923)', *Ayer*, 36 (1999), pp. 105–29.

12. T. Carnero, 'Elite gobernante dinástica e igualdad política en España, 1898–1914, *Historia Contemporánea*, 8 (1992), pp. 46–8; B. de Riquer, 'La débil nacionalización española del siglo XIX', *Historia Social*, 20 (1994), pp. 103–12.

13. S. Balfour, *The End of the Spanish Empire, 1898–1923* (Oxford: Oxford University Press, 1997), p. 99.

14. France had 45 per cent of her active population in the primary sector while Britain had 12 per cent. Infant mortality in both countries was approximately 146 per 1000. The proportion of the population aged 18 or under receiving school tuition was 59 per cent in France and 52 in Britain. See L. Prados de la Escosura, *De imperio a nación: Crecimiento y atraso económico en España, 1870–1930* (Madrid: Alianza, 1988), p. 56.

15. G. Tortella, 'Agriculture: A Slow Moving Sector, 1830–1935', in N. Sánchez Albornoz (ed.), *The Economic Modernization of Spain, 1830–1930* (New York: New York University Press, 1987), p. 55.

16. F. J. Romero Salvadó, *Twentieth-Century Spain: Politics and Society in Spain, 1898–1998* (London: Macmillan, 1999), pp. 2–4.

17. A social reforms commission was created in 1883 to recommend labour policies. It was re-named as the *Instituto de Reformas Sociales* in 1902 and was meant to advise on and promote social legislation. Despite its good intentions, the *Instituto* remained grossly underfunded and labour inspections were too few to accomplish their tasks. Furthermore, their legislative recommendations were normally met with hostility or not implemented by the employers. See B. Martin, *The Agony of Modernization: Labor and Industrialization in Spain* (Ithaca, NY: Cornell University Press, 1990), pp. 61–5.

18. P. Heywood, *Marxism and the Failure of Organised Socialism in Spain, 1879–1936* (Cambridge: Cambridge University Press, 1990), pp. 1–18; M. Pérez Ledesma, *Pensamiento Socialista español a comienzos de siglo* (Madrid: Centro, 1974), pp. 26–54; S. Juliá, *Los Socialistas en la política española, 1879–1982* (Madrid: Taurus, 1997), pp. 15–49.

19. For the Basque Country, see J. P. Fusi, *Política obrera en el Pais Vasco, 1880–1923* (Madrid: Tuner, 1975), pp. 82–103; J. M. Eguiguren, *El PSOE en el País Vasco, 1886–1936* (San Sebastián: Haramburu, 1984), pp. 25–6; For Asturias, see A. Shubert, *The Road to Revolution in Asturias: the Coal Miners of Asturias, 1860–1934* (Chicago: University of Illinois Press, 1987), pp. 111–12.

20. S. Castillo (ed.), *Historia de la Unión General de Trabajadores* (Madrid: Unión, 1998), vol. 1, pp. 107–8.

21. X. Cuadrat, *Socialismo y Anarquismo en Cataluña, 1890–1911* (Madrid: Revista de Trabajo, 1976), pp. 26–41, 80–9, 321; A. Balcells, 'El Socialismo en Cataluña hasta la Guerra Civil', in *Anales de la historia*, vol. 3 (Madrid: Pablo Iglesias, 1988), pp. 9–14; A. Smith, 'Anarchism, the General Strike and the Barcelona Labour Movement, 1899–1914', *European History Quarterly*, vol. 27 (1997), pp. 14–23.

22. J. J. Morato, *Pablo Iglesias* (Barcelona: reprinted by Ariel, 2000), pp. 91–2, 162.

23. M. Bookchin, *The Spanish Anarchists* (New York: Free Life, 1976), J. Alvarez Junco, *La ideología política del anarquismo español, 1868–1910* (Madrid: Siglo XXI, 1976), pp. 592–4; G. R. Esenwein, *Anarchist Ideology and the Working-class Movement in Spain, 1868–98* (Berkeley: University of California Press, 1989), pp. 29–30.

24. On the violence, see J. Casanova, 'La cara oscura del anarquismo', in S. Juliá (ed.), *Violencia política en la España del Siglo XX* (Madrid: Taurus, 2000), p. 67; W. L. Bernecker, 'Acción Directa y violencia en el anarquismo español', *Ayer*, 13 (1994), pp. 151–4, 165–6.

25. The *Lliga* entered coalition governments in the years 1917, 1918, 1921 and 1931. B. de Riquer, *Regionalistes i Nacionalistes, 1898–1931* (Barcelona: Dopesa, 1979), pp. 42–9.

26. Lerroux's ability to create a modern political party by mobilising elements of the proletariat and petty bourgeoisie, who were formerly underrepresented within the political system, cannot be denied. It does

not seem that Lerroux was sent to Barcelona by Madrid in 1901, but his success encouraged Liberal governments to prop him up. This is well documented in the private papers of leading Restoration politicians held at the Biblioteca de la Real Academia de la Historia. For instance, it seems from *Natalio Rivas's Diaries* (hereafter ANR), Leg. 11–8898, that Natalio Rivas, a leading figure in the then Liberal administration of Segismundo Moret, met Lerroux in his house and handed over 3500 pesetas for the latter's brother-in-law (on 26 January 1910); the Conservative Augusto Besada told Rivas that, in conversation with the King, he had assured the monarch that a revolution could not take place in Spain, as the only able leader would be Lerroux and he could be bought (27 January 1910). A balanced accounts of Lerroux's political talent and populist demagoguery can be found in J. Alvarez Junco, *El Emperador del Paralelo: Lerroux y la demagogia populista* (Madrid: Alianza, 1990), especially, pp. 169–70, 216–7, 270–3, 334–6.

27. C. Seco Serrano, *Militarismo y civilismo en la España contemporánea* (Madrid: Instituto de Estudios Económicos, 1984), p. 233.

28. Political crises were known as '*orientales*', as they were generally produced and resolved at the Palace of Oriente, Alfonso's residence.

29. The cartoon portrayed the dialogue between a civilian and a soldier, who were watching the crowds entering a big stadium. The soldier asked what was being celebrated and the civilian replied that it was a 'victory banquet'. 'Well then,' said the soldier, 'they must be civilians.'

30. Ballbé, *Orden público*, pp. 273–7.

31. A treaty signed in Algeciras in 1906, confirmed one year later at the Conference of Cartagena, allotted Spain a strip of land in northern Morocco where she already possessed the coastal enclaves of Ceuta and Melilla.

32. On 31 May 1906, the day of the wedding of King Alfonso and the English Princess Victoria Eugénie of Battenberg, Mateo Morral, a former teacher in Ferrer's school, had hurled a bomb at the royal carriage. The royal couple escaped unhurt but twenty people were killed and over one hundred were injured. In order to avoid capture, Morral shot himself the following morning. Ferrer was tried but had to be released because of a lack of evidence. The best study of the Tragic Week remains J. Connelly Ullman, *The Tragic Week: A Study of Anticlericalism in Spain, 1875–1912* (Cambridge, MA: Harvard University Press, 1968), pp. 167–282.

33. This can be measured by the huge number of reports located in the Archive of the Royal Palace, (Caja 15,418, Exp. 8).

34. G. Maura and M. Fernández Almagro, *Por qué cayó Alfonso XIII* (Madrid: Ambos Mundos, 1948), p. 155.

35. F. J. Romero Salvadó, *Spain 1914–1918: Between War and Revolution* (London: Routledge, 1999), pp. 6–16. There were important exceptions. For instance, General Miguel Primo de Rivera was a well-known

Francophile. There was also a huge gap between the positions endorsed by most Carlists and *Mauristas* and their respective leaders, the pro-Russian Carlist Pretender and Maura's moderate neutralism. Unlike the Socialists, who were dominated by a vehement pro-Allied leadership, the CNT adhered to an internationalist position denouncing the war as a 'capitalist' struggle.

36.  G. Meaker, 'A Civil War of Words', in H. A. Schmitt (ed.), *Neutral Europe between War and Revolution, 1917–1923* (Charlottesville: University of Virginia Press, 1988), pp. 1–2, 6–7.

37.  F. J. Romero Salvadó, 'Fatal Neutrality: Pragmatism or Capitulation? Spain's Foreign Policy during the Great War', *European History Quarterly*, 33, 3 (July 2003), pp. 299–300. The collusion between Germans and Anarcho-syndicalists was recognised by Angel Pestaña, one of the CNT's most influential leaders, in his memoirs *Lo que aprendí en la vida* (Murcia: reprinted by Zero, 1971, vol. 1, pp. 66–74). The CNT organ, *Solidaridad Obrera*, received German financing. After Pestaña and a new team replaced its former staff, this newspaper provided, on 9 June 1918, documentary evidence that Barcelona's police inspector, Manuel Bravo Portillo, and other agents had relayed information on the movements of Spanish vessels which, later, were sunk by German submarines. Portillo also played a crucial part in the killing of José Barret, a leading Catalan metalwork owner and exporter to France.

38.  M. Tuñón de Lara, *Historia del movimiento obrero español* (Madrid: Taurus, 1972), pp. 550–72.

39.  Heywood, *Marxism*, pp. 40–1.

40.  B. Márquez and J. Capó, *Las juntas militares de defensa* (La Habana: Porvenir, 1923), p. 24; C. B. Boyd, *Praetorian Politics in Liberal Spain* (Chapel Hill: University of North Carolina Press, 1979), pp. 53–60.

41.  F. Cambó, *Memorias* (Madrid: Alianza, 1987), pp. 223–4; M. Cabrera, F. Comín and J. L. García Delgado, *Santiago Alba: un programa de reforma económica en la España del primer tercio del Siglo XX* (Madrid: Instituto de Estudios Fiscales, 1989), pp. 251–426.

42.  Romanones's openly pro-Allied position was an exceptional case within the governing elites. As early as August 1914, he had shocked the governing class when he stated these views in an editorial called 'Fatal Neutralities'. The scandalous sinking of the Spanish vessel *San Fulgencio* in April 1917 was, for the count, the right psychological moment to break off diplomatic relations with Germany. However, he met with opposition from the King and was replaced in office by the Marquis of Alhucemas, the leader of the neutralist section of the Liberal Party.

43.  M. Burgos y Mazo, *Páginas históricas de 1917* (Madrid: Núñez Samper, 1918), pp. 54–9, 73–4.

44.  J. A. Lacomba, *La crisis española de 1917* (Málaga, Ciencia Nueva, 1970), pp. 165–212.

45.  J. Ferrer, *Simó Piera, perfil d'un sindicalista: Records i experiencies d'un dirigent de la CNT* (Barcelona: Portic, 1975), p. 143.

46.  F. J. Romero Salvadó, 'Spain and the First World War: The Structural Crisis of the Liberal Monarchy', *European History Quarterly*, vol. 25, 4 (October 1995), p. 543.

47.  L. Simarro, *Los sucesos de agosto en el parlamento* (Madrid: n.p., 1918), pp. 13–20, 50–1.

48.  The official figures confirmed a total of 71 dead, 200 wounded and 2000 arrested. In reality, the casualties were probably higher than this. See Lacomba, *La crisis española*, pp. 213–84.

49.  The *Lliga*'s objectives were achieved: the monopoly of politics enjoyed by the *turno* had been broken and now Catalan Regionalists held two portfolios that included control of the economy.

50.  Abundant evidence of this witch-hunt of foreigners for the period 1919–23 can be found in Archivo Histórico Nacional, *Serie Gobernación*, Leg. 2A, Exp. 16; Leg. 3A, Exp. 15; Leg. 17A, Exp. 1; and Leg. 35A, Exp. 1 (1920–23); and in Archivo del Ministerio de Asuntos Exteriores, H2766.

51.  Borodin was helped by the Indian Communist M. N. Roy and Jesús Ramírez (pseudonym of the US Communist Charles Francis Phillips). Reports of their activities can be found in Fundación Pablo Iglesias, *Internacional Comunista. Informes de España* (AAVV-CV-16).

52.  G. Meaker, *The Revolutionary Left in Spain, 1914–23* (Stanford, CA: Stanford University Press, 1974), pp. 478–83.

53.  J. Díaz del Moral, *Historia de las agitaciones campesinas andaluzas* (Madrid: 4th edn, Alianza, 1995), pp. 267–73.

54.  A. Balcells, *El sindicalisme a Barcelona, 1916–1923* (Barcelona: Nova Terra, 1965), pp. 73–82.

55.  However, the CNT would subsequently withdraw from the Comintern at the Conference of Zaragoza in June 1922. See A. Bar, *La CNT en los años rojos, 1910–26* (Madrid: Akal, 1981), pp. 489–555; and F. J. Romero Salvadó, 'The Views of an Anarcho-syndicalist on the Soviet Union: The Defeat of the Third International in Spain', *Revolutionary Russia*, vol. 8, 1 (June 1995), pp. 33–5.

56.  For the *Libres* see C. Winston, *Workers and the Right in Spain, 1900–1936* (Princeton, NJ: Princeton University Press, 1984), pp. 108–71. An excellent analysis of the alliance between the Catalan bourgeoisie and the military may be found in S. Bengoechea, *El Locaut de Barcelona, 1919–20* (Barcelona: Curial, 1998), pp. 75–234.

57.  A. Balcells, 'Violencia y terrorismo en la lucha de clases en Barcelona de 1913 a 1923' and F. del Rey Reguillo, 'Ciudadanos honrados y somatenistas. El orden y la subversión en la España de los años 20', both in *Estudios de Historia Social*, nos. 42–43 (July–December 1987), pp. 37–79, 97–150; E. González Calleja, *El Mauser y el sufragio: Orden público, subversión y violencia política en la crisis de la Restauración, 1917–1923* (Madrid: CSIC, 1999), pp. 127–226.

58. P. La Porte, *La Atracción del imán; El desastre de Annual y sus repercusiones en la política europea, 1921–1923* (Madrid: Biblioteca Nueva, 2001), pp. 63–88.
59. The manifesto of Primo de Rivera is in *El ABC* (14 September 1923).
60. M. Maura, *Así cayó Alfonso XIII* (Barcelona, 7th edn: Ariel, 1995), p. 39; S. Ben-Ami, *The Origins of the Second Republic in Spain* (Oxford: Oxford University Press, 1978), pp. 8–9.
61. J. L. Gómez Navarro, *El régimen de Primo de Rivera* (Madrid: Cátedra, 1991), pp. 53–66.
62. In the station gathered, amongst others, Josep Puig i Cadafalch (president of the local administrative institution *La Mancomunitat*), the Marquis of Alella (Barcelona's Mayor), the Marquis of Comillas (ultra-Catholic magnate and ship-owner), the Viscount of Cusso (president of the industrialists' confederation, *Fomento del Trabajo Nacional*) and the *Lliga's* leading politician, Joan Ventosa.
63. M. T. González Calbet, *La Dictadura de Primo de Rivera* (Madrid: El Arquero, 1987), pp. 79–84.
64. Heywood, *Marxism*, pp. 95–7.
65. This was not the case in rural Spain, where paternalistic social legislation was not introduced.
66. Martin, *Agony*, pp. 281–4.
67. Worried by the successes of the natives led by Abd-el-Krim, the French and Spanish armies agreed in the summer of 1925 to a joint military operation. Thus, the rebels found themselves caught in a vice, squeezed between Spanish troops coming from the north and the French from the south. By the spring of 1926, Morocco had been pacified.
68. S. Ben-Ami, *Fascism from Above: The Dictatorship of Primo de Rivera in Spain, 1923–1930* (Oxford: Oxford University Press, 1983), pp. 127–60.
69. Up to 1925, owing to Primo's sympathy towards *abandonismo* (that is, favouring withdrawal from Morocco), opposition had come basically from the *Africanistas*. However, after the conclusion of the successful campaign there, Primo was not only reconciled with them but even began to promote colonial officers to key positions. Additionally, the dictator's introduction of promotion by special selection incensed the metropolitan *Junteros* who defended the closed scale (that is, the system of strict promotion by seniority). The Liberal leader Count Romanones and the Conservative J. Sanchez Guerra played a major role in these rebellions. See ANR, Legs. 11-8917–8920.
70. J. Harrison, *The Spanish Economy in the Twentieth Century* (London: Croom Helm, 1985), pp. 69–70.
71. S. Ben-Ami, 'The Republican "Take-over": Prelude to Inevitable Catastrophe?', in P. Preston (ed.), *Revolution and War in Spain, 1931–1939* (London: Methuen, 1984), pp. 15–16.
72. Romero Salvadó, *Twentieth-Century Spain*, p. 62.

73. An excellent analysis of monarchist disarray is in S. Ben-Ami, 'The Crisis of the Dynastic Elite in the Transition from Monarchy to Republic, 1929–1931', in P. Preston and F. Lannon (eds), *Elites and Power in Twentieth-Century Spain: Essays in Honour of Sir Raymond Carr* (Oxford: Oxford University Press, 1990), pp. 72–7.

74. E. Montero, 'Reform Idealized: The Intellectual and Ideological Origins of the Second Republic', in H. Graham and J. Labanyi (eds), *Spanish Cultural Studies* (Oxford: Oxford University Press, 1995), p. 129.

75. Maura, *Así cayó Alfonso*, pp. 69–72.

76. In a final attempt to delay Galán's rebellion, the Provisional Government sent one of their members, the Galician Republican Santiago Casares Quiroga, to detain him but he arrived too late. Ben-Ami, *Origins*, pp. 94–9.

77. Maura, *Así cayó Alfonso*, pp. 132–7.

78. Maura and Fernández Almagro, *Por qué cayó Alfonso XIII*, p. 387.

79. The last prime minister, Admiral Aznar, admitted this defeat. Asked by journalists if there was a crisis, he retorted that there could be no bigger crisis than that of a country that went to bed Monarchist and woke up Republican. Romanones's visit in the afternoon of 14 April to Alcalá Zamora, in order to negotiate a political truce, confirmed to the Republicans that victory was theirs. An emboldened Alcalá demanded the King's departure from the country before sunset. Earlier in the morning, General Sanjurjo, head of the Civil Guard, had gone to the house of Miguel Maura to assert the loyalty of that institution to the Republic. See Maura, *Así cayó Alfonso*, pp. 149–69.

## 2   The Second Republic (1931–1936): A Brief Essay in Democracy

1. A. Lerroux, *Al servicio de la República* (Madrid: Morata, 1930), p. 353. The establishment of the Republic was greeted enthusiastically by the crowds. Many appeared to believe that magically overnight all the existing problems would disappear – a sentiment echoed in Lerroux's writing.

2. S. Juliá, *Madrid, 1931–34: De la fiesta popular a la lucha de clases* (Madrid: Siglo XXI, 1984), pp. 2, 7–11.

3. J. Palafox, *Atraso económico y democracia; La Segunda República y la economía española, 1892–1936* (Barcelona: Crítica, 1991), pp. 127, 148–50, 173.

4. N. Townson, *The Crisis of Democracy in Spain: Centrist Politics under the Second Republic, 1931–1936* (Brighton: Sussex Academic Press, 2000), p. 19. If elements of the old regime remained well entrenched in the judiciary, civil service and police, that was not the case for the traditional political class. Even though, at least in theory, they had obtained large majorities in rural Spain during the April municipal

elections, the old governing elites soon lost control of their strongholds. In many localities they were unceremoniously expelled from their posts – either by pro-republican crowds or by newly appointed civil governors who replaced them with temporary committees.

5. Count Romanones, for example, would be returned as an independent monarchist deputy in the three elections of the Second Republic.
6. M. Tuñón de Lara, *La II República*, vol. 1 (Madrid: Siglo XXI, 1976), p. 76.
7. Juliá, *Los Socialistas*, pp. 152–7, 165–6; Heywood, *Marxism*, pp. 117–20.
8. C. P. Boyd, *Historia Patria: Política, historia e identidad nacional en España, 1875–1975* (Barcelona: Pomares, 2000), p. 175.
9. The two first ministers of education were intellectuals: the Radical-Socialist Marcelino Domingo was a journalist and essayist; the Socialist Fernando de los Ríos was a professor at the University of Granada. There were many other outstanding examples, such as Julián Besteiro (a professor at the University of Madrid) and Manuel Azaña (a former president of the Ateneo, the cultural centre of the capital).
10. P. B. Radcliff, *From Mobilization to Civil War: The Politics of Polarization in the Spanish City of Gijón, 1900–1937* (Cambridge: Cambridge University Press, 1996), p. 36.
11. C. Cobb, 'The Republican State and Mass Educational–Cultural Activities, 1931–36', in Graham and Labanyi (eds), *Spanish Cultural Studies*, p. 133.
12. Juliá, *Los Socialistas*, pp. 180–1.
13. Cobb, 'The Republican State', p. 136.
14. S. Juliá, *Manuel Azaña: Una biografía política* (Madrid: Alianza, 1991), pp. 98–110; G. Cardona, *Poder militar en la España contemporánea hasta la Guerra Civil* (Madrid: Siglo XXI, 1983), pp. 123–4, 138–66.
15. Martin, *Agony*, p. 305.
16. E. Malefakis, *Agrarian Reform and Peasant Revolution in Spain* (London: Yale University Press, 1970), pp. 166–71.
17. *Ezquerra Republicana* (an alliance of the Nationalist *Estat Catalá* and the *Partit Republicá Catalá*) rushed, in April 1931, to declare the existence of a Catalan Republic within Spain's new Federal Republic. After a visit by a governmental delegation, they were persuaded to wait and to recognise the faculty of the Spanish parliament to grant autonomy to Cataluña. *Ezquerra* now emerged as the hegemonic Catalan political force, replacing the *Lliga*. One of the *Ezquerra* leaders, Lluís Companys, became a minister in the central government in 1933.
18. The right of women to vote was supported by Socialists and rightwing parties. Most republicans were opposed or lukewarm, believing that most women were Catholic and therefore too easily influenced by the clergy.
19. Maura, *Así cayó Alfonso*, pp. 84–93, also cited by F. Largo Caballero, *Mis recuerdos: Cartas a un amigo* (México: Ed. Unidas, 1976), p. 99. Lerroux was finally offered the Foreign Office.

20. Former monarchist *caciques* and even entire local organisations flocked into republican parties with the objective of maintaining their power. In return, republicans could then bolster their meagre standing in many areas. However, the Radicals' political ambiguity meant that, by and large, they benefited the most from this 'sudden republican conversion'. Townson, *Crisis of Democracy*, pp. 32, 40–2, 49.

21. As early as July 1931, Prieto had stated that the PSOE would neither back nor trust a cabinet presided over by Lerroux. The Radical leader was furious, feeling that Azaña, a newcomer to politics, had usurped the premiership when he did not give way to a new cabinet led by the most senior republican figure, himself. See Juliá, *Manual Azaña*, pp. 116–21, 155.

22. S. Juliá, 'Sistema de partidos y problemas de consolidación de la democracia', in S. Juliá (ed.), *Política en la Segunda República, Ayer*, 20 (1995), p. 125.

23. F. Lannon, *Privilege, Persecution and Prophecy: The Catholic Church in Spain, 1875–1975* (Oxford: Oxford University Press, 1987), p. 181.

24. Boyd, *Historia Patria*, p. 178.

25. Lannon, *Privilege*, p. 185. Ironically, the Law of Congregations (finally passed in May 1933) that determined the end of teaching by Catholic orders in January 1934 was not implemented, as by then a new administration had taken over. Other laws, such as the secularisation of cemeteries in January 1933, were definitely motivated by revenge rather than mere modernist feelings. See J. Avilés Farré, *La Izquierda burguesa en la II República* (Madrid: EspasaCalpe, 1985), p. 128. Religion becoming a rallying banner for the Right is recognised in J. M. Gil Robles, *No fue posible la paz* (Madrid: Planeta, 1998), p. 53.

26. Maura (*Así cayó Alfonso*, pp. 293–306) stressed that the subversive activities of influential elements in the Church hierarchy left him with no option but their expulsion from the country.

27. H. Raguer, *La Pólvora y el incienso: La Iglesia y la Guerra Civil Española, 1936–1939* (Barcelona: Península, 2001), p. 48.

28. Azaña's insensitive remark that all the convents of Madrid were not worth the life of one republican (following, as it did, the burning of religious buildings in several cities after monarchist provocation in May 1931) provided crucial ammunition to those in the Catholic establishment eager to combat the Republic. In fact, the minister of the interior, Miguel Maura, was given full powers to deal vigorously with those causing disorder and arson. Martial law was declared and the army called out to restore order and protect Church property. The three Socialist ministers did not hesitate to back energetic measures. See Maura, *Así cayó Alfonso*, pp. 249–53; and N. Alcalá Zamora, *Memorias* (Madrid: Planeta, 1998), pp. 291–2.

29. Ironically, Azaña's radical speech (which included the dissolution of the Jesuits and deprived the religious orders of their teaching functions) was

a successful effort to seek Socialist support and at the same time to isolate his more anticlerical colleagues of the PRRS, who pursued the dissolution of all orders.

30. Lannon, *Privilege*, p. 18.
31. Ibid., pp. 163–4.
32. There were, indeed, large numbers of masons in the republican parties. See Avilés Farré, *La Izquierda burguesa*, pp. 85–6.
33. P. Preston, *The Coming of the Spanish Civil War: Reform, Reaction and Revolution in the Second Republic* (London: Routledge, 1994), p. 5.
34. According to Palafox (*Atraso económico*, p. 180), between 14 April and 30 June 1931 alone, 917 million pesetas (13 per cent of the total deposits) had been withdrawn.
35. M. Cabrera, *La patronal ante la II República* (Madrid: Siglo XXI, 1983), pp. 204–6, 215–8.
36. Malefakis, *Agrarian Reform*, p. 170.
37. P. Preston, 'The Agrarian War in the South', in Preston (ed.), *Revolution and War*, p. 159.
38. C. Gil Andrés, *Echarse a la calle: Amotinados, huelguistas y revolucionarios, La Rioja, 1890–1936* (Zaragoza: Prensas Universitarias, 2000), pp. 194–7.
39. J. M. Macarro, *Socialismo, República y revolución en Andalucía, 1931–36* (Seville: Universidad de Sevilla, 2000), pp. 117–19, 165–7.
40. The UGT membership went from some 300,000 in December 1930 to more than a million in June 1932. The sudden growth of the FNTT was greatly out of proportion with the overall growth of the UGT. The FNTT constituted about 10 per cent of the total UGT membership in 1930, two years later it was nearly 40 per cent.
41. Cabrera, *La patronal*, pp. 63–5.
42. Macarro, *Socialismo*, pp. 73, 101–2.
43. Preston, *The Coming*, p. 82.
44. A. Elorza and M. Bizcarrondo, *Queridos camaradas: La Internacional Comunista y España, 1919–1939* (Madrid: Planeta, 1999), pp. 71–4, 78.
45. The PCE remained a small party, with some 3,000 members in May 1931 and close to 12,000 two years later, financially dependent on the Comintern and tutored by its delegates in Spain. Indeed, rather than ideological conflicts, the fall of the Bullejos leadership was caused by constant disputes with the Comintern's delegate, the Argentinian Victorio Codovilla. See Elorza and Bizcarrondo, *Queridos camaradas*, pp. 146–53, 161–70; and R. Cruz, *El Partido Comunista de España en la II República* (Madrid: Alianza, 1987), pp. 31-2, 116.
46. Some of the well-known action groups, such as *Los Solidarios* (which included Joan García Oliver, Francisco Ascaso, Ricardo Sanz and Buenaventura Durruti) did not join the FAI until 1933.
47. J. Casanova, *De la calle al frente. El anarcosindicalismo en España 1931–1939* (Barcelona: Crítica, 1997), pp. 13–15.

48. J. García Oliver, *El eco de los pasos* (Paris: Ruedo Ibérico, 1978), p. 115.
49. The FAI launched a vicious campaign against well-known 'moderate' leaders such as Joan Peiró, Angel Pestaña and Camil Piñón. M. Lladonosa, *Sindicalistes i Llibertaris: L'experiencia de Camil Piñón* (Barcelona: Rafael Dalmau, 1989), pp. 54–6.
50. J. M. Macarro, 'Sindicalismo y política', in Juliá (ed.), *Política*, pp. 144–5.
51. C. Ealham, 'Revolutionary Gymnastics and the Unemployed. The Limits of the Spanish Anarchist Utopia, 1931–37', in K. Flett and D. Renton (eds), *The Twentieth Century. A Century of Wars and Revolutions?* (London: Rivers Oram, 2000), pp. 142–3.
52. Juliá, *Los Socialistas*, pp. 168–72.
53. Macarro, 'Sindicalismo', p. 152.
54. Ealham, 'Revolutionary Gymnastics', p. 136.
55. The Assault Guards were well trained and at least 1.80 metres in height and they carried a small gun and truncheon instead of the Civil Guard's traditional long rifle, the Mauser. E. González Calleja, 'El estado ante la violencia', in Juliá (ed.), *Violencia*, pp. 382–3.
56. Gil Andrés, *Echarse a la calle*, p. 198.
57. In the summer of 1933, the *Ley de Vagos y Maleantes* (Law against Vagrants and Idlers) was passed. It allowed the arrest of those who could not prove that they had legal means to support themselves. Many in the CNT believed it was directed at them since it could lead to the imprisonment of those collecting dues to sustain the direct action of their unions. See C. Lorenzo, *Los anarquistas españoles y el poder* (Paris: Ruedo Ibérico, 1972), pp. 59–60.
58. Ferrer, *Simó Piera*, p. 139.
59. Lladonosa, *Sindicalistes*, p. 58.
60. Ballbé, *Orden público*, p. 342.
61. Joan Peiró and the editorial board of the CNT's newspaper, *Solidaridad Obrera*, had to resign in September 1931. Pestaña lost his post of secretary general in March 1932. Accused of reformism, the trade unions of Sabadell (Barcelona) were expelled in September 1932. During the following months, other unions were also expelled or left the CNT. See E. Vega, *Anarquistas y sindicalistas, 1931–1936* (Valencia: Alfons el Magnánim, 1987), pp. 56–7.
62. Casanova, *De la calle*, pp. 28, 84–5.
63. If Lerroux's personal stance was not above suspicion, this was not the case of many Radicals. In Sevilla, the party leader, Diego Martínez Barrios, immediately placed himself at the disposal of the government. See Townson, *Crisis of Democracy*, pp. 134–43. M. Azaña, *Diarios, 1932–3* (Madrid: Crítica, 1997), p. 3, states how the government had known of the coup since late July and was prepared to crush it. The lover of one of the compromised officers had alerted the authorities (p. 13). Azaña's opinion (p. 38) on Lerroux was that he was '*un bruto, un loco o un malvado*' ('brutal, crazy or wicked'). With the exception of the

interior minister, Santiago Casares Quiroga, the government voted to commute all the death sentences, so as not to stain the regime with blood (pp. 44–8).

64. Juliá, *Manuel Azaña*, p. 183.
65. Azaña (*Diarios*, p. 407) wrote in July 1933 that Domingo's initiatives left him desolate.
66. The best analysis of the agrarian reform can be found in Malefakis, *Agrarian Reform*, pp. 200–35, 243–57.
67. In April 1932 *Acción Nacional* had changed its name to *Acción Popular*.
68. The Agrarian Party was founded in January 1934 and led by a well-known Monarchist, José Martínez de Velasco. Dominated by land-owners from Castilla, the members of this party had been part of the Agrarian minority, an umbrella coalition of right-wing deputies. They normally collaborated with the CEDA.
69. Gil Robles (*No fue posible*, p. 788) in a letter of 13 January 1933 to the Monarchist leader, A. Goicoechea, affirmed: 'It should remain very clear that our incompatibility is not due to political differences but reasons of strategy.'
70. Azaña (*Diarios*, p. 138) noted in his diary about the difficulties created by this *tenaza* (pincer) of Monarchists and Anarchists.
71. Malefakis, *Agrarian Reform*, pp. 258–9.
72. The leader of the platoon of Assault Guards, Captain Rojas, told reporters that he had received orders to take 'neither wounded nor prisoners' and that even Azaña had used the term 'shoot them in the belly'. The subsequent investigation exonerated the government but the director general of security, Arturo Menéndez, was forced to resign. Rojas and his chief lieutenant were relieved of duty. Rojas was eventually brought to trial in May 1934 and sentenced to 21 years in prison, the only member of the security personnel prosecuted for police atrocities under the Republic. See S. Payne, *Spain's First Democracy. The Second Republic, 1931–6* (Madison: University of Wisconsin Press, 1993), pp. 131–2. Azaña stated how all the ministers (including the Socialists Largo and de los Ríos) believed that rigorous measures were needed to put down the revolt, but when Rojas was interviewed by the prime minister, he denied shooting anyone in cold blood. See Azaña, *Diarios*, pp. 136, 198–9.
73. Azaña (*Diarios*, p. 186) was disgusted by this campaign of 'bringing corpses to the chamber' in which both Radicals and rightists collaborated.
74. Palafox, *Atraso económico*, p. 193. In a year unemployment had gone up from 440,000 to 600,000.
75. Macarro, *Socialismo*, pp. 168–9.
76. Shubert, *The Road*, pp. 142–3.
77. In the Thirteenth Congress of the PSOE, in October 1932, the followers of Largo Caballero and those of Prieto collaborated in defeating

Besteiro. Caballero became the PSOE's President. The *Besteiristas* were finally ousted from the UGT's leadership in January 1934, when a new executive dominated by *Caballeristas* was appointed. See Juliá, *Los Socialistas*, pp. 201–3.

78. This sector was an exception in the dismal record of the CNT's loss of membership. As the depression worsened, bringing about a sharp increase in unemployment, the CNT's strategy of mobilisation (as opposed to the UGT's reliance on negotiation) appealed to the unskilled construction workers, many of whom had only quite recently arrived in Madrid, during the boom of the Dictatorship years. The general strike of September 1933 forced construction employers to recognise the CNT, thus putting an end to a Socialist monopoly. See Juliá, *Madrid*, pp. 169–71, 240–58.

79. Heywood, *Marxism*, p. 130.

80. Azaña (*Diarios*, p. 254) called them the most reactionary provinces in the country.

81. Avilés Farré, *La izquierda burguesa*, pp. 174, 191–6.

82. Azaña (*Diarios*, pp. 277, 307–8, 316) complained about the behaviour of Alcalá, who was lecturing ministers while plotting behind their backs. He forced a government reshuffle in June and then, insisting that the left-wing composition of parliament did not respond to the will of the country, he brought the government down (p. 366).

83. Largo viewed the end of Socialist participation in government as a betrayal of the former republican partners. See F. Largo Caballero, *Escritos de La República* (Madrid: Pablo Iglesias, 1985), p. 32.

84. In 1933, Gil Robles (*No fue posible*, pp. 90, 96–8) had attended the Nazi rallies at Nuremberg and had learnt from their mass appeal choreography.

85. Tuñón de Lara, *La II República*, vol. 2, pp. 12–5.

86. He nevertheless resisted all the pressures from members of the previous administration to cancel the results. Alcalá Zamora, *Memorias*, pp. 298–301.

87. Townson, *Crisis of Democracy*, pp. 127, 205, 208–10.

88. Ibid., pp. 257–8.

89. Juliá, *Madrid*, p. 345.

90. Payne, *Spain's First Democracy*, p. 185.

91. Juliá, 'Sistema', p. 130.

92. Townson, *Crisis of Democracy*, p. 221.

93. Alcalá Zamora, *Memorias*, p. 307.

94. Avilés Farré, *La izquierda burguesa*, pp. 238, 246–8.

95. Martin, *Agony*, p. 338.

96. Ballbé, *Orden público*, p. 364.

97. Juliá, *Los Socialistas*, p. 211.

98. Cabrera, *La patronal*, pp. 21, 161.

99. Preston, 'Agrarian War', pp. 174–6.

100. Companys had become president of the *Generalitat* and leader of *Ezquerra* after the death of Francesc Maciá in December 1933.

101. G. Jackson, *The Spanish Republic and the Civil War, 1931–9* (Princeton, NJ: Princeton University Press, 1967), p. 148.

102. S. Juliá, 'Preparados para cuando la ocasión se presente: Los socialistas y la revolución', in Juliá (ed), *Violencia*, p. 176. Largo Caballero (*Escritos*, pp. 140–9) portrayed the revolutionary preparations as chaotic, with arms purchases ending in losses, swindles or police confiscations.

103. Largo Caballero (*Mis recuerdos*, pp. 127–8) wrote that, when questioned by the military judge, he denied being the leader of the revolutionary movement and affirmed that he had nothing to do with the general strike. He had slept the first two nights at Prieto's house, moving then to the homes of a doctor and a journalist before returning home. There is no mention, in this book, of any revolutionary strategy. Hardly the image one has of Lenin on the eve of the October Revolution!

104. S. Balfour, *Deadly Embrace: Morocco and the Road to the Spanish Civil War* (Oxford: Oxford University Press, 2002), p. 256.

105. Members of the Foreign Legion assassinated Luis Sirval, a journalist who dared to report the brutalities committed in Asturias.

106. Tuñón de Lara, *La II República*, vol. 2, p. 96.

107. Cabrera, *La patronal*, p. 242.

108. Malefakis, *Agarian Reform*, pp. 347–55.

109. Gil Robles (*No fue posible*, pp. 138–43, 205) contends that for the three Catalan officers involved in the October events, Lerroux was prepared to back the death sentence but the government was stopped by 'the regrettable politics of Alcalá Zamora', then 'the gravest danger for the peace of Spain'. Such was the anger of the CEDA that they sounded the possibility of a military coup but they were dissuaded by the negative response of the generals.

110. Ballbé, *Orden público*, pp. 378–80.

111. Gil Robles, *No fue posible*, pp. 256–7.

112. Malefakis, *Agarian Reform*, pp. 355–60.

113. Townson, *Crisis of Democracy*, pp. 315–36. The so-called *straperlo* gambling fraud exploded in October. It involved several ministers (and even Lerroux's stepson) and an international swindler, the Dutchman Daniel Strauss, who was granted a licence for his fixed roulette (known as *straperlo* from the name of its inventors Strauss and Perl) to operate in San Sebastián and Formentor (Mallorca). When the licence was withdrawn, an infuriated Strauss, failing to obtain an indemnity for all his expenses, dispatched a full dossier to the president of the republic. Alcalá refused to ignore the matter, forcing the creation of a parliamentary commission that condemned several leading Radicals. One month later, a new scandal broke out. It involved the connivance

of Lerroux himself in irregular payments from colonial funds, the so-called 'Treasure of Guinea', to a bankrupt company for former services in that colony. See also Alcalá Zamora, *Memorias*, pp. 353–7.

114. Preston, *The Coming*, p. 200.
115. Gil Robles (*No fue posible*, pp. 352–8) wrote that no punches were pulled in his conversation with the president. When Alcalá argued that the government of the Republic could not be entrusted to someone who had not sworn the constitution, the Catholic leader replied that the president of the Republic had sworn loyalty to the Monarchy. Gil Robles was aware that the government, at this time, had ordered police forces to surround the War Ministry and other strategic posts.
116. Gil Robles (*No fue posible*, p. 476) called Alcalá 'an Andalusian *cacique*'.
117. It was in the elections of November 1933 that the PNV, with 30 per cent of the vote, emerged as the main Basque political force in Vizcaya and Guipúzcoa. However, the CEDA's rejection of the Basque statute in 1934, added to the conflict of the central government with the Catalan *Generalitat*, convinced the PNV that nothing could be gained from right-wing governments in Madrid.
118. Gil Robles, *No fue posible*, pp. 369–71, 391–6.
119. P. Preston, 'The Creation of the Popular Front in Spain', in Graham and Preston (eds), *Popular Front*, p. 84.
120. IR resulted from the merging of Azaña's own party (AR) with the section of the PRRS led by Marcelino Domingo and the Galician Republicans of Santiago Casares Quiroga.
121. Azaña had written to Prieto in April 1935 enquiring about the possibilities of renewing the coalition with the Socialists. See Juliá, *Manuel Azaña*, pp. 411–20.
122. S. Juliá, *Orígenes del Frente Popular en España, 1934–6* (Madrid: Siglo XXI, 1979), pp. 44–5. A summary of this work, in English, is in S. Juliá, 'The Origins of the Spanish Popular Front', in M. S. Alexander and H. Graham (eds), *The French and Spanish Popular Fronts* (Cambridge: Cambridge University Press, 1989), pp. 24–37.
123. Preston, *The Coming*, pp. 211–38.
124. Cruz, *El partido Comunista*, pp. 189, 230.
125. The PCE's sudden about turn began officially with a speech by José Díaz in Madrid in June 1935. See Elorza and Bizcarrondo, *Queridos camaradas*, pp. 245–50.
126. Avilés Farré, *La izquierda burguesa*, p. 371; Elorza and Bizcarrondo, *Querido camaradas*, pp. 259–63.
127. Even FAI hardliners like García Oliver (*El eco de los pasos*, p. 163) agreed to refrain from asking for electoral abstention.
128. Tuñón de Lara, *La II República*, vol. 2, p. 166.
129. Both Alcalá Zamora (*Memorias*, pp. 393–4) and Gil Robles (*No fue posible*, pp. 481–6) agreed that an overwhelmed prime minister hastened to transfer the 'worries of government' on to Azaña's shoulders.

130. Malefakis, *Agrarian Reform*, pp. 368–74; Avilés Farré, *La izquierda burguesa*, pp. 295–8.

131. Hitler's occupation of the Rhineland in March 1936 confirmed the Comintern in its strategy of Popular Fronts, and Communists became earnest defenders of bourgeois democracy against the risk of Fascism. See Elorza and Bizcarrondo, *Queridos camaradas*, pp. 279–86. During the spring and summer months of 1936, the PCE became a staunch supporter of the Republican government, stressing its opposition to abusive labour demands.

132. Casanova, *De la calle*, pp. 147–9.

133. Jackson, *The Spanish Republic*, p. 209.

134. H. Graham, 'The Spanish Popular Front and the Civil War', in Graham and Preston (eds), *Popular Front*, p. 110.

135. Largo Caballero, *Recuerdos*, p. 141.

136. Prieto's speech in Cuenca (1 May 1936) to this effect is in I. Prieto, *Discursos fundamentales* (Madrid: Turner, 1975), p. 272.

137. For Miguel Maura (*Así cayó Alfonso*, p. 222) the Socialist veto on Prieto was a catastrophe which inevitably sealed the end of the Republic.

138. Gil Robles, *No fue posible*, p. 697.

139. Gil Andrés, *Echarse a la calle*, p. 251.

140. Despite all his denials of direct involvement in the conspiracy, Gil Robles (*No fue posible*, pp. 707–8) was kept informed by some of his party colleagues who were fully committed to the plot. Less easy to explain (ibid., p. 775) is how he donated, in early July, 500,000 pesetas from the electoral funds to General Mola.

141. Preston, *The Coming*, p. 265.

142. The killers of Calvo Sotelo belonged to the elite police unit based in the Pontejos barracks, next to the ministries. They were joined by one of the few left-wing officers in the Civil Guard, Captain Fernando Condés, a personal friend of Lieutenant Castillo. In the nocturnal raid, members of the Socialist militia known as *La Motorizada* took part. It is possible that Calvo was only meant to be arrested but was then killed, on the spur of the moment, by a highly excitable young Socialist, Victoriano Cuenca. The body was then dumped in the morgue of Madrid's cemetery. No member of the government or leading left-wing politician was party to the events. See Payne, *Spain's First Democracy*, pp. 353–9.

143. Gil Robles, *No fue posible*, pp. 797–807.

## 3   The Distorting Mirror: The International Dimension of the Spanish Civil War

1. C. Palacio in 1939, 'Song of the International Brigades', in *Songs of Battle, 1936–1939* (Valencia: Dahiz, 2001), pp. 51–2. In the autumn

of 1936 Madrid became the symbol of popular resistance to the advance of Fascism, the place where the International Brigades first entered into battle.

2. A. Beevor, *The Spanish Civil War* (London: Cassell, 1999), p. 53.

3. *The Times* (8 September 1936), cited by E. Moradiellos, 'El espejo deformante: Las dimensiones internacionales de la Guerra Civil', in *Revista de Extremadura*, 21 (September–December 1996), p. 55.

4. J. E. Dreifort, *Yvon Delbos at the Quai d'Orsay: French Foreign Policy during the Popular Front, 1936–1938* (Lawrence: University Press of Kansas, 1973), p. 34; J. Avilés Farré, *Pasión y farsa: Franceses y británicos ante la guerra civil* (Madrid: Eudema, 1994), p. 8.

5. R. Miralles, 'La política exterior de la República española hacia Francia durante la guerra civil', *Historia Contemporánea*, 10 (1993), p. 29.

6. Although there is no written proof of these hints, it is difficult to believe that during this summit, at the highest level, the rebellion in Spain was not discussed. The British leaders must have stated their antagonistic feelings to any French support for the Republic or, at least, they must have been conveyed via the French ambassador Charles Corbin. This is the opinion of Robert Blum, the Premier's son, in P. Renouvin and R. Rémond (eds), *Léon Blum* (Paris: Presses de la Fondation Nationales des Sciences Politiques, 1967), p. 356. In his hotel room, Blum received the visit of the French journalist André Géraud 'Pertinax' who warned him that military aid to the Republic would not be well received by the British. See *L'Oeuvre de Léon Blum*, vol. IV, 2 (Paris: Albin Michel, 1965), p. 374; and J. Lacouture, *Léon Blum* (New York: Holmes & Meier, 1982), pp. 307–8.

7. There were numerous violent right-wing groups active in France (such as *Le Cagoule, Le Croix de Feu, Les Jeunes Patriotes* and *Les Camelots du Roi*) which resorted to terrorist methods in their best efforts to destroy the Republic. Blum himself was badly beaten up in February 1936.

8. P. Jackson, 'French Strategy and the Spanish Civil War', in C. Leitz and D. J. Dunthorn (eds), *Spain in an International Context, 1936–1959* (Oxford: Berghahn, 1999), pp. 55–63.

9. *L'Oeuvre de Léon Blum*, pp. 374–5; W. L. Shirer, *The Collapse of the Third Republic* (London: Cox & Wyman, 1970), pp. 280–1.

10. Renouvin and Rémond, *Léon Blum*, p. 372.

11. Unlike the French government, which did not seem to have foreseen the army's insurrection, the British administration was fully informed by detailed diplomatic and intelligence reports of the deteriorating political situation.

12. E. Moradiellos, *Neutralidad benévola: El Gobierno británico y la insurrección militar española de 1936* (Oviedo: Pentalfa, 1990), pp. 119–26. Some elements of this work are available in English as 'The Origins of British Non-Intervention in the Spanish Civil War: Anglo-Spanish

Relations in Early 1936', *European History Quarterly* vol. 21, no. 3 (1991), pp. 339–64 and 'British Political Strategy in the face of the Military Rising of 1936 in Spain', *Contemporary European History*, vol. 1, no. 2 (1992), pp. 123–37. See also D. Little, *Malevolent Neutrality: The United States, Great Britain, and the Origins of the Spanish Civil War* (Ithaca: Cornell University Press, 1985), pp. 23–4, 184–6, 191–219.

13. J. Edwards, *The British Government and the Spanish Civil War* (London: Macmillan, 1979), pp. 4–9; Moradiellos, *Neutralidad*, pp. 149–53, 165–8.

14. Moradiellos, *Neutralidad*, pp. 97–102.

15. E. Moradiellos, 'The Gentle General: The Official British Perception of General Franco during the Spanish Civil War', in P. Preston and A. L. Mackenzie (eds), *The Republic Besieged* (Edinburgh: Edinburgh University Press, 1996), pp. 6–7.

16. E. Moradiellos *La Perfidia de Albión: El Gobierno británico y la guerra civil española* (Madrid: Siglo XXI, 1996), p. 44. A condensed English version of this work is 'Appeasement and Non-Intervention: British Policy during the Spanish Civil War', in P. Catterall and C. J. Morris (eds), *Britain and the Threat to Stability in Europe, 1918–45* (Leicester: Leicester University Press, 1993).

17. Little, *Malevolent Neutrality*, p. 240.

18. Moradiellos, *Neutralidad*, pp. 158–64.

19. Quoted in Moradiellos, *La Perfidia*, pp. 51, 58.

20. T. Jones, *A Diary with Letters* (Oxford: Oxford University Press, 1954), p. 231.

21. Moradiellos, *La Perfidia*, pp. 94–5.

22. A. Pena Rodríguez, *El gran aliado de Franco: Portugal y la guerra civil española, prensa, radio, cine y propaganda* (Coruña: Castro, 1998), pp. 45–9, 174–5; M. Alpert, *A New International History of the Spanish Civil War* (London: Macmillan 1994), pp. 54–5.

23. Britain was the main investor in Spain with 687.5 million pesetas, followed by France with 439.6 million. Germany's capital investments amounted to only 10.3 million pesetas. See A. Viñas, *Franco, Hitler y el estallido de la guerra civil* (Madrid: Alianza, 2001), p. 236.

24. *Documents on German Foreign Policy 1918–1945*, Series D, vol. 3: *Germany and the Spanish Civil War* (hereafter *DGFP*), (London: His Majesty's Stationery Office, 1951), Doc. 10 (Memo of the Director of the Political Department, 25 July 1936), pp. 10–11.

25. Viñas, *Franco*, pp. 344–75; R. H. Whealey, *Hitler and Spain* (Lexington: University Press of Kentucky, 1989), pp. 6–7.

26. Viñas, *Franco*, p. 430.

27. Ibid., pp. 385–97.

28. C. Leitz, 'Nazi Germany and Francoist Spain, 1936–45', in S. Balfour and P. Preston (eds), *Spain and the Great Powers* (London: Routledge, 1996), p. 129.

29. Whealey, *Hitler and Spain*, pp. 1, 9, 28–30; C. Leitz, *Economic Relations between Nazi Germany and Franco's Spain, 1936–1945* (Oxford: Oxford University Press, 1996), p. 15.

30. I. Saz, *Mussolini contra la II República* (Valencia: Alfons el Magnánim, 1986), pp. 30–1, 39–42, 69–74, 138–42, 171–8.

31. J. Coverdale, *Italian Intervention in the Spanish Civil War* (Princeton, NJ: Princeton University Press, 1975), p. 74.

32. Saz, *Mussolini*, pp. 179–210, 228–9; P. Preston, 'Mussolini's Spanish Adventure: From Limited Risk to War', in Preston and Mackenzie (eds), *The Republic Besieged*, pp. 23–45. See also M. Heiberg, *Emperadores del Mediterráneo: Franco, Mussolini y la guerra civil española* (Barcelona: Crítica, 2004), pp. 57–65. Heiberg agrees with Saz and Preston on the opportunist character of the Italian intervention. However, he stresses particularly the role played by the optimistic reports sent by the Italian diplomats in Morocco (Luccardi and del Rossi) in persuading Mussolini to take his final decision.

33. Coverdale, *Italian Intervention*, p. 87.

34. Ibid., p. 4.

35. Dreifort, *Yvon Delbos*, pp. 43–4.

36. Saz, *Mussolini*, pp. 203–5, 210.

37. Dreifort, *Yvon Delbos*, p. 45.

38. Moradiellos, *La Perfidia*, p. 66.

39. *L'Oeuvre de Léon Blum*, pp. 377–8.

40. Asúa believed that Blum should resign but he was overruled by the new Spanish ambassador in Paris, Alvaro de Albornoz. Backed by Madrid, the latter argued that a friendly government in France led by Blum, even with its hands tied, was better than a potentially hostile new administration. Asúa's testimony is in Renouvin and Rémond, *Léon Blum*, pp. 409–11; see also Lacouture, *Léon Blum*, pp. 311–2.

41. The devastating effect of the British Ambassador's threat of rupture between the two allies is underlined by the then Socialist minister Georges Monnet in Renouvin and Rémond, *Léon Blum*, p. 360.

42. Dreifort, *Yvon Delbos*, p. 46–7.

43. G. Howson, *Arms for Spain: The Untold Story of the Spanish Civil War* (London: John Murray, 1998), pp. 48–56, 255–6.

44. Lacouture, *Léon Blum*, pp. 332–3.

45. Blum confided to Eden that he was convinced that a non-intervention agreement was the best means to help the Republic, since the dictatorships could supply arms much more readily than France. See A. Eden, *Facing the Dictators* (London: Cassell, 1962), p. 409.

46. A. Adamthwaite, *France and the Coming of the Second World War, 1936–1939* (London: Frank Cass, 1977), p. 44.

47. J. Alvarez del Vayo, *Freedom's Battle* (London: Heinemann, 1940), p. 70.

48. Edwards, *The British Government*, pp. 30–5.

49.  R. P. Traina, *American Diplomacy and the Spanish Civil War* (Blooming-ton: Indiana University Press, 1968), pp. 52–3, 84, 100.
50.  Alpert, *A New International History*, p. 60.
51.  Edwards, *The British Government*, pp. 40–7.
52.  I. Maisky, *Spanish Notebooks* (London: Hutchinson, 1966), p. 33.
53.  Edwards, *The British Government*, p. 33.
54.  Moradiellos, *La Perfidia*, p. 85.
55.  *DGFP*, Doc. 73 (Germany's director of the legal department mentioned that the objective pursued by Italy and German was to give the NIC's activities a purely platonic character, 5 September 1936), p. 75; Doc. 79 (Germany's chargé d'affaires in London noted that the real objective of the NIC was to pacify the Left in Western countries, 9 September 1936), p. 84; and Doc. 131 (Germany's chargé d'affaires in London indicated that for the British government the NIC was a useful instrument to encourage dilatory solutions to avoid conflict and work as a shield against parliamentary pressure, 27 November 1936), pp. 141–2.
56.  H. Thomas, *The Spanish Civil War* (London: Penguin, 3rd edn, 1986), p. 396.
57.  In July 1934, the attempted coup by the Austrian Nazis, which produced the killing of the pro-Italian chancellor Dollfuss, had brought both Germany and Italy close to hostilities.
58.  Whealey, *Hitler and Spain*, pp. 14, 44.
59.  G. Ciano, *Diplomatic Papers* (London: Odham Press, 1948), con-versation between the *Duce* and Nazi minister of justice Hans Frank, 23 September 1936, pp. 43–6, and between Hitler and Ciano, 24 October 1936, pp. 56–7.
60.  Thomas, *The Spanish Civil War*, p. 376.
61.  Whealey, *Hitler and Spain*, p. 8.
62.  Coverdale, *Italian Intervention*, pp. 106, 127–46.
63.  Little, *Malevolent Neutrality*, p. 261.
64.  T. G. Powell, *Mexico and the Spanish Civil War* (Albuquerque: Uni-versity of New Mexico Press, 1981), pp. 58–60, 71–5, 96–9; M. Ojeda-Revah, 'Mexico and the Spanish Republic, 1931–9' (University of London Ph.D. thesis, 2002), pp. 6–7, 140–1, 147–88.
65.  British examples can be found in T. Buchanan, *Britain and the Spanish Civil War* (Cambridge: Cambridge University Press, 1997), pp. 93–102.
66.  R. Skoutelsky, *L'Espoir guidait leur pas: Les volontaires français dans les Brigades Internationales, 1936–1939* (Paris: Grasset, 1998), pp. 34–40, 109–11.
67.  John Steinbeck, William Faulkner, Aldous Huxley, Arthur Miller, Dashiell Hammet, Lillian Hellman, Melvyn Douglass, Joan Crawford, Fredric March, Bette Davis, Franchot Tone, Charles Chaplin and Orson Welles were amongst the most openly vocal supporters of the Republic. Actors such as Humphrey Bogart, Gregory Peck, Gary Cooper, Orson

Welles, Charles Boyer, Paul Lukas, Paul Muni, Ray Milland and John Garfield would star in films (before the reaction of the McCarthy era) playing the roles of foreign idealists or adventurers who fought in the Spanish Civil War. See D. Pastor Petit, *Hollywood responde a la guerra civil* (Barcelona: Tempestad, 1998), pp. 85, 102, 107–8, 153, 229.

68. R. Radosh et al. (eds), *Spain Betrayed: The Soviet Union in the Spanish Civil War* (London: Yale University Press, 2001), Doc. 10, p. 21.
69. D. Kowalsky, *La Unión Soviética y la guerra civil española* (Barcelona: Crítica, 2004), pp. 25, 77–80; D. Smyth, 'We Are with You: Solidarity and Self-Interest in Soviet Policy towards Republican Spain, 1936–1939', in Preston and Mackenzie (eds), *The Republic Besieged*, p. 88; E. H. Carr, *The Comintern and the Spanish Civil War* (London: Macmillan, 1984), pp. 15–16.
70. The reports sent by the Comintern delegate, the Argentinian Victorio Codovilla, during the first weeks of the conflict indicated that the Republicans were in control of the situation. See Elorza and Bizcarrondo, *Queridos camaradas*, pp. 294–7.
71. Maisky, *Spanish Notebooks*, p. 47.
72. J. Haslam, *The Soviet Union and the Struggle for Collective Security in Europe, 1933–1939* (London: Macmillan, 1984), p. 110; Kowalsky, *La Unión Soviética*, pp. 28–31, 43–6.
73. Smyth, 'We Are With You', pp. 98–100.
74. Howson, *Arms for Spain*, pp. 125–6, 136–7.
75. Skoutelsky, *L'Espoir*, pp. 53–4.
76. M. Jackson, *Fallen Sparrows: The International Brigades in the Spanish Civil War* (Philadelphia: Amer Philosophical Society, 1994), pp. 31, 45.
77. J. Gurney, *Crusade in Spain* (Newton Abbot: Faber & Faber, 1974), p. 36.
78. Skoutelsky, *L'Espoir*, pp. 119–21.
79. Thomas, *The Spanish Civil War*, p. 432.
80. *El Mundo Obrero* (23 November 1936), cited by Skoutelsky, *L'Espoir*, p. 174. See also Carr, *Comintern*, p. 27.
81. C. Blanco Escolá, *La incompetencia militar de Franco* (Madrid: Alianza, 2000), pp. 294–5, 306–7.
82. Ojeda-Revah, 'Mexico', p. 14.
83. Jackson, *Fallen Sparrows*, pp. 16–7.
84. P. Montoliú, *Madrid en la Guerra Civil*, 2 vols. (Madrid: Silex, 1998), vol. 1, pp. 191–210; G. Cardona, 'Las operaciones militares', in M. Tuñón de Lara et al., *La Guerra Civil Española 50 años después* (Barcelona: Labor, 1986), pp. 215–9.
85. E. Toller, 'Madrid–Washington' in V. Cunningham (ed.), *Spanish Front: Writers on the Civil War* (Oxford: Oxford University Press, 1986), p. 73.
86. This was the view of the German chargé d'affaires in Spain. With Republican resistance stiffening, Madrid could no longer be captured. He saw two clear solutions: either to abandon the Spanish adventure or

to throw in additional forces. *DGFP*, Doc. 144 (5 December 1936), pp. 154–5; see also Blanco Escolá, *La incompetencia militar*, p. 324.

87.  *L'Oeuvre de Léon Blum*, p. 379.

88.  Testimony of Pierre Cot in Renouvin and Rémond, *Léon Blum*, p. 368.

89.  M. Thomas, *Britain, France and Appeasement* (Oxford: Berg, 1996), p. 95.

90.  R. García Pérez, *Franquismo y Tercer Reich* (Madrid: Centro de Estudios Constitucionales, 1994), p. 55.

91.  Whealey, *Hitler and Spain*, pp. 53–4.

92.  Ciano, *Diplomatic Papers*, pp. 75–7.

93.  I. Saz and J. Tusell (eds), *Fascistas en España* (Madrid: CSIC, 1981), p. 27.

94.  Coverdale, *Italian Intervention*, p. 180.

95.  Saz and Tusell, *Fascistas*, pp. 29–32.

96.  Cardona, 'Las operaciones', pp. 220–1; Thomas, *The Spanish Civil War*, pp. 488–95.

97.  B. Alexander, *British Volunteers for Liberty* (London: Lawrence & Wishart, 1983), pp. 93–107; M. Merriman and W. Lerude, *Robert Hale Merriman and the Abraham Lincoln Brigade* (Reno: University of Nevada Press, 1986), pp. 114, 118.

98.  Gurney, *Crusade in Spain*, p. 108.

99.  Cardona, 'Las operaciones', pp. 221–4.

100.  Saz and Tusell, *Fascistas*, p. 43.

101.  Ibid., pp. 52–3.

102.  Coverdale, *Italian Intervention*, pp. 225–48.

103.  Saz and Tusell, *Fascistas*, pp. 63–4.

104.  P. Preston, *A Concise History of the Spanish Civil War* (London: HarperCollins, 1996), p. 98.

105.  Alvarez del Vayo, *Freedom's Battle*, pp. 72, 222, 227–8.

106.  The shipment of gold to Russia was decided by the prime minister, Largo Caballero, and the minister of finance, Juan Negrín. Only a very small group of highly-placed officials were aware of the operation. Certainly the decision was not taken under pressure from Moscow and not even the leadership of the PCE knew about it. A. Viñas, 'Gold, the Soviet Union and the Spanish Civil War', in M. Blinkhorn (ed.), *Spain in Conflict, 1931–1939: Democracy and its Enemies* (London: Sage, 1986), pp. 224–34.

107.  Howson, *Arms for Spain*, p. 74.

108.  Whealey, *Hitler and Spain*, p. 56.

109.  C. Leitz, 'Nazi Germany's Intervention in the Spanish Civil War', in Preston and Mackenzie (eds), *The Republic Beseiged*, pp. 62–81.

110.  All the figures for foreign aid are in E. Moradiellos, *El reñidero de Europa: Las dimensiones internacionales de la guerra civil española* (Barcelona: Península, 2001), pp. 261–3. However, Kowalsky (*La*

*Unión Sovietica*, pp. 201–2, 212–18) shows that there remain wide discrepancies on the total amounts of Soviet *matériel*.

111.  A. Hitler, *Hitler's Table Talk, 1941–1944* (London: Weidenfeld & Nicolson, 1953), pp. 569, 607, 687.

112.  W. Krivitsky, *I was Stalin's Agent* (Cambridge: Ian Faulkner, 1992) p. 89.

113.  An account of Nationalist volunteers is in J. Keene, *Fighting for Franco: International Volunteers in Nationalist Spain During the Spanish Civil War, 1936–39* (London: Leicester University Press, 2001).

114.  M. R. de Madariaga, 'The Intervention of Moroccan Troops in the Spanish Civil War: A Reconsideration', *European History Quarterly*, vol. 22 (1992), pp. 78–9.

115.  Coverdale, *Italian Intervention*, pp. 181–6.

116.  An exception was the air squadron hired by Malraux at the start of the war.

117.  Merriman and Lerude, *Robert Hale Merriman*, p. 82.

118.  Skoutelsky, *L'Espoir*, pp. 82, 85, 95–6, 262.

119.  As in the case of the military attaché Barroso in Paris, the defection of the diplomatic corps was a deadly blow for the Republic. There were even embassies and consulates whose officials, by claiming their loyalty to the Republic, could actually continue to deceive the Spanish government.

120.  Howson, *Arms for Spain*, pp. 107–13, 138–40, 146–52; Kowalsky, *La Unión Soviética*, pp. 218–24, 238–40.

## 4  Apocalypse in 1936 Spain

1.  A. Malraux, *L'Espoir* (Paris: Gallimard, 1987), pp. 136–40. First published in 1937, this was Malraux's fictional account of his experiences in Spain. The French author and pilot's call for the 'organisation of the apocalypse' can be seen as an endorsement of the Republican–Communist line.

2.  K. W. Watkins, *The Effects of the Spanish Civil War on British Political Opinion* (Edinburgh: R. & R. Clark, 1963), pp. 239–44. The most competent analysis and demolition of the conspiracy theory is in H. R. Southworth, *Conspiracy and the Spanish Civil War: The Brainwashing of Francisco Franco* (London: Routledge, 2002).

3.  Southworth, *Conspiracy*, pp. 1–8, 71–2.

4.  Ibid., p. 87.

5.  Ibid., pp. 122–3.

6.  A. Reig Tapia, *Violencia y terror* (Madrid: Akal, 1990), pp. 17, 22.

7.  A. Reig Tapia, *Ideología e historia* (Madrid: Akal, 1986), p. 38–42.

8. Reig, *Violencia*, pp. 26–31.
9. P. Preston, *¡Comrades!: Portraits from the Spanish Civil War* (London: HarperCollins, 1999), pp. 3–4.
10. Balfour, *Deadly Embrace*, p. 262.
11. Cardona, *Poder*, pp. 307–9; S. Juliá, 'De "guerra contra el invasor" a "guerra fratrícida" ', in S. Juliá (ed.), *Víctimas de la guerra civil* (Madrid: Temas de Hoy, 1999), p. 16.
12. R. Fraser, *Blood of Spain* (Harmondsworth: Penguin, 1981), p. 51; H. Graham, *The Spanish Republic at War* (Cambridge: Cambridge University Press, 2002), p. 81.
13. J. Zugazagoitia, *Guerra y vicisitudes de los españoles* (Madrid: Tusquets, 2001), p. 152; Preston, *¡Comrades!*, pp. 226–28.
14. Zugazagoitia, *Guerra*, p. 68.
15. A. Barea, *The Clash* in A. Barea, *The Forging of a Rebel* (London: Granta Books, 2001), pp. 522–3; Zugazagoitia, *Guerra*, p. 73; Thomas, *The Spanish Civil War*, pp. 228–30.
16. In the dialectical battle, the insurgents, in an attempt to be identified with the nation/motherland, called themselves '*nacionales*'. Those defending the republican legality they termed simply '*los rojos*' (the Reds). In turn, the Republicans called their enemies 'rebels' or 'Fascists'. R. Abella, *La vida cotidiana durante la guerra civil: La España Nacional* (Barcelona: Planeta, 5th edn, 1976), pp. 29–30.
17. M. Blinkhorn, *Carlism and Crisis in Spain* (Cambridge: Cambriege University Press, 1975), p. 259; Fraser, *Blood*, pp. 64–5; 70–1; J. Casanova, *La Iglesia de Franco* (Madrid: Temas de Hoy, 2001), p. 55.
18. Malraux, *L'Espoir*, pp. 11–18.
19. Fraser, *Blood*, p. 106.
20. P. Pagés, *La Guerra Civil Espanyola a Catalunya, 1936–9* (Barcelona: A. Romero, 2nd edn, 1997), pp. 37–40; Fraser, *Blood*, pp. 63–9.
21. J. Cervera, *Madrid en guerra* (Madrid: Alianza, 1998), pp. 41–8; Montoliú, *Madrid*, vol. 1, pp. 61–73; Zugazagoitia, *Guerra*, pp. 79–85.
22. J. Ortiz Villalba, *Sevilla 1936* (Sevilla: Vistalegre, 1998), pp. 111–44; J. Cifuentes and M. P. Maluenda, 'De las urnas a los cuarteles: La destrucción de las bases sociales republicanas en Zaragoza', in J. Casanova et al., *El pasado oculto: Fascismo y violencia en Aragón, 1936–1939* (Zaragoza: Mira, 2nd edn, 1999), pp. 44–7; Fraser, *Blood*, pp. 69–70.
23. Pagés, *La Guerra Civil*, pp. 55–8.
24. Blinkhorn, *Carlism*, pp. 254–5.
25. Cardona, 'Operaciones', pp. 206–11.
26. Thomas, *The Spanish Civil War*, p. 227.
27. Juliá, 'De "guerra contra el invasor" ', p. 20.
28. J. Aróstegui, 'Los componentes sociales y políticos', in Tuñón de Lara et al., *La Guerra Civil*, p. 60.

29. Reig, *Violencia*, pp. 64–5.
30. J. Tusell, 'La Junta de Defensa de Burgos', in *Historia 16, La Guerra Civil*, 6 (1986), pp. 56–64; Abella, *La España Nacional*, pp. 32–4.
31. Graham, *The Spanish Republic*, p. 96.
32. E. Malefakis, 'La revolución social', in E. Malefakis (ed.), *La guerra de España, 1936–39* (Madrid: Taurus, 1996), pp. 424–5.
33. Zugazagoitia, *Guerra*, p. 76.
34. W. L. Bernecker, 'La revolución social', in S. Payne and J. Tusell (eds), *La Guerra Civil* (Madrid: Temas de Hoy, 1996), pp. 489–90; Aróstegui, 'Los componentes', pp. 53–4.
35. A. Balcells, 'España entre dos gobiernos', in *Historia 16, La Guerra Civil*, 6 (1986), p. 42.
36. M. Alpert, *El ejército republicano en la Guerra Civil* (Madrid: 2nd edn, Siglo XXI, 1989), p. 30.
37. There is a large amount of bibliography on collectivisation. For instance, J. Casanova (ed.), *El sueño igualitario: Campesinado y colectivizaciones en la España Republicana, 1936–1939* (Zaragoza: Fernando el Católico, 1989); W. L. Bernecker, *Colectividades y revolución social* (Barcelona: Crítica, 1982); A. Bosch, *Colectivistas, 1936–39* (Valencia: Almudín, 1980); G. Leval, *Collectives in the Spanish Revolution* (London: Freedom Press, 1975).
38. Jackson, *The Spanish Republic*, pp. 276–83.
39. G. Orwell, *Homage to Catalonia* (Harmondsworth: Penguin, 1987), pp. 8–9.
40. R. Abella, *La vida cotidiana durante la guerra civil: La España Republicana* (Barcelona: Planeta, 1975), pp. 15–16.
41. Balcells, *España*, pp. 8, 38–42; M. Tuñón de Lara, 'Los mecanismos del estado en la zona republicana', in *Anales de la Historia*, vol. 2, *Socialismo y Guerra Civil* (Madrid: Pablo Iglesias, 1987), pp. 124–6.
42. Martin, *Agony*, p. 380.
43. Juliá, *Los Socialistas*, p. 242.
44. S. Juliá, 'De la division orgánica al gobierno de unidad nacional', in *Anales*, p. 234.
45. G. Esenwein and A. Shubert, *Spain at War: The Spanish Civil War in Context, 1931–1939* (London: Longman, 1995), p. 110.
46. Lladonosa, *Sindicalistes*, pp. 66, 72.
47. García Oliver, *El eco*, p. 190.
48. Lorenzo, *Los Anarquistas*, pp. 82–4.
49. Casanova, *De la calle*, pp. 156–8.
50. J. Vilarroya and J. M. Solé i Sabaté, 'La represión en la zona rebelde', in *Historia 16, La Guerra Civil*, 6 (1986), pp. 100–2.
51. Cervera, *Madrid*, p. 48, Montoliú, *Madrid*, vol. 1, p. 69.
52. J. Casanova, 'Rebelión y revolución', in Juliá, *Víctimas*, pp. 86–7, 93–5, 104.

53. The term is borrowed from Gramsci. See Q. Hoare and G. Nowell Smith (eds), *Selections from the Prison Notebooks of Antonio Gramsci* (London: Lawrence and Wishart, 1986), pp. 5–7.
54. Casanova, *La Iglesia*, pp. 38–9.
55. The case of Mosén Puig is cited in Julio de la Cueva Merino, 'Si los curas y frailes supieran', in Juliá (ed.), *Violencia*, pp. 191–2; see also Casanova, 'Rebelión', pp. 127, 139, 153–5; Abella, *La España Republicana*, pp. 100–2; and Casanova, *La Iglesia*, pp. 154–9, 171–93.
56. Juliá, 'De "guerra contra el invasor"', p. 25.
57. Abella, *La España Republicana*, p. 48.
58. García Oliver, *El eco*, pp. 195–6.
59. Fraser, *Blood*, p. 142; Graham, *The Spanish Republic*, pp. 87–8.
60. S. Payne, *Fascism in Spain, 1923–77* (Madison: University of Wisconsin Press, 1999), pp. 254–6; Abella, *La España Nacional*, p. 96.
61. Casanova, 'Rebelión', pp. 69–73, 117–21; Balcells, *España*, pp. 28–9; Abella, *La España Republicana*, pp. 94–6.
62. Montoliú, *Madrid*, vol. 1, pp. 81–97; Cervera, *Madrid*, pp. 56–74.
63. Barea, *The Forging*, pp. 542, 554–5, 559–61; similar cases are cited by Zugazagoitia, *Guerra*, pp. 90–1 and Abella, *La España Republicana*, p. 98.
64. Barea, *The Forging*, p. 548.
65. Zugazagoitia, *Guerra*, p. 89; Reig, *Ideología*, pp. 131–7; Pagés, *La Guerra Civil*, pp. 72–3.
66. Raguer, *La pólvora*, pp. 198–204; Cervera, *Madrid*, pp. 347–50, 369–74; Montoliú, *Madrid*, vol. 1, pp. 106–7.
67. Reig, *Violencia*, pp. 114–15; Casanova, 'Rebelión', pp. 161–3; Abella, *La España Republicana*, p. 40.
68. García Oliver, *El eco*, pp. 347–8.
69. A. Reig Tapia, *Memoria de la Guerra Civil* (Madrid: Alianza, 1999), pp. 230–1; Montoliú, *Madrid*, vol. 1, pp. 234–8; Cervera, *Madrid*, pp. 84–99.
70. J. M. Solé i Sabaté, 'Las represiones', in Payne and Tusell (eds), *La Guerra Civil*, pp. 600–1; Reig, *Violencia*, p. 16.
71. Vilarroya and Solé i Sabaté, 'La represión en la zona rebelde', p. 100; Reig, *Violencia*, p. 107; Casanova, 'Rebelión', p. 59.
72. A fact recognised by R. Serrano Suñer, *Memorias* (Barcelona: Planeta, 1977), pp. 245–7.
73. Juliá, 'De "guerra contra el invasor"', p. 26; Reig, *Violencia*, p. 14.
74. Reig, Violencia, p. 110; Casanova, 'Rebelión', p. 81; H. Southworth, *El mito de la cruzada de Franco* (Barcelona: Plaza and Janés, 1986), pp. 215–17.
75. P. Preston, *The Politics of Revenge: Fascism and the Military in Twentieth-Century Spain* (London: Routledge, 1995), p. 3; F. Espinosa, 'Julio 1936', in J. Casanova et al., *Morir, matar, sobrevivir: La violencia en la dictadura de Franco* (Barcelona: Crítica, 2002), p. 115; A. Cenarro, 'Matar, vigilar y

delatar: La quiebra de la sociedad civil durante la guerra y la posguerra en España, 1936–48', *Historia Social*, 44 (2002), pp. 70–2.

76.  A. Cenarro, 'Muerte y subordinación en la España franquista: El imperio de la violencia como base del nuevo estado', *Historia Social*, 30 (1998), p. 13.

77.  M. Richards, *A Time of Silence: Civil War and the Culture of Repression in Franco's Spain, 1936–1945* (Cambridge: Cambridge University Press, 1998), p. 9; Casanova, 'Rebelión', p. 64; Abella, *La España Nacional*, p. 81.

78.  Vilarroya and Solé i Sabaté, 'La represión en la zona rebelde', p. 104.

79.  Espinosa, 'Julio 1936', pp. 90, 117.

80.  Zugazagoitia, *Guerra*, p. 94; Casanova, 'Rebelión', p. 76.

81.  Preston, *Concise History*, p. 89.

82.  M. R. de Madariaga, *Los Moros que trajo Franco: La intervención de tropas coloniales en la guerra civil* (Barcelona: Martínez Roca, 2002), pp. 304–8; Balfour, *Deadly Embrace*, pp. 291, 293; Espinosa, 'Julio 1936', pp. 69–71.

83.  Southworth, *El mito*, pp. 217–31; Reig, *Memoria*, pp. 115–8, 124–38; Espinosa, 'Julio 1936', pp. 75–7.

84.  Casanova, 'Rebelión', pp. 112–14; Raguer, *La Pólvora*, pp. 204–11.

85.  Reig Tapia, *Ideología*, pp. 144–7.

86.  Reig Tapia, *Memoria*, p. 130.

87.  Ibid., p. 228; Abella, *La España Republicana*, p. 38.

88.  Cited by Preston, *¡Comrades!*, p. 331.

89.  Reig Tapia, *Memoria*, pp. 80–1.

90.  A. Reig Tapia, *Franco Caudillo: Mito y realidad* (Madrid: Tecnos, 1995), pp. 117–18; J. Casanova, 'Una dictadura de cuarenta años', in Casanova et al., *Morir*, p. 21.

91.  In general, I have used the term 'apocalypse' in its wider meaning of mayhem. In this subheading, it is employed following Malraux's definition of revolutionary fervour following the coup.

92.  Thomas, *The Spanish Civil War*, pp. 282–3.

93.  Preston, *Concise History*, pp. 179–80.

94.  H. Graham, *Socialism and War: The Spanish Socialist Party in Power and Crisis, 1936–1939* (Cambridge: Cambridge University Press, 1991), p. 88.

95.  H. Graham, 'The Eclipse of the Socialist Left: 1934–37', in Preston and Lannon (eds), *Elites*, p. 128.

96.  Tuñón de Lara, 'Los mecanismos', p. 127.

97.  Martin, *Agony*, pp. 381.

98.  Juliá, *Los Socialistas*, p. 250.

99.  F. Fernández Bastarreche, 'La estrategia militar republicana durante la guerra civil', in *Anales*, pp. 50–1; H. Graham, 'Mobilize and Survive: A Story from the Spanish Civil War', *History Teaching Review Year Book*, vol. 10 (1996), p. 33.

100. Fraser, *Blood*, pp. 134–6; Thomas, *The Spanish Civil War*, pp. 316–22, 400.
101. Abella, *La España Republicana*, p. 27; Alpert, *El ejército republicano*, p. 31.
102. Graham, 'Mobilize', p. 39.
103. J. Casanova, *Anarquismo y revolución en la sociedad rural aragonesa* (Madrid: Siglo XXI, 1985), pp. 148–50; Martin, *Agony*, p. 383.
104. Casanova, *De la calle*, p. 177. Lorenzo (*Los Anarquistas*, pp. 182–90) explained how the central issue was not whether to join the government but how to obtain as many portfolios as possible. Horacio Prieto even managed to get Azaña's support in his bargaining with Largo Caballero.
105. Fraser, *Blood*, p. 372.
106. Alpert, *El ejército republicano*, pp. 50–2, 68–82.
107. Thomas, *The Spanish Civil War*, p. 299.
108. Graham, *The Spanish Republic*, p. 130.
109. Preston, *Concise History*, p. 145.
110. P. Preston, *Franco* (London: HarperCollins, 1993), pp. 16–21; J. Tusell, *Franco en la Guerra Civil* (Madrid: Tusquets, 1993), p. 16.
111. Blanco Escolá, *La Incompetencia*, pp. 81–101, 121–146.
112. Southworth, *Conspiracy*, p. 177.
113. Preston, *Franco*, pp. 103–5.
114. Blanco Escolá, *La Incompetencia*, pp. 194–211; S. Ellwood, *Franco* (London: Longman, 1994), pp. 52–65; Preston, *Franco*, pp. 131–3.
115. Serrano Suñer, *Memorias*, p. 121.
116. Blanco Escolá, *La Incompetencia*, pp. 212–17; Reig, *Franco*, pp. 73–6; Preston, *Franco*, pp. 134–43.
117. Ellwood, *Franco*, pp. 76, 79–85; Preston, *Concise History*, pp. 83–4.
118. The legend fabricated around the siege of the *Alcázar* is analysed in depth by Southworth, *El mito*, pp. 93–116; and more recently, by Reig, *Memorias*, pp. 156–87.
119. Tusell, *Franco*, pp. 52–6; Preston, *Franco*, pp. 176–84.
120. Abella, *La España Nacional*, p. 48.
121. Raguer, *La Pólvora*, pp. 69–75, 84.
122. Casanova, 'Una Dictadura', p. 33.
123. Casanova, *La Iglesia*, p. 14; Lannon, *Privilege*, pp. 199–200.
124. Reig, *Violencia*, pp. 41–3; Raguer, *La pólvora*, pp. 107–8.
125. Casanova, *La Iglesia*, pp. 14, 109–11, 204.
126. Reig, *Memoria*, pp. 280–99.

## 5   Breaking the Stalemate (December 1936–March 1938)

1. A. Hitler, *Hitler's Table Talk, 1941–1944* (London: Weidenfeld and Nicolson, 1953), p. 608. Franco's hesitation to join openly the Axis on

the Second World War confirmed Hitler's already low opinion of the *Caudillo* as a military leader during the Spanish Civil War.

2.  M. Azaña, *Memorias políticas y de la Guerra* (Barcelona: Crítica, 1978), vol. 2, pp. 64–5. The Spanish president of the Republic's sarcastic comments could not highlight better the hypocrisy of the Non-Intervention Agreement.

3.  Blanco Escolá, *La Incompetencia*, pp. 19–25.

4.  P. Preston, 'Francisco Franco: política y estrategia en la Guerra Civil', *Revista de Extremadura*, 21 (September–December 1996), pp. 6, 14, 17.

5.  Serrano Suñer, *Memorias*, pp. 127–50.

6.  Ibid., pp. 157–9.

7.  I. Saz, 'La peculiaritat del feixisme espanyol', *Afers* 25 (1996), pp. 629–31 and I. Saz, 'Salamanca, 1937: los fundamentos de un régimen', *Revista de Extremadura*, 21 (September–December 1996), pp. 83–4.

8.  Abella, *La España Nacional*, p. 100.

9.  Serrano Suñer, *Memorias*, p. 163.

10.  Preston, *Franco*, pp. 209–10.

11.  Blinkhorn, *Carlism*, pp. 276–7; Tusell, *Franco*, pp. 70–5.

12.  Saz, 'Salamanca', p. 89.

13.  Saz, 'La peculiaritat', p. 633.

14.  Zugazagoitia, *Guerra*, p. 270.

15.  S. Ellwood, *Spanish Fascism in the Franco Era* (London: Macmillan, 1987), pp. 36–7; Preston, *¡Comrades!*, pp. 101–7; Payne, *Fascism*, pp. 209–36.

16.  Serrano Suñer, *Memorias*, pp. 169–70; Preston, *Franco*, pp. 193–7; Thomas, *The Spanish Civil War*, pp. 498–500.

17.  Serrano Suñer, *Memorias*, p. 170.

18.  Preston, *Franco*, pp. 260–5; Tusell, *Franco*, pp. 125–30.

19.  Serrano Suñer, *Memorias*, pp. 174, 187.

20.  Payne, *Fascism*, pp. 270–1; Preston, *Franco*, pp. 267–70.

21.  Blinkhorn, *Carlism*, pp. 293–5.

22.  Saz, 'Salamanca', p. 89.

23.  Ellwood, *Franco*, p. 45.

24.  Two Cardinals, six Archbishops, thirty-five Bishops and five Vicars-General signed the letter. Only two refused to endorse it: Francesc Vidal i Barraquer, the Catalan Archbishop of Tarragona, and Mateo Múgica, the Basque Bishop of Vitoria.

25.  Casanova, *La Iglesia*, pp. 78–81.

26.  Preston, *Franco*, pp. 188–9, 273.

27.  Abella, *La España Nacional*, p. 181.

28.  Preston, *¡Comrades!*, p. 53.

29.  Preston, *Franco*, pp. 290–1.

30.  Ibid., pp. 295–6.

31.  Abella, *La España Republicana*, pp. 266, 285–96.

32.  Graham, *Socialism*, p. 67; Juliá, *Los Socialistas*, p. 253.

33.  Juliá, 'De la división', pp. 241–2; Graham, *Socialism*, pp. 88–9.

34. Graham, *The Spanish Republic*, pp. 145, 181–4, 213–4.
35. Aróstegui, 'Los componentes sociales', p. 72.
36. Graham, *The Spanish Republic*, p. 140.
37. Jackson, *The Spanish Republic*, pp. 341–2.
38. In *Mis recuerdos* (p. 180) Largo called Miaja a prima donna who had joined the PCE. Azaña (*Memorias*, p. 39) found Largo's views shocking.
39. Elorza and Bizcarrondo, *Queridos camaradas*, pp. 325, 340. Radosh et al., *Spain*; Doc. 34, pp. 135–7 and Doc. 37, pp. 149–50; Carr, *Comintern*, pp. 37–40; Graham, *The Spanish Republic*, pp. 140–1, 207–8.
40. Juliá, *Los Socialistas*, p. 250.
41. Montoliú, *Madrid*, vol. 1, pp. 239–42; Abella, *La España Republicana*, pp. 204–5.
42. H. Graham, 'Against the State: A Genealogy of the Barcelona May Days', *European History Quarterly*, 29, 4 (October 1999), p. 496.
43. Graham, *The Spanish Republic*, pp. 218–20.
44. The largest of all the parties forming the PSUC was the *Unió Socialista de Catalunya* (USC), a splinter group of the PSOE's Catalan section in 1923. See A. Balcells, *Trabajo industrial y organización obrera en la Cataluña contemporánea, 1900–1936* (Barcelona: LAIA, 1974), pp. 151–2.
45. D. Ballester, *Marginalidades y hegemonías: La UGT de Cataluña, 1888–1936* (Barcelona: Bronce, 1996), pp. 200–10.
46. Lorenzo, *Los anarquistas*, pp. 103–6.
47. See, for example, L. Trotsky, *The Spanish Revolution, 1931–39* (New York: 4th edn, Pathfinder, 1986), pp. 207–21, 245–50.
48. B. Bolloten, *The Spanish Revolution* (Chapel Hill: University of North Carolina Press, 1979), p. 381.
49. Casanova, *De la calle*, pp. 211–12.
50. Elorza and Bizcarrondo, *Queridos camaradas*, pp. 347–54.
51. Lorenzo, *Los Anarquistas*, p. 212.
52. Pelai Pagés, *La Guerra Civil Espanyola a Catalunya (1936–1939)* (Barcelona: Romero, 1997), pp. 103–4.
53. Casanova, *De la calle*, pp. 216–8.
54. Ibid., pp. 219–20.
55. Graham, 'Against the State', p. 524.
56. A. Guillamón, *The Friends of Durruti Group, 1937–1939* (Edinburgh: AK Press, 1996), p. 22.
57. Pagés, *La Guerra Civil*, pp. 106–7.
58. The best updated version of the May Days is in Graham, 'Against the State', pp. 486–542.
59. Casanova, *De la calle*, pp. 222–4.
60. Azaña, *Memorias*, pp. 22–3.
61. In fact, Franco and his brother boasted before the German ambassador Wilhem Faupel that 13 Nationalist agents had organised the affair. See *DGFP*, Doc. 254, p. 286. This, though, is hardly credible.
62. Orwell, *Homage*, pp. 146–7.

63. Guillamón, *The Friends of Durruti Group*, p. 53.
64. Elorza and Bizcarrondo, *Queridos camaradas*, pp. 358–62.
65. Graham, 'Against the State', pp. 522–3.
66. Radosh et al., *Spain Betrayed*, Doc. 41, pp. 181–2, Doc. 43, pp. 195–8 and Doc. 44, pp. 206–7.
67. T. Rees, 'The Highpoint of Communist Influence? The Communist Party and the Civil War in Spain', in T. Rees and A. Thorpe (eds), *International Communism and the Third International, 1919–43* (Manchester: Manchester University Press, 1998), pp. 145, 159.
68. Azaña, *Memorias*, p. 23.
69. Ibid., p. 26.
70. Graham, 'Against the State', pp. 526–7.
71. Lorenzo, *Los Anarquistas*, p. 220.
72. Azaña, *Memorias*, pp. 46–53.
73. Ibid., pp. 42–3.
74. Juliá, *Los Socialistas*, p. 265; Graham, *Socialism*, pp. 126–31, 167–81.
75. The view of Negrín as 'the Moscow man' brought together during the Cold War Francoists, Anarchists and some Socialists. It was advanced in academic circles mainly by Burnett Bolloten: see *The Spanish Revolution*, pp. 451–7 and 'Negrín: El hombre de Moscú', *Historia 16* (January 1986), pp. 11–24. Despite the fact that there is glaring evidence against this case in the documents they themselves reproduce, Radosh et al. (*Spain Betrayed*, pp. 171–6) have recently endorsed it. A recent revaluation of Negrín can be found in the new biography of the Spanish prime minister by R. Miralles, *Juan Negrín* (Madrid: Temas de Hoy, 2003); and the chapter devoted to him in E. Moradiellos, *1936: Los mitos de la Guerra Civil* (Barcelona: Península, 2004), pp. 171–94. For other responses to Bolloten, see H. R. Southworth, 'The Grand Camouflage: Julián Gorkin, Burnett Bolloten and the Spanish Civil War', and H. Graham, 'War, Modernity and Reform: The Premiership of Juan Negrín, 1937–39', both in Preston and Mackenzie (eds), *The Republic Besieged* (pp. 261–310 and 163–96, respectively); J. Aróstegui, 'Burnett Bolloten y la Guerra Civil Española: La persistencia del Gran Engaño', *Historia Contemporánea*, 3 (1990), pp. 151–77; R. Miralles, 'Juan Negrín, ¿resistir, para qué?, *Historia 16*, 253 (May, 1997), pp. 8–23; and M. Tuñón de Lara et al., *Juan Negrín, el hombre necesario* (Las Palmas: Gobierno Canario, 1996), pp. 13–17, 191–2.
76. Miralles, *Juan Negrín*, pp. 49–69; Tuñón de Lara et al., *Juan Negrín*, pp. 19–39, 168.
77. Azaña, *Memorias*, pp. 55–7.
78. Graham, *The Spanish Republic*, pp. 297–8.
79. Zugazagoitia, *Guerra*, p. 303.
80. Radosh et al., *Spain Betrayed*, Doc. 46, p. 220 and Doc. 63, pp. 396–7.
81. Tuñón de Lara et al., *Juan Negrín*, p. 186.
82. Miralles, *Juan Negrín*, pp. 361–65.

83. Ibid., pp. 72–4, 140.
84. Miralles, 'Juan Negrín: ¿resistir, para qué?', p. 9; Moradiellos, *1936*, pp. 182–3.
85. Casanova, *De la calle*, pp. 227–8.
86. F. Godicheau, 'Los hechos de mayo de 1937 y los presos antifascistas: Identificación de un fenómeno represivo', *Historia Social*, 44 (2002), pp. 39–63.
87. A list of reprisals against CNT militants is in J. Peirats, *La CNT en la revolución española* (Paris: Ruedo Ibérico, 1971), vol. 2, pp. 156–64.
88. Orwell, *Homage*, p. 34.
89. Casanova, *Anarquismo*, pp. 228–9, 253, 268–77; Fraser, *Blood*, pp. 390–4.
90. Guillamón, *The Friends of Durruti Group*, p. 61.
91. Casanova, *Anarquismo*, pp. 278–9, 293–4.
92. Orwell, *Homage*, pp. 174–6.
93. Azaña (*Memorias*, p. 165) commented that it all sounded like a novel when Negrín told him the police had arrested the POUM leaders after documents in secret ink had been found incriminating the party. Nin was also supposed to have broken out of jail, helped by a Gestapo squad. For a further analysis of Nin's assassination, see Graham, *The Spanish Republic*, pp. 287–9.
94. Elorza and Bizcarrondo, *Queridos Camaradas*, pp. 374–5, 380–3; Graham, *The Spanish Republic*, p. 284. Even Orwell (*Homage*, p. 168) noted that Negrín kept his head and refused to stage a wholesale massacre of 'Trotskyists'.
95. Cardona, 'Las operaciones', p. 232.
96. J. P. Fusi, 'El País Vasco durante la guerra', in Malefakis (ed.), *La Guerra*, p. 310.
97. Blanco Escolá, *La Incompetencia*, pp. 361–5.
98. Azaña, *Memorias*, p. 98.
99. Fusi, 'El País Vasco', pp. 305–6.
100. Jackson, *The Spanish Republic*, p. 385.
101. H. R. Southworth, *La Destrucción de Guernica* (Paris: Ruedo Ibérico, 1977), pp. 48–50, 487, 499–503; Reig, *Violencia*, pp. 140–64.
102. Fusi, 'El País Vasco', pp. 317–8.
103. Cardona, 'Las operaciones', pp. 239–40.
104. Azaña, *Memorias*, p. 154.
105. Fusi, 'El País Vasco', pp. 319–20; Coverdale, *Italian Intervention*, pp. 285–94.
106. Cardona, 'Las operaciones', pp. 242–3.
107. Preston, *Concise History*, p. 203.
108. Blanco Escolá, *La Incompetencia*, pp. 417–19.
109. Cardona, 'Las operaciones', pp. 243–5.
110. Thomas, *The Spanish Civil War*, pp. 797–803.
111. Graham, 'War', p. 193.
112. Preston, *Concise History*, pp. 4, 190.

113. Moradiellos, *Neutralidad*, pp. 249–50, 306–13.
114. *DGFP*, Doc. 506, p. 564.
115. Alpert, *A New International History*, pp. 113, 116; Howson, *Arms*, pp. 230–1.
116. Azaña, *Memorias*, p. 64.
117. Orwell, *Homage*, p. 241.
118. Maisky, *Spanish Notebooks*, pp. 145–6.
119. Ciano, *Diplomatic Papers*, pp. 75–7.
120. Eden, *Facing the Dictators*, pp. 412, 430–6, 451.
121. Ciano, *Diplomatic Papers*, pp. 83–6; *DGFP*, Doc. 202 (Telegram from German Foreign Minister Constantin Neurath, 14 January 1937), p. 225, and Doc. 204 (Memo from Ulrich Hassell, German Ambassador in Italy, 15 January 1937), pp. 226–7.
122. Eden, *Facing the Dictators*, pp. 439–41; Maisky, *Spanish Notebooks*, p. 125; *DGFP*, Doc. 239 (30 March 1937), pp. 262–5.
123. J. F. Berdah, *La Democracia asesinada: La República española y las grandes potencias, 1931–1939* (Barcelona: Crítica, 2002), pp. 284–5.
124. Southworth, *La Destrucción*, 255–73, 281–300.
125. Zugazagoitia, *Guerra*, p. 304; Radosh et al., *Spain Betrayed*, Doc. 55, orders conveyed by Soviet Minister of Defence Voroshilov and stressing that Stalin himself opposed the bombing of foreign ships, pp. 275–6.
126. *DGFP*, Doc. 264, Neurath to Embassy in Great Britain (23 June 1937), p. 369.
127. Cited by E. Moradiellos, *El reñidero*, p. 163.
128. *DGFP*, Docs. 407 and 408, German Diplomatic Personnel in Italy confirming Italian agreement to comply with Franco's request of blocking routes to Spain (3 and 5 August 1937), pp. 432–3.
129. Ciano, *Diplomatic Papers*, p. 137.
130. *DGFP*, Doc. 418 (12 September 1937), p. 443; G. Ciano, *Diary, 1937–43* (London: Phoenix, 2002), p. 5.
131. Dreifort, *Yvon Delbos*, pp. 62–9.
132. Eden, *Facing the Dictators*, pp. 465–70.
133. Haslam, *The Soviet Union*, p. 148.
134. Ciano, *Diary*, pp. 8, 14–15.
135. Azaña, *Memorias*, pp. 119–20.
136. Miralles, *Juan Negrín*, pp. 268–70.
137. Avilés Farré, *Pasión*, pp. 105–6, 113.
138. Cited by Miralles, 'La política exterior', p. 48.

## 6  The Republic's Defeat (March 1938–March 1939): Chronicle of a Death Foretold?

1. The bitterness of the retreat across the Pyrenees and the taste of defeat are captured in Barea, *The Forging*, p. 750.

2. Zugazagoitia, *Guerra*, p. 377; Abella, *La España Republicana*, pp. 371–4, 380.
3. Azaña, *Memorias*, pp. 38, 121.
4. Moradiellos, *El reñidero*, pp. 144–7.
5. Zugazagoitia, *Guerra*, pp. 445, 460; Jackson, *The Spanish Republic*, pp. 441–2, 456; P. Preston, 'A Pacifist in War: The Tragedy of Julián Besteiro', in Preston, *¡Comrades!*, p. 178.
6. Miralles, *Juan Negrín*, pp. 153–5, 356–8.
7. Zugazagoitia, *Guerra*, p. 441.
8. Azaña, *Memorias*, pp. 278; Alpert, *El ejército republicano*, pp. 185–6, 224.
9. P. Preston, 'A Life Adrift: Indalecio Prieto', in Preston, *¡Comrades!*, p. 270.
10. Zugazagoitia, *Guerra*, p. 411.
11. Elorza and Bizcarrondo, *Queridos camaradas*, pp. 412–13; Miralles, *Juan Negrín*, pp. 195–6.
12. Casanova, *De la calle*, p. 235.
13. Tuñón de Lara et al., *Juan Negrín*, p. 81.
14. I. Prieto, *Yo y Moscú* (Madrid: Nos, 1955), p. 139. As Graham (*The Spanish Republic*, p. 333; and *Socialism*, pp. 136–7) notes, a large part of Prieto's post-war anti-Communist writings were connected with Cold War politics, when it was hoped that the adoption of this position would help the Republicans to attract Western support against Franco. See also Preston, 'A Life', p. 272.
15. The Italian Communist Palmiro Togliatti became, by the summer of 1937, the Comintern's leading man in Spain. The highly unpopular Argentinian Victorio Codovilla was recalled to Moscow. See Elorza and Bizcarrondo, *Queridos camaradas*, p. 455.
16. Ibid., pp. 409–10.
17. Alvarez del Vayo, *Freedom's Battle*, pp. 215–16.
18. Azaña, *Memorias*, p. 396.
19. Tuñón de Lara et al., *Juan Negrín*, p. 92; Cardona, 'Las operaciones militares', pp. 248–9.
20. An emphasis on Franco's desire to prolong the war can be found in Preston, 'Francisco Franco', pp. 24–5. The belief in the Nationalist intention of not alarming France is in M. Alonso Baquer, *El Ebro: La batalla decisiva de los cien días* (Madrid: La Esfera de los Libros, 2003), pp. 220–2. Blanco Escolá (*La incompetencia*, pp. 442–3, 449, 453–5, 462) emphasises Franco's military incompetence.
21. Eden, *Facing the Dictators*, p. 571.
22. Moradiellos, *El reñidero*, pp. 184–5.
23. Eden, *Facing the Dictators*, pp. 554, 574–5, 589–92; Ciano *Diplomatic Papers*, pp. 164, 172–84. See also Moradiellos, *La Perfidia*, pp. 186–8, 197–200, 221–40; and Alpert, *A New International History*, pp. 152–4.
24. Dreifort, *Yvon Delbos*, p. 101.
25. Ciano, *Diary*, p. 61.

26. Heiberg, *Emperadores*, pp. 128, 133. The Italian bombing campaign of eastern Spanish cities in the first half of 1938 totalled 782 raids and left 2618 civilians dead and 5678 wounded. In Barcelona alone, the raids of 16–18 March killed 550 people and left 689 wounded.
27. *DGFP*, Doc. 539 (28 February 1938), pp. 610–12.
28. *DGFP*, Doc. 548 (21 March 1938), p. 622.
29. Moradiellos, *El reñidero*, pp. 193, 202; see also Buchanan, *Britain*, p. 60.
30. Miralles, *Juan Negrín*, p. 183; Avilés Farré, *Pasión*, p. 134.
31. *L'Oeuvre de Léon Blum*, pp. 398–9; see also Lacouture, *Léon Blum*, pp. 346–9.
32. Miralles, *Juan Negrín*, p. 219.
33. Berdah (*La democracia*, p. 371) notes that there had been British pressure to persuade Daladier to replace the persona non grata Boncour by Georges Bonnet, a known supporter of appeasement, at the Quai d'Orsay.
34. Ibid., p. 376.
35. Cited in Moradiellos, 'The Gentle General', p. 16.
36. Bonnet's identification with the British line was complete: like London, he espoused the elimination of the Spanish obstacle in order to improve relations with the dictators and he desired neutralism in central Europe. Daladier personally gave the news to Marcelino Pascua, formerly the Spanish ambassador in the Soviet Union and then in France since April 1938. He claimed that he could no longer resist the pressure of the British, with whom, he noted, France needed to be on good terms. See Miralles, 'La política', pp. 42–6; and Moradiellos, *El reñidero*, pp. 209–10.
37. Ciano, *Diplomatic Papers*, p. 211; Moradiellos, *La Perfidia*, pp. 285–97; Tusell, *Franco*, pp. 198–9.
38. Cited in Moradiellos, *El reñidero*, p. 214 (my own emphasis). Sir Eric Phipps replaced Sir George Clerk as British ambassador to Paris in February 1937.
39. Graham, *The Spanish Republic*, p. 366.
40. García Oliver, *El eco*, p. 503. See also Casanova, *De la calle*, p. 236.
41. Miralles, *Juan Negrín*, pp. 208–9; Thomas, *The Spanish Civil War*, p. 820.
42. J. M. Reverte, *La Batalla del Ebro* (Barcelona: Crítica, 2003), pp. 11, 19–22; Alpert, *El ejército republicano*, p. 203.
43. A detailed account of the Ebro battle can be found in the already-mentioned texts by Reverte and Alonso Baquer. See also Servicio Histórico Militar, *La Batalla del Ebro*, no. 13 (Madrid: San Martín, 1988); Blanco Escolá, *La Incompetencia*, pp. 471–502; and Cardona, 'Las operaciones', pp. 249–54.
44. Reverte, *La Batalla*, pp. 280–4; Servicio Histórico Militar, *La batalla*, p. 200; Thomas, *The Spanish Civil War*, p. 848.
45. *DGFP*, Doc. 660, report by Stohrer (19 September 1938); Berti's instructions to Franco are in *DGFP*, Doc. 654 (22 August 1938), pp. 736–7; Ciano, *Diary*, p. 119.

46. Until the end of the war, the Nationalists counted over 30,000 Italians as well as thousands of Moorish mercenaries and German pilots, advisers and specialists manning tanks and artillery among their ranks. See Reverte, *La Batalla*, pp. 5–6.
47. Thomas, *The Spanish Civil War*, pp. 851–2.
48. Alexander, *British Volunteers*, p. 240.
49. Preston, *Franco*, p. 312.
50. German understanding can be found in *DGFP*, Docs. 666 and 669, (28 September 1938), pp. 749–50, 752; Ciano, *Diary*, p. 132.
51. The unfavourable odds facing the Nationalists if a general war broke out are well examined by the German chargé d'affaires in Spain, Erich Heberlein in *DGFP*, Doc. 657 (12 September 1938), p. 740; and the German ambassador, von Stohrer, *DGFP*, Doc. 658 (16 September 1938), p. 741. The French military plans are discussed in Reverte, *La Batalla*, pp. 344–5; and Avilés Farré, *Pasión*, p. 163.
52. Cited in Moradiellos, *La Perfidia*, p. 321.
53. Reverte, *La Batalla*, p. 563; Blanco Escolá, *La incompetencia*, pp. 481, 502.
54. There are wide disparities in the final number of casualties. I have used those given by Servicio Histórico Militar, *La Batalla*, pp. 300–3; and Reverte, *La Batalla*, p. 571.
55. Cited in Moradiellos, *El reñidero*, p. 232.
56. Cervera, *Madrid*, pp. 119, 376–7.
57. This letter can be found in S. Alvárez, *Negrín, personalidad histórica* (Madrid: Ediciones de la Torre, 1994), Doc. 8, pp. 45–54.
58. Only a few Soviet planes crossed the border but they soon flew back to France as Cataluña was about to be seized by the Nationalists. See Kowalsky, *La Unión Soviética*, pp. 228–31. See also Alpert, *A New International History*, pp. 166, 168. For Cisneros's mission see Alvárez del Vayo, *Freedom's Battle*, Doc. 9, pp. 55–60.
59. Moradiellos, *La Perfidia*, pp. 326–9.
60. Ciano, *Diary*, p. 162.
61. Coverdale, *Italian Intervention*, pp. 371–2; Tusell, *Franco*, pp. 213–14.
62. The German conditions for the supply of their military equipment can be found in *DGFP*, Doc. 674 (5 October 1938), pp. 758–60; Doc. 679 (14 October 1938), pp. 767–8; Doc. 682 (18 October 1938), pp. 769–71; Doc. 691 (7 November 1938), pp. 784–7. The Nationalist compliance is in *DGFP*, Doc. 698 (18 November 1938), pp. 795–6. See also Leitz, *Economic Relations*, pp. 85–90; and Tusell, *Franco*, p. 346.
63. Cardona, 'Las operaciones', pp. 254–6.
64. Servicio Histórico Militar, *La Lucha por la Victoria*, no. 17, vol. 1 (Madrid: San Martín, 1985), pp. 47–73.
65. Avilés Farré, *Pasión*, p. 178.
66. Ciano, *Diary*, pp. 173, 179.
67. Miralles, *Juan Negrín*, p. 287.

68. Abella, *La España Republicana*, p. 428.
69. Ibid., pp. 432–3.
70. Alvárez del Vayo, *Freedom's Battle*, Doc. 10, pp. 67–92. Azaña, *Memorias*, p. 438.
71. The successful conclusion of the Bérard mission can be found in *DGFP*, Doc. 745, Stohrer's report to Berlin (26 February 1939), pp. 855–6. See also Moradiellos, *El reñidero*, p. 247.
72. Cited in Moradiellos, *El reñidero*, p. 241; and Edwards, *The British Government*, pp. 211–12.
73. Moradiellos, *1936*, p. 97.
74. Alvárez del Vayo, *Freedom's Battle*, p. 252.
75. Ibid., p. 281.
76. Cited in Alvárez del Vayo, *Freedom's Battle*, p. 160.
77. Graham, *The Spanish Republic*, p. 399.
78. Zugazagoitia, *Guerra*, pp. 557–8.
79. Graham, *Socialism*, p. 150.
80. Miralles, 'Juan Negrín, resistir, ¿para qué?', p. 19.
81. Preston, *Franco*, pp. 319–20.
82. Miralles, *Juan Negrín*, p. 312.
83. Graham, *The Spanish Republic*, p. 352.
84. For the meeting in Los Llanos see Zugazagoitia, *Guerra*, p. 562–3. Negrín's secret contacts with the enemy are in Miralles, *Juan Negrín*, p. 358; and Thomas, *The Spanish Civil War*, p. 821.
85. Graham, *Socialism*, p. 233.
86. Zugazagoitia, *Guerra*, pp. 492, 536.
87. Graham, *The Spanish Republic*, p. 405; Servicio Histórico Militar, *La lucha*, p. 125.
88. Cervera, *Madrid*, pp. 379–80; Alpert, *El ejército*, p. 286; and Servicio Histórico Militar, *La Lucha*, p. 149.
89. Cervera, *Madrid*, pp. 383–7.
90. Miralles, *Juan Negrín*, p. 317.
91. Azaña, *Memorias*, 409–10. Rivas's opinion is cited in Tuñón de Lara et al., *Juan Negrín*, p. 140. The first official contact between Besteiro and Casado took place on 3 February 1939 at the former's home. They agreed on everything but Besteiro declined the post of president of the new administration, arguing that an army officer should occupy it. See A. Bahamonde and J. Cervera, *Así terminó la guerra de España* (Madrid: Marcial Pons, 1999), p. 302.
92. Preston, 'A Pacifist', pp. 179–81, 186–7. Among the leading members of the fifth column were Antonio Luna García, a professor in the Madrid faculty of law, and Julio Palacios, the vice-rector of the central university. See Bahamonde and Cervera, *Así terminó la guerra*, pp. 256–7.
93. Ibid., pp. 350–1.
94. Servicio Histórico Militar, *La Lucha*, p. 153.

95. Bahamonde and Cervera, *Así terminó la guerra*, pp. 52, 245–6.
96. Ibid., pp. 217–18, 326, 468–9; Servicio Histórico Militar, *La Lucha*, pp. 93–101; Thomas, *The Spanish Civil War*, pp. 898–9.
97. The myth of a Communist takeover is perfectly explained in Alpert, *El ejército republicano*, p. 290; Miralles, *Juan Negrín*, pp. 318–20; Tuñón de Lara et al., *Juan Negrín*, p. 138; and Bahamonde and Cervera, *Así terminó la guerra*, pp. 340–4. On 3 March 1939, Colonel Francisco Galán, Lieutenant Colonel Etelvino Vega, Lieutenant Colonel Leocadio Mendiola and Major Inocencio Curto were given command of the Cartagena naval base, Alicante, Murcia and Albacete respectively.
98. Servicio Histórico Militar, *La Lucha*, pp. 193–233.
99. Zugazagoitia, *Guerra*, p. 574; Miralles, *Juan Negrín*, pp. 322–3.
100. Graham, *The Spanish Republic*, pp. 404–6; Tuñón de Lara et al., *Juan Negrín*, p. 190; Alpert, *El ejército republicano*, p. 230; Bahamonde and Cervera, *Así terminó la guerra*, p. 377.
101. Graham, *The Spanish Republic*, pp. 409–10.
102. Servicio Histórico Militar, *La Lucha*, pp. 264–87; Bahamonde and Cervera, *Así terminó la guerra*, pp. 377–404.
103. Zugazagoitia, *Guerra*, p. 600. See also Servicio Histórico Militar, *La lucha*, pp. 294–314.
104. Thomas, *The Spanish Civil War*, pp. 900–15.
105. Ciano, *Diary*, p. 209.
106. Cited in Preston, *Concise History*, pp. 214–15.

## 7  Epilogue: The Legacy of the Spanish Civil War

1. Azaña, *Memorias*, pp. 312–13. Given the central role played by the army and the Church in the Nationalist camp, Azaña believed that Spain's new order would consist of a traditional reactionary dictatorship different from the 'modernising' features of Fascism.
2. Largo Caballero, *Mis recuerdos*, p. 163.
3. Preston, *The Politics of Revenge*, p. 38; Richards, *A Time of Silence*, pp. 16–17; Reig Tapia, *Franco*, pp. 78; and Moradiellos, *1936*, pp. 19–25. Naturally, there were attempts by the vanquished in exile to write a Manichean interpretation of the Civil War. Yet, their bickering and internal divisions made it impossible to present a coherent and all-embracing view.
4. Preston, *The Politics of Revenge*, p. 56; J. Tusell, *Franco, España y la II Guerra Mundial. Entre el Eje y la Neutralidad* (Madrid: Temas de Hoy, 1995), p. 13.
5. S. Hoare, *Ambassador on Special Mission* (London: Collins, 1946), pp. 22–3, 29–32, 47, 60–1. For Franco's pro-Nazi stance, see Preston, *The Politics of Revenge*, pp. 56–7; Tusell, *Franco*, pp. 45–6, 646, 649.

6.  Reig Tapia, *Franco*, pp. 280–1; Preston, *The Politics of Revenge*, pp. 57–68, 73–4, 84; Tusell, *Franco*, pp. 138–9, 144, 160–2, 200.
7.  Preston, *The Politics of Revenge*, p. 76.
8.  Q. Ahmad, *Britain, Franco Spain and the Cold War, 1945–1950* (London: Garland, 1992), p. 63; F. Portero, *Franco aislado. La cuestión española, 1945–1950* (Madrid: Aguilar, 1989), pp. 128, 212.
9.  Reig Tapia, *Franco*, p. 202.
10. I. Saz, *Fascismo y Franquismo* (Valencia: Universitat de València, 2004), pp. 82–3, 88–9, 155.
11. Preston, *The Politics of Revenge*, p. 37; Reig Tapia, *Franco*, p. 187.
12. Richards, *A Time of Silence*, p. 7; J. Casanova, 'Una dictadura de 40 años', in Casanova et al., *Morir*, pp. 5–9, 13; F. Moreno, 'La represión en la posguerra', in Juliá (ed.), *Víctimas*, pp. 277–8; Reig Tapia, *Franco*, pp. 61, 199–200 and *Memoria*, pp. 11, 22, 70.
13. Of course, the Nazi holocaust was an atrocity without possible comparisons. However, Nazi repression against Germans for political motives was far less widespread than that of Franco's Spain. The number of executions in Spain for political reasons (more than 150,000) was ten times larger than that in Nazi Germany and 1000 times larger than in Fascist Italy. In 1945, six years after the Nationalist victory, there were still over 43,000 political prisoners in Spain, a figure ten times greater than that in Germany in 1937. See Saz, *Fascismo*, pp. 14–15, 179. As Reig Tapia (*Franco*, p. 89) noted, Franco signed more death sentences than any previous head of state in Spain. When he visited Spain in July 1939, Ciano (*Diplomatic*, p. 294) was shocked at the savage repression. He wondered how in Sevilla, which had never been in the hands of 'Reds', could there still be 80 executions daily.
14. Still in present days victims of the Nationalist repression are being dug up in Spain. An updated summary on the Francoist regime repression is in C. Mir Curcó, 'El estudio de la represión franquista: una cuestión sin agotar', in C. Mir Curcó (ed.), *La Represión bajo el Franquismo, Ayer*, 43 (2001), pp. 11–35. The impossibility of finding out the final figures of the repression is stressed by Mir Curcó, 'La represión franquista en la Cataluña rural', in Casanova et al., *Morir*, p. 130. See also Casanova, 'Una dictadura', pp. 8, 20–1.
15. F. Vilanova i Vila-Abadal, 'En el exilio: De los campos franceses al umbral de la deportación', in C. Molinero, M. Sala and J. Sobrequés (eds), *Una inmensa prisión: Los campos de concentración y las prisiones durante la guerra civil y el franquismo* (Barcelona: Crítica, 2003), pp. 81–115.
16. An excellent account of the Republicans' ordeal in German-occupied Europe, and particularly of the horrors of Mauthausen, can be found in D. W. Pike, *Spaniards in the Holocaust: Mauthausen, the Horror on the Danube* (London: Routledge, 2000).
17. J. Cercas, *Soldados de Salamina* (Barcelona: 21st edn, 2002), pp. 156–60.
18. A good summary of the guerrilla war can be found in F. Moreno

Gómez, 'Huidos, guerrilleros, resistentes: La oposición armada a la dictadura', in Casanova et al., *Morir*, pp. 197–295.

19. A selection of thought-provoking articles on the question of penal repression and social persecution is in Molinero, Sala and Sobrequés (eds), *Una inmensa prisión*. See also Richards, *A Time of Silence*, pp. 26–7, 31; and Moreno, 'La represión', pp. 279, 288–9, 298–9.

20. I am indebted to my great-aunt, Carmen Salvadó, for having shown me the letters from her husband while he was in a concentration camp. It was the first time she had shared them with anyone.

21. Richards, *A Time of Silence*, p. 73.

22. Moreno, 'La represión', pp. 298–9.

23. Ibid., pp. 351–9; Casanova, *La Iglesia*, pp. 243–53. Reminiscent of the times of the *Reconquista*, many priests were the first to demand punishment for the 'Red rabble and Godless men' who fought for the Republic. Rafael Puerta, one of the Republican soldiers captured in Teruel and then recycled to fight for the Nationalists, still remembers with dismay how, before an offensive, the clergy acted as political commissars, rousing the spirit of the 'Christian army' and, with pistols in hand, called for the extermination of the faithless 'Communist scum'.

24. Cenarro, 'Matar', pp. 78–81.

25. A. Cenarro, 'Memory Beyond the Public Sphere: The Francoist Repression remembered in Aragon', in R. Rein (ed.), *Spanish Memories: Images of a Contested Past*; *History and Memory*, vol. 44 (Fall 2002), p. 167; Casanova, 'Una dictadura', p. 15; Richards, *A Time of Silence*, pp. 24, 28–9.

26. V. M. Pérez-Díaz, *The Return of Civil Society. The Emergence of Democratic Spain* (Cambridge: Harvard University Press, 1993), pp. 12–13; P. Preston, *The Triumph of Democracy in Spain* (London: Methuen, 1986), pp. 11–13; D. Gilmour, *The Transformation of Spain. From Franco to the Constitutional Monarchy* (London: Quartet, 1985), p. 33.

27. P. Aguilar Fernández, *Memoria y olvido de la Guerra Civil española* (Madrid: Alianza, 1996), pp. 34–5, 47, 56–7.

# Select Bibliography

The Spanish Civil War has generated a massive amount of literature in many languages. Although the majority of the texts are in Spanish, many important works have been translated into English and some of the most significant academic contributions to the debate have been produced in Britain and the United States. The following bibliography is designed for an English-speaking audience, although it also contains some crucial works in Spanish and other languages. Its purpose is to offer the reader a concise but useful point of departure.

## The origins of the Civil War

Two classic texts on the origins of the Spanish Civil War are G. Brennan, *The Spanish Labyrinth: An Account of the Social and Political Background of the Spanish Civil War* (New York: Canto edn, 1990; first published in 1943) and R. Carr, *Spain, 1808–1975* (Oxford: Clarendon Press, 1982). A good social history background is A. Shubert, *A Social History of Modern Spain* (London: Unwin Hyman, 1990). Good introductions to economic history are N. Sánchez Albornoz (ed.), *The Economic Modernization of Spain, 1830–1930* (New York: New York University Press, 1987); J. Harrison, *The Spanish Economy in the Twentieth Century* (London: Croom Helm, 1985); and J. Palafox, *Atraso económico y democracia: La Segunda República y la economía española, 1892–1936* (Barcelona: Crítica, 1991).

There are many excellent studies of Spain's organised labour movement from the monarchy to the republic. A comprehensive exploration of working-class divisions and radicalisation during the last years of the Liberal monarchy can be found in G. Meaker, *The Revolutionary Left in Spain, 1914–1923* (Stanford, CA: Stanford University Press, 1974). Covering the period from the nineteenth century to the civil war is the sober and well-argued text by B. Martin, *The Agony of Modernization:*

*Labor and Industrialization in Spain* (Ithaca, NY: Cornell University Press, 1990). For the Socialist movement, see P. Heywood, *Marxism and the Failure of Organised Socialism in Spain, 1879–1936* (Cambridge: Cambridge University Press, 1990). On the Anarcho-syndicalist movement there are some outstanding studies in Spanish, such as A. Bar, *La CNT en los años rojos, 1910–26* (Madrid: Akal, 1981) and J. Casanova, *De la calle al frente: El anarcosindicalismo en España, 1931–1939* (Barcelona: Crítica, 1997). In contrast, texts in English are often partisan and lacking in any great academic value. Exceptions include the works of C. Ealham, such as 'Anarchism and Illegality in Barcelona, 1931–1937', *Contemporary European History*, vol. 4, 2 (1995); 'Revolutionary Gymnastics and the Unemployed: The Limits of the Spanish Anarchist Utopia, 1931–37', in K. Flett and D. Renton (eds), *The Twentieth Century: A Century of Wars and Revolutions?* (London: Rivers Oram, 2000) and 'Class and the City: Spatial Memories of Pleasure and Danger in Barcelona, 1914–23', *Oral History*, vol. 29, 1 (Spring 2001). An interesting collection of essays on Catalan labour can also be found in A. Smith (ed.), *Red Barcelona: Social Protest and Mobilization in the Twentieth Century* (London: Routledge, 2002). On right-wing tradeunionism there is the original contribution, although baffling in some of its conclusions, by C. Winston, *Workers and the Right in Spain, 1900–1936* (Princeton, NJ: Princeton University Press, 1984).

On the army, see S. Payne, *Politics and the Military in Modern Spain* (Stanford, CA: Stanford University Press, 1967); C. P. Boyd, *Praetorian Politics in Liberal Spain* (Chapel Hill: University of North Carolina Press, 1979); and M. Ballbé, *Orden público y militarismo en la España constitucional, 1812–1983* (Madrid: Alianza, 1985). A lucid exploration of the ideology and role played by the colonial army is in S. Balfour, *Deadly Embrace: Morocco and the Road to the Spanish Civil War* (Oxford: Oxford University Press, 2002). A classic study of the crucial issue of land reform and rural disturbances is E. Malefakis, *Agrarian Reform and Peasant Revolution in Spain* (London: Yale University Press, 1970). On the Catholic Church the most thorough analyses are in F. Lannon, *Privilege, Persecution and Prophecy: The Catholic Church in Spain, 1875–1975* (Oxford: Oxford University Press, 1987) and H. Raguer, *La pólvora y el incienso: La Iglesia y la guerra civil española, 1936–1939* (Barcelona: Península, 2001).

The growing political turmoil and social upheaval following the First World War is examined in F. J. Romero Salvadó, *Spain 1914–1918: Between War and Revolution* (London: Routledge, 1999). The dictatorship of Primo de Rivera is studied by S. Ben-Ami in *The Origins of the Second Republic in Spain* (Oxford: Oxford University Press, 1978) and *Fascism from Above: The Dictatorship of Primo de Rivera in Spain, 1923–1930* (Oxford: Oxford University Press, 1983). However, more up-to-date studies can be found in Spanish works such as M. T. González Calbet, *La Dictadura de Primo de Rivera* (Madrid: El Arquero, 1987) and J. L. Gómez Navarro, *El régimen de Primo de Rivera* (Madrid: Cátedra, 1991). An excellent analysis of the breakdown of the Second Republic is P. Preston, *The Coming of the Spanish Civil War: Reform, Reaction and Revolution in the Second Republic* (London: Routledge, 1994). An alternative view, sympathetic to the CEDA, can be found in S. Payne, *Spain's First Democracy: The Second Republic, 1931–6* (Madison: University of Wisconsin Press, 1993). The failure of centrist politics is examined in N. Townson, *The Crisis of Democracy in Spain: Centrist Politics under the Second Republic, 1931–1936* (Brighton: Sussex Academic Press, 2000). An interesting study of political radicalism and social polarisation, focusing on the Asturian city of Gijón, can be found in P. B. Radcliff, *From Mobilization to Civil War: The Politics of Polarization in the Spanish City of Gijón, 1900–1937* (Cambridge: Cambridge University Press, 1996). For this period, S. Juliá is the author of a series of extremely useful works in Spanish: *Madrid, 1931–34: De la fiesta popular a la lucha de clases* (Madrid: Siglo XXI, 1984); *Orígenes del Frente Popular en España, 1934–6* (Madrid: Siglo XXI, 1979); *Manuel Azaña: Una biografía política* (Madrid: Alianza, 1991). He is also the editor of an important collection of essays in *Política en la Segunda República*, *Ayer*, 20 (1995).

Although unfortunately not translated into English, there are a number of crucial memoirs of and accounts by protagonists: J. M. Gil Robles, *No fue posible la paz* (Madrid: Planeta, 1998); M. Maura, *Así cayó Alfonso XIII* (Barcelona, 7th edn: Ariel, 1995); N. Alcalá Zamora, *Memorias* (Madrid: Planeta, 1998); F. Largo Caballero, *Mis recuerdos. Cartas a un amigo* (México: Ed. Unidas, 1976) and *Escritos de La República* (Madrid: Pablo Iglesias, 1985); and M. Azaña, *Diarios, 1932–3* (Madrid: Crítica, 1997).

**General surveys**

Three of the pioneer narratives of the civil war still remain very useful: H. Thomas, *The Spanish Civil War* (London: Penguin, 3rd edn; 1986, first published in 1961); G. Jackson, *The Spanish Republic and the Civil*

*War, 1931–39* (Princeton, NJ: Princeton University Press, 1967); and R. Carr, *The Spanish Tragedy: The Civil War in Perspective* (London, 1977, reprinted by Sterling, 2002). Much more outdated is the classic text by the French authors, P. Broué and E. Témime, *The Revolution and the Civil War in Spain* (London: Faber, 1972). There are a number of more recent and concise synthetic studies: H. Browne, *Spain's Civil War* (Harlow: Longman, 1983); S. Ellwood, *The Spanish Civil War* (Oxford: Blackwell, 1991); G. Esenwein and A. Shubert, *Spain at War: The Civil War in Context 1931–1939* (London: Longman, 1995); P. Preston, *A Concise History of the Spanish Civil War* (London: HarperCollins, 1996); A. Beevor, *The Spanish Civil War* (London: Cassell, 1999); and F. Lannon, *The Spanish Civil War, 1936–1939* (Oxford: Osprey, 2002). Collections of edited articles dealing with a variety of important aspects of both the Second Republic and the Civil War can be found in P. Preston (ed.), *Revolution and War in Spain, 1931–1939,* (London: Methuen, 1984); M. Blinkhorn (ed.), *Democracy and Civil War in Spain, 1931–1939: Democracy and its Enemies* (London: Routledge, 1988); and P. Preston and A. Mackenzie (eds), *The Republic Besieged: Civil War in Spain, 1936–1939* (Edinburgh: Edinburgh University Press, 1996). A thought-provoking work based on oral history is R. Fraser, *Blood of Spain: An Oral History of the Spanish Civil War* (Harmondsworth: Penguin, 1981). There are, naturally, a large number of texts in Spanish. Of great value, for instance, due to the quality of the contributors, are the collection of articles in M. Tuñón de Lara et al., *La Guerra Civil Española 50 años después* (Barcelona: Labor, 1986); E. Malefakis (ed.), *La guerra de España, 1936–39* (Madrid: Taurus, 1996); and S. Payne and J. Tusell (eds), *La Guerra Civil* (Madrid: Temas de Hoy, 1996). The most recent important analytical study is E. Moradiellos, *1936: Los mitos de la Guerra Civil* (Barcelona: Península, 2004).

## The Republican zone

The most competent and well-argued analysis of the impact of the war upon the Republic is in H. Graham, *The Spanish Republic at War, 1936–39* (Cambridge: Cambridge University Press, 2002). Graham is also the author of the best and most cogent account of the Republic's internal tensions, as shown in the May Days of 1937: 'Against the State: A Genealogy of the Barcelona May Days', *European History Quarterly*, Vol. 29, 4 (October 1999). On the issue of war and revolution, the monumental work by B. Bolloten is still important: *The Grand Camouflage* (New York: Prager, 1968). Bolloten's volume was later revised and expanded in successive publications: *The Spanish Revolution* (Chapel Hill: University of North Carolina Press, 1979) and *The Spanish Civil War: Revolution and Counterrevolution*, (Hemel Hempstead: Harvester Wheatsheaf, 1991). However, Bolloten's powerful indictment of the Communist Party and of prime minister Negrín has been challenged by more recent works, including the clinical and detailed study by H. R. Southworth: 'The Grand Camouflage: Julián Gorkin, Burnett Bolloten and the Spanish Civil War', in Preston and Mackenzie (eds), *The Republic Besieged*. A similar assault on Bolloten's thesis can be found in J. Aróstegui, 'Burnett Bolloten y la Guerra Civil Española: La persistencia del Gran Engaño', in *Historia Contemporánea*, 3 (1990). In turn, Bolloten's characterisation of Negrín as little more than a puppet of Moscow has been demolished by the powerful studies of M. Tuñón et al., *Juan Negrín, el hombre necesario* (Las Palmas: Gobierno Canario, 1996) and R. Miralles, *Juan Negrín* (Madrid: Temas de Hoy, 2003). A good English-language version of the reassessment of Negrín can be found in H. Graham, 'War, Modernity and Reform: The Premiership of Juan Negrín, 1937–39', in Preston and Mackenzie (eds), *The Republic Besieged*; see also H. Graham, 'The Spanish Socialist Party in Power and the Government of Juan Negrín', *European History Quarterly*, Vol. 18, 2 (1988).

An interesting account of daily life in the Republican zone can be found in R. Abellá, *La vida cotidiana durante la guerra civil: La España Republicana* (Barcelona: Planeta, 1975). However, the memoirs of protagonists are indispensable to understand the traumatic times undergone by the Republic during the war: M. Azaña, *Memorias políticas y de la Guerra* (Barcelona: Crítica, 1978); J. Zugazagoitia, *Guerra y vicisitudes de los españoles* (Madrid: Tusquets, 2001); F. Largo Caballero, *Mis recuerdos. Cartas a un amigo* (México: Ed. Unidas, 1976); J. Alvarez del Vayo, *Freedom's Battle* (London: Heinemann, 1940); and A. Barea, *The Clash*, as part of his important trilogy, *The Forging of a Rebel* (London: Granta Books, 2001). An excellent biographical study of leading Republican politicians – Manuel Azaña, Julián Besteiro and Indalecio Prieto – is in P. Preston, *¡Comrades! Portraits from the Spanish Civil War* (London: HarperCollins, 1999).

The most thorough study of the CNT during the war is that already mentioned by J. Casanova, *De la calle al frente*. A brief version of Casanovas's work in English can be found in his 'Anarchism and Revolution in the Spanish Civil War: The Case of Aragon', *European*

*History Quarterly*, vol. 17, 4 (October 1987). Other works on the Anarcho-syndicalist movement are: R. J. Alexander, *The Anarchists in the Spanish Civil War*, 2 vols. (London: Janus, 1999); J. Brademas, *Anarcosindicalismo y revolución en España, 1930–1937* (Barcelona: Ariel, 1974); G. Kelsey, *Anarchosyndicalism, Libertarian Communism and the State: The CNT in Zaragoza and Aragón* (Amsterdam: Institute for Social History, 1991); and J. Peirats, *Anarchists in the Spanish Revolution* (London: Freedom Press, 1990). Also of interest is the autobiography of J. García Oliver: *El eco de los pasos* (Paris: Ruedo Ibérico, 1978); and the study of the Anarchist leader Buenaventura Durruti by A. Paz, *Durruti: The People Armed* (Montreal: Black Rose Books, 1976).

The Socialist movement is studied in H. Graham, *Socialism and War: The Spanish Socialist Party in Power and Crisis, 1936–1939* (Cambridge: Cambridge University Press, 1991). In turn, the growing influence of the PCE in the Republican camp can be found in A. Elorza and M. Bizcarrondo, *Queridos camaradas: La Internacional Comunista y España, 1919–1939* (Madrid: Planeta, 1999) and T. Rees, 'The Highpoint of Communist Influence? The Communist Party and the Civil War in Spain', in T. Rees and A. Thorpe (eds), *International Communism and the Third International, 1919–43* (Manchester: Manchester University Press, 1998). It is also worth looking at the view offered by the Communist leader Dolores Ibarruri in *They Shall Not Pass: The Autobiography of La Pasionaria* (London: Allen & Unwin, 1966); and R. Low, *La Pasionaria: The Spanish Firebrand* (London: Random House 1992).

On the difficulties of creating a Republican army, see M. Alpert, *El ejército republicano en la Guerra Civil* (Madrid: 2nd edn, Siglo XXI, 1989). For the process of collectivisation, see: J. Casanova (ed.), *El sueño igualitario* (Zaragoza: Fernando el Católico, 1989); W. L. Bernecker, *Colectividades y revolución social* (Barcelona: Crítica, 1982); A. Bosch, *Colectivistas, 1936–39* (Valencia: Almudín, 1980); and G. Leval, *Collectives in the Spanish Revolution* (London: Freedom Press, 1975). There are an increasing number of books dealing with the changing role of women in the Republic: M. A. Ackelsberg, *Free Women of Spain: Anarchism and the Struggle for the Emancipation of Women* (Bloomington: Indiana University Press, 1991); M. Nash, *Defying Male Civilization: Women in the Spanish Civil War* (Denver, CO: Arden Press, 1995); P. Preston, *Doves of War: Four Women of Spain* (London: HarperCollins, 2002); and A. Jackson, *British Women and the Spanish Civil War* (London: Routledge, 2002).

The best analysis of the last days of the war is A. Bahamonde and J. Cervera, *Así terminó la guerra de España* (Madrid: Marcial Pons,

1999). Casado's version of the events can be found in English: *The Last Days of Madrid* (London: Peter Davies, 1939). The delusions and despair reflected in the behaviour of Julián Besteiro is perfectly illustrated in the chapter devoted to him in Preston, *¡Comrades!*

## The Nationalist zone

Once the vast number of apologist narratives and the Francoist propaganda are eliminated, there are far fewer academic studies on Nationalist than on Republican Spain. An exception is the significant number of important biographical studies of the *Caudillo*. The most thorough and far-reaching work is P. Preston, *Franco* (London: HarperCollins, 1993). Preston is also the author of a brief study of the Spanish dictator, together with studies of General Millán Astray and José Antonio Primo de Rivera in his *¡Comrades!* Other valuable biographies are J. P. Fusi, *Franco: A Biography* (London: Unwin Hyman, 1987); S. Ellwood, *Franco* (London: Longman, 1994); and G. Ashford Hodges, *Franco* (London: Weidenfeld & Nicolson, 2000). The most competent study in Spanish of Franco's rise during the civil war is J. Tusell, *Franco en la Guerra Civil* (Madrid: Tusquets, 1993). A very interesting study of Franco's military shortcomings can be found in C. Blanco Escolá, *La incompetencia militar de Franco* (Madrid: Alianza, 2000). The most outstanding analyses of the mythical foundations of the Nationalist crusade and of Franco's rise to power are the works by H. R. Southworth, *El mito de la cruzada de Franco* (Barcelona: Plaza & Janés, 1986) and *Conspiracy and the Spanish Civil War: The Brainwashing of Francisco Franco* (London: Routledge, 2002); and those by A. Reig Tapia, *Ideología e historia* (Madrid: Akal, 1986) and *Franco Caudillo: Mito y realidad* (Madrid: Tecnos, 1995).

To compliment his similar study of the Republic, R. Abellá is the author of an interesting account of quotidian life in Franco's Spain: R. Abellá, *La vida cotidiana durante la guerra civil: La España Nacional* (Barcelona: Planeta, 5th edn, 1976). A detailed study of Carlism in the 1930s can be found in M. Blinkhorn, *Carlism and Crisis in Spain, 1931–39* (Cambridge: Cambridge University Press, 1975). On the Falange, the most competent works are those by S. Ellwood, *Spanish Fascism in the Franco Era* (London: Macmillan, 1987); S. Payne, *Fascism in Spain, 1923–77* (Madison: University of Wisconsin Press, 1999); and J. Thomas, *La Falange de Franco. Fascismo y fascistización en el régimen franquista, 1937–1945* (Barcelona: Plaza & Janés, 2001). Crucial analyses of the Catholic Church and the civil war are the aforementioned volume by Raguer, *La pólvora y el incienso*, and J. Casanova, *La Iglesia de Franco* (Madrid: Temas de Hoy, 2001). The political foundations of the Nationalist state are well analysed by I. Saz in *España contra España: Los nacionalismos franquistas* (Madrid: Marcial Pons, 2003) and *Fascismo y Franquismo* (Valencia: Universitat de València, 2004).

**Military history**

The literature in English focusing on the military aspects and key battles of the war has become outdated by the publication of more recent and well-researched Spanish works. An exception is the lucid study of war in the air by G. Howson, *Aircraft of the Spanish Civil War, 1936–1939* (London: Putnam, 1990) and the thorough analysis of the bombing of Guernica by H. R. Southworth, *Guernica! Guernica! A Study of Journalism, Diplomacy, Propaganda and History* (Berkeley: California University Press, 1977).

Narratives in English of the battle and siege of Madrid, such as R. G. Colodny, *The Struggle for Madrid* (New York, Payne-Whitman, 1958) and D. Kurzman, *Miracle of November* (New York: Putnam, 1980), have been superseded by Spanish works such as J. Aróstegui and J. A. Martínez, *La Junta de Defensa de Madrid* (Madrid: Comunidad de Madrid, 1984) and J. M. Reverte, *La batalla de Madrid* (Barcelona: Crítica, 2004). The same can be said on the advance of the Army of Africa. Old texts, such as H. G. Cardozo, *The March of a Nation: My Year of Spain's Civil War* (London: Right Book Club, 1937) and C. Gerahty, *The Road to Madrid* (London: Hutchinson, 1937), look very outdated compared to new contributions such as F. Espinosa Maestre, *La columna de la muerte. El avance del ejército franquista de Sevilla a Badajoz* (Barcelona: Crítica, 2003).

A number of volumes dealing with every major battle have been produced by the Spanish military archives (the Servicio Histórico Militar). A very coherent summary of the military aspects of the war can be found in G. Cardona, 'Las operaciones militares', in M. Tuñón de Lara et al., *La guerra civil española*. The Battle of the Ebro, the longest-lasting and bloodiest battle of the war, has been examined thoroughly from different perspectives by J. M. Reverte, *La batalla del Ebro* (Barcelona: Crítica, 2003) and M. Alonso Baquer, *El Ebro: La batalla decisiva de los cien días* (Madrid: La Esfera de los Libros,

2003). A very interesting dissection of every battle (comparing the strategies followed by General Franco and the chief of the Republic's general staff, General Rojo) can be found in the aforementioned Blanco Escolá, *La incompetencia militar de Franco*.

## Foreign intervention

The international dimension of the war is the field best covered by English-language publications. An interesting pioneer survey is D. A. Puzzo, *Spain and the Great Powers* (New York: Columbia University Press, 1962). Slightly more outdated is P. van der Esch, *Prelude to War* (The Hague: Martinus Nijhoff, 1951). A more recent and reader-friendly overview can be found in M. Alpert, *A New International History of the Spanish Civil War* (London: Macmillan, 1994). An extremely original work (focusing on the hitherto neglected but crucial area of arms dealers and the procurement of weapons) is G. Howson, *Arms for Spain: The Untold Story of the Spanish Civil War* (London: John Murray, 1998). The best survey in Spanish is E. Moradiellos, *El reñidero de Europa: Las dimensiones internacionales de la guerra civil española* (Barcelona: Península, 2001). Also interesting is the work, originally published in French, by J. F. Berdah, *La democracia asesinada: La república española y las grandes potencias, 1931–1939* (Barcelona: Crítica, 2002).

For Britain's position during the Spanish Civil War, texts worth reading are K. W. Watkins, *The Effects of the Spanish Civil War on British Political Opinion* (Edinburgh: R. & R. Clark, 1963); J. Edwards, *The British Government and the Spanish Civil War* (London: Macmillan, 1979); and D. Little, *Malevolent Neutrality: The United States, Great Britain and the Origins of Non-Intervention* (Ithaca, NY: Cornell University Press, 1981). A recent work more sympathetic to the British government is T. Buchanan, *Britain and the Spanish Civil War* (Cambridge: Cambridge University Press, 1997). However, the best analyses can be found in Spanish: J. Avilés Farré, *Pasión y farsa: Franceses y británicos ante la guerra civil* (Madrid: Eudema, 1994); E. Moradiellos, *Neutralidad benévola* (Oviedo: Pentalfa, 1990); and E. Moradiellos *La Perfidia de Albión* (Madrid: Siglo XXI, 1996). Fortunately, there are versions of Moradiellos's works in English: 'The Origins of British Non-Intervention in the Spanish Civil War: Anglo-Spanish Relations in Early 1936', *European History Quarterly* vol. 21, 131 (1991); 'British Political Strategy in the Face of the Military

Rising of 1936 in Spain', *Contemporary European History*, vol. 1, 2 (1992); 'Appeasement and Non-Intervention: British Policy during the Spanish Civil War', in P. Catterall and C. J. Morris (eds), *Britain and the Threat to Stability in Europe, 1918–45* (Leicester: Leicester University Press, 1993); and 'The Gentle General: The Official British Perception of General Franco during the Spanish Civil War', in Preston and Mackenzie (eds), *The Republic Besieged*.

The French attitude is examined in J. E. Dreifort, *Yvon Delbos at the Quai d'Orsay: French Foreign Policy during the Popular Front, 1936–1938* (Lawrence: University Press of Kansas, 1973); J. Lacouture, *Léon Blum* (New York: Holmes & Meier, 1982); and P. Jackson, 'French Strategy and the Spanish Civil War', in C. Leitz and D. J. Dunthorn (eds), *Spain in an International Context, 1936–1959* (Oxford: Berghahn, 1999). Very revealing are the texts in French: *L'Oeuvre de Léon Blum*, vol. IV, 2 (Paris: Albin Michel, 1965); P. Renouvin and R. Rémond (eds), *Léon Blum, chef du gouvernement, 1936–1937* (Paris: Presses de la Fondation Nationale des Sciences Politiques, 1967); D. W. Pike, *Les Français et la guerre d'Espagne* (Paris: Presses Universitaires de France, 1975); and J. Sagnes and S. Caucanas, *Les Français et la guerre d'Espagne* (Perpignan: Université de Perpignan, 1990). In Spanish, there is the important contribution already mentioned by J. Avilés Farré, *Pasión y farsa*, and the brief, but very thorough, essay by R. Miralles, 'La política exterior de la República española hacia Francia durante la guerra civil', *Historia Contemporánea*, 10 (1993).

On the role of the Soviet Union in the Spanish Civil War, the pioneer work by E. H. Carr, *The Comintern and the Spanish Civil War* (London: Macmillan, 1984), is now largely outdated. The most recent and most wide-ranging analysis is in D. Kowalsky, *La Unión Soviética y la guerra civil española* (Barcelona: Crítica, 2004). However, a very succinct and clear essay on the reasons for Soviet involvement can be found in D. Smyth, 'We Are with You: Solidarity and Self-Interest in Soviet Policy towards Republican Spain, 1936–1939', in Preston and Mackenzie (eds), *The Republic Besieged*. Also worth reading are S. Payne, *The Spanish Civil War, the Soviet Union and Communism* (New Haven, CT: Yale University Press, 2004); G. Roberts, 'Soviet Foreign Policy and the Spanish Civil War, 1936–1939', in C. Leitz and D. J. Dunthorn (eds), *Spain in an International Context, 1936–1959* (Oxford: Berghahn, 1999); and J. Haslam, *The Soviet Union and the Struggle for Collective Security in Europe, 1933–1939* (London: Macmillan, 1984). A large number of original documents from Soviet archives have been published and edited by R. Radosh et al. in *Spain Betrayed: The Soviet*

*Union in the Spanish Civil War* (London: Yale University Press, 2001). The aforementioned works by Elorza and Bizcarrondo, *Queridos camaradas,* and Rees, 'The Highpoint of Communist Influence?' also draw upon the Soviet archives. The views of the Soviet ambassador in London, I. Maisky, *Spanish Notebooks* (London: Hutchinson, 1966) make for very useful reading.

For Germany's intervention, the *Documents on German Foreign Policy 1918–1945,* Series D, vol. 3: *Germany and the Spanish Civil War* (London: HMSO, 1951) are indispensable. The best study of Hitler's decision to intervene in Spain is A. Viñas, *Franco, Hitler y el estallido de la guerra civil* (Madrid: Alianza, 2001). Other texts worth reading are R. H. Whealey, *Hitler and Spain: The Nazi Role in the Spanish Civil War* (Lexington: University Press of Kentucky, 1989) and R. Proctor, *Hitler's Luftwaffe in the Spanish Civil War* (Westport, CT: Greenwood Press, 1983). C. Leitz is the author of a series of cogent analyses on the economic aspects of the Nazi intervention: *Economic Relations between Nazi Germany and Franco's Spain, 1936–1945* (Oxford: Oxford University Press, 1995); 'Nazi Germany's Intervention in the Spanish Civil War and the Foundation of HISMA/ROWAK', in Preston and Mackenzie (eds), *The Republic Besieged*; and 'Nazi Germany and Francoist Spain, 1936–45', in S. Balfour and P. Preston (eds), *Spain and the Great Powers* (London: Routledge, 1999).

On Italy's role, the work by J. Coverdale, *Italian Intervention in the Spanish Civil War* (Princeton, NJ: Princeton University Press, 1975) is still very useful. However, Coverdale's explanations for Mussolini's original motives to intervene in Spain have been successfully challenged – firstly by I. Saz, *Mussolini contra la II República* (Valencia: Alfons el Magnánim, 1986) and then by P. Preston, in 'Mussolini's Spanish Adventure: From Limited Risk to War', in Preston and Mackenzie (eds), *The Republic Besieged* and 'Italy and Spain in Civil War and World War', in S. Balfour and P. Preston (eds), *Spain and the Great Powers.* A competent overview can be found in M. Heiberg, *Emperadores del Mediterráneo: Franco, Mussolini y la guerra civil española* (Barcelona: Crítica, 2004). The writings of the Italian foreign minister, G. Ciano, are extremely revealing: *Diplomatic Papers* (London: Odham Press, 1948) and *Diary, 1937–43* (London: Phoenix, 2002).

On the role of the United States, the most recent contribution is the already-mentioned work by D. Little, *Malevolent Neutrality: The United States, Great Britain and the Origins of Non-Intervention.* Very outdated are the texts by A. Guttmann, *American Neutrality and the Spanish Civil War* (Bloomington: Indiana University Press, 1963) and R. P. Traina, *American Diplomacy and the Spanish Civil War* (Bloomington: Indiana University Press, 1968). An interesting eye-witness account is given by the US Ambassador C. Bowers in *My Mission to Spain* (London: Gollancz, 1954). On Portuguese intervention, the traditional work is G. Stone, *The Oldest Ally: Britain and the Portuguese Connection, 1936–1941* (Woodbridge: Royal Historical Society, 1994). On the role of Mexico, see T. G. Powell, *Mexico and the Spanish Civil War* (Albuquerque: University of New Mexico Press, 1981). M. R. de Madariaga has provided the most far-reaching literature on the crucial role played by the Moorish mercenaries in the war: *España y el Rif* (Málaga: Centro Asociado de Melilla, 2nd edn, 2000) and *Los Moros que trajo Franco: La intervención de tropas coloniales en la guerra civil* (Barcelona: Martínez Roca, 2002). A brief version of her work can be found in English: 'The Intervention of Moroccan Troops in the Spanish Civil War: A Reconsideration', *European History Quarterly*, vol. 22, 3 (1992).

**Intellectuals and international volunteers**

The International Brigades have generated an enormous amount of literature. However, some of the traditional works have been proven to be highly distorted and even inaccurate. Among such publications are V. Brome, *The International Brigades* (London: Heinemann, 1965); V. B. Johnson, *Legions of Babel: The International Brigades in the Spanish Civil War* (University Park: Pennsylvania State University Press, 1967); and R. D. Richardson, *Comintern's Army: The International Brigades and the Spanish Civil War* (Lexington: University Press of Kentucky, 1982). A much better effort is M. Jackson, *Fallen Sparrows: The International Brigades in the Spanish Civil War* (Philadelphia, PA: American Philosophical Society, 1994). Although focusing mainly on the French contingent, the best up-to-date overall view of the International Brigades is R. Skoutelsky, *L'Espoir guidait leur pas: Les volontaires français dans les Brigades Internationales, 1936–1939* (Paris: Grasset, 1998). For the British Brigadiers, a very thorough analysis can be found in R. Baxell, *British Volunteers in the Spanish Civil War: The British Battalion in the International Brigades* (London: Routledge, 2004). For the Americans, the most competent work is P. N. Carroll, *The Odyssey of the Abraham Lincoln Brigade: Americans in the Spanish Civil War* (Stanford, CA: Stanford University Press, 1994). An interesting account of volunteers in Nationalist Spain can be found in J. Keene, *Fighting for Franco: International Volunteers in Nationalist Spain during the Spanish Civil War* (London: Leicester University Press, 2001). There is a vast number of individual volunteers' personal recollections. For instance: J. Gurney, *Crusade in Spain* (Newton Abbot: Faber & Faber, 1974); B. Alexander, *British Volunteers for Liberty* (London: Lawrence & Wishart, 1983); M. Merriman and W. Lerude, *American Commander in Spain: Robert Hale Merriman and the Abraham Lincoln Brigade* (Reno: University of Nevada Press, 1986); Walter Gregory, *The Shallow Grave* (Gollancz, 1986); and M. Wolff, *Another Hill* (Chicago: University of Illinois Press, 1994).

Regarding intellectuals and the war, probably the best-known recollection of his experiences is that of G. Orwell, *Homage to Catalonia* (Harmondsworth: Penguin, 1987). Equally interesting, however, are the works by F. Borkenau, *The Spanish Cockpit: An Eyewitness Account of the Political and Social Conflicts of the Spanish Civil War* (London: Pluto Press, 1986) and A. Koestler, *Dialogue with Death* (London: Papermac, 1983). Examples of fictional accounts of the war are E. Hemingway, *For Whom the Bell Tolls* (London: Scribner, 1995) and the superb novel (loosely based on his experiences in the Republican air force) by A. Malraux, *L'Espoir* (Paris: Gallimard, 1987), translated into English as *Days of Hope* (London: Hamilton, 1968). Good compilations of essays and writings by various intellectuals about the Spanish Civil War can be found in V. Cunningham (ed.), *Spanish Front: Writers on the Civil War* (Oxford: Oxford University Press, 1986) and J. Pérez and W. Aycock (eds), *The Spanish Civil War in Literature* (Lubbock, TX: Tech University Press, 1990).

**The legacy of the war**

Since the mid-1980s, the wealth of Spanish scholarship focusing on provincial studies has been vital in unearthing hitherto concealed and crucial aspects of the war and the subsequent repression. Some of these groundbreaking works have been brought together in edited collections of essays. Among the most wide-ranging are: S. Juliá (ed.), *Víctimas de la guerra civil* (Madrid: Temas de Hoy, 1999); J. Casanova et al., *Morir, matar, sobrevivir: La violencia en la dictadura de Franco* (Barcelona: Crítica, 2002); and C. Molinero, M. Sala and J. Sobrequés (eds), *Una inmensa prisión: Los campos de concentración y las prisiones durante la guerra civil y el franquismo* (Barcelona: Crítica, 2003). Other excellent works on the question of Francoist repression are A. Cazorla Sánchez, *Las políticas de la victoria. La consolidación del Nuevo Estado franquista (1938–1953)* (Madrid: Marcial Pons, 2000); and the essays by A. Cenarro: 'Muerte y subordinación en la España franquista: El imperio de la violencia como base del nuevo estado', *Historia Social*, 30 (1998) and 'Matar, vigilar y delatar: La quiebra de la sociedad civil durante la guerra y la posguerra en España, 1936–48, *Historia Social*, 44 (2002). A crucial analysis of the Francoist legacy of propaganda manipulation and myth creation is A. Reig Tapia, *Memoria de la Guerra Civil* (Madrid: Alianza, 1999).

Apart from Franco's biographies and some general surveys of the Francoist regime, there is a very small bibliography in English on the repression and legacy of the war. However, although limited, this literature is excellent. The crucial works are P. Preston, *The Politics of Revenge: Fascism and the Military in 20th Century Spain* (London: Routledge, 1995); M. Richards, *A Time of Silence: Civil War and the Culture of Repression in Franco's Spain, 1939–1945* (Cambridge: Cambridge University Press, 1998); and H. Graham, 'Spain's Memory Wars', *History Today*, May 2004. An extremely moving account of the fate of Spanish Republicans in occupied France can be found in D. W. Pike, *Spaniards in the Holocaust: Mauthausen, the Horror on the Danube* (London: Routledge, 2000). Finally, we can also find some important works originally in Spanish but translated into English: A. Cenarro, 'Memory Beyond the Public Sphere: The Francoist Repression remembered in Aragon', in R. Rein (ed.), *Spanish Memories: Images of a Contested Past; History and Memory*, vol. 44 (Fall 2002) and P. Aguilar Fernández, *Memory and Amnesia: The Role of the Spanish Civil War in the Transition to Democracy* (New York: Berghahn, 2002).

# Index